VICO   *A Study of the 'New Science'*

VICO
A Study of the 'New Science'

SECOND EDITION

LEON POMPA

Professor of Philosophy, University of Birmingham

The right of the University of Cambridge to print and sell all manner of books was granted by Henry VIII in 1534. The University has printed and published continuously since 1584.

CAMBRIDGE UNIVERSITY PRESS

Cambridge

New York   Port Chester

Melbourne   Sydney

Published by the Press Syndicate of the University of Cambridge
The Pitt Building, Trumpington Street, Cambridge CB2 1RP
40 West 20th Street, New York, NY 10011, USA
10 Stamford Road, Oakleigh, Melbourne 3166, Australia

First published 1975
Second edition 1990

Printed in Great Britain at
the University Press, Cambridge

British Library cataloguing in publication data
Pompa, L. (Leon)
Vico: a study of the 'New Science'. – 2nd edn.
1. Historiology. Philosophical perspectives. Vico,
Giambattista, 1668–1744. Scienza nuova – Critical studies
I. Title
901

Library of Congress cataloguing in publication data
Pompa, Leon.
Vico: a study of the 'New Science' / Leon Pompa. – 2nd edn.
p.   cm.
Bibliography.
Includes index.
ISBN 0-521-38217-3. – ISBN 0-521-38871-6 (pbk.)
1. Vico, Giambattista, 1668–1744. Principi di una scienza nuova.
2. Philosophy. 3. History – Philosophy. I. Title.
B3581.P73P65 1990
195 – dc20   89-35786 CIP

ISBN 0 521 38217 3 hard covers
ISBN 0 521 38871 6 paperback
(First edition ISBN 0 521 20584 0 hard covers)

To Carol

CONTENTS

vii

PREFACE

This book is intended both to offer an interpretation of the main theories in Vico's *Scienza Nuova* and to serve as an analytic introduction to its text. When the first edition was published in 1975, there had already been a considerable re-awakening of interest in Vico's thought. Nevertheless, as was noted at the time, in the two centuries since the appearance of the *Scienza Nuova*, there had not been a single analytic commentary or monograph devoted exclusively to it, i.e. a monograph which attempted, on the basis of a close examination of the text, to locate and analyse the philosophical foundations of Vivo's thought and to show that, despite the many obscurities, digressions and eccentricities, not to mention outright mistakes, which it contains, his great 'science' was more than a series of brilliant *aperçus* spread over a variety of essentially disconnected subjects.

It was not the case, however, that there had been no earlier attempts to establish the fundamental philosophical tenets which underlay and were brought together in the *Scienza Nuova*. A number of such works already existed. In Italy there was, in general, a division between an essentially quasi-Hegelian approach and a Catholic tradition of interpretation. Unquestionably the most important of either kind was Benedetto Croce's pioneering volume, *La Filosofia Di Giambattista Vico*. First published in 1911 and fairly continuously reprinted since then, this consolidated the late nineteenth-century idealist interpretation of Vico and became the most influential reading for nearly half a century. The alternative Catholic viewpoint was most fully developed in an excellent, though somewhat neglected, monograph by F. Amerio, *Introduzione allo Studio di G. B. Vico*, published in 1947. This is still, in my view, the most comprehensive and philosophically interesting statement of the Catholic interpretation of Vico. Outside Italy, however, philosophical interest in Vico in the twentieth century was extremely limited until T. G. Bergin and Max H. Fisch produced their translations of Vico's Autobiography in 1944 and then of the *Scienza Nuova* in 1948. From that point onwards, interest in English-speaking countries quickened considerably. Fisch himself had written a most illuminating account of Vico's thought in the Introduction to the translation of the Autobiography and, more recently, Sir Isaiah Berlin had given a series of lectures at the Italian Institute in London, which were published under the title 'The Philosophical Ideas of Giambattista Vico' in *Art and Ideas in Eighteenth-Century Italy* in 1960. Beyond this, however, there had also been very considerable research, primarily on the part of Italian scholars, into the historical and cultural context within which Vico wrote, the most important fruits of which were probably Fausto Nicolini's various historical essays, culminating in his massive *Commento Storico alla Seconda 'Scienza Nuova'* in 1949–50, and Nicola Badaloni's equally erudite *Introduzione a G. B. Vico* of 1961. But these were only some of many historically orientated enquiries which had been appearing in Italy, since Croce's first volume had had such a powerful impact upon Vico research.

Nevertheless, where the present volume differed from these works and where, I believe, it was unique, is that it was the first to attempt to lay bare the philosophical foundations of the *Scienza Nuova* by a systematic analysis of the text, in which particular attention was paid to the relation of the various parts to the whole, i.e. of the relationship between Vico's treatment of its particular subject matters to the body of philosophical theory, extending from epistemology and metaphysics to questions of methodology, upon which, as he constantly, if somewhat obscurely, insisted, the whole 'science' rested. Despite all the research which had been done upon the *Scienza Nuova* the problem, as I perceived it, was that it was still very difficult to gain any clear ideas as to what in the work was philosophically fundamental and what was less so, what was philosophical or theoretical, in some or other sense, as against what was empirical, what was concerned with principles of interpretation as against what was concerned with principles of verification and how, if at all, these distinctions operated in connection with the concept of a single science.

The present study differed from those which had preceded it, therefore, in that it was the first to be devoted exclusively to an analysis of the text of the *Scienza Nuova*, with the aim of ascertaining the body of theory which gave coherence to its structure as a whole. It was not suggested, nor would it have been possible without writing a book of much greater length, that it could cover the total contents of the *Scienza Nuova*. In any case this seemed unwise. For not only was it explicitly intended as an introduction, but I felt that, in striking out in a relatively new direction, there was a very real possibility of mistakes of judgement and of balance on my part. My hope was that other scholars who detected these might also go on to correct them, thus leading to a better understanding of what Vico was doing than I had achieved.

Since then there has been an enormous increase in Vico studies, some idea of the extent of which can be gathered by even the most cursory glance through the many bibliographies of books and articles on him or on themes to which his work is directly relevant. Covering, as it does, almost everything pertinent to understanding his thought, including continued detailed study of his historical and cultural context, analytic research into the thinkers by whom he was influenced, the nature and course of the development of his own thought and the effect which his ideas have had upon later thinkers, it would not be possible here to give an account of the various trends and changes of interest and emphasis to be discerned in it. The results have, however, undoubtedly been of great importance in helping to appreciate Vico's conception of the particular subject matters which are discussed in the *Scienza Nuova* and his contribution to our own understanding of these subjects as such. Thus his contribution to our conceptions of historical and comparative linguistics, of cultural and social anthropology, of developmental psychology, of social and political theory and of culture and of history have been increasingly clarified and appreciated. Experts in these various fields, who have no reason to interest themselves in Vico as a thinker in his own right, have consequently found themselves increasingly drawn to his work, both for the stimulus which it can give to their own thought and for the light which it can help to throw upon the historical development of their own discipline.

There remains, nevertheless, one peculiarity in this general trend towards a greater appreciation of Vico as a thinker. Although he may now be discussed in relation to many more diverse areas of knowledge than was previously the case, it is still frequent to find him either omitted in histories of philosophy or, at best, alluded to as an eccentric figure of little intrinsic interest. This, indeed, was the position when the first edition of this work was published and it is little altered today. The concentration of studies upon Vico's contribution to various non-philosophical areas of thought has done little to increase recognition of his merits as a philosopher. Nor is this too surprising. For in the midst of this large and varied body of research, there has been one notable omission: continued enquiry into the nature of the philosophical basis of the different doctrines within the *Scienza Nuova*, to which, correctly or incorrectly, Vico ascribed the over-all coherence which he claimed for it.

This generalisation is, of course, subject to certain reservations. It is certainly not the case that there has been no work done upon this aspect of Vico's thought. But this has tended to fall into two categories. On the one hand there has been a fairly large number of relatively brief essays, which both recognise the importance of philosophy in Vico's work and offer accounts of how he conceived of philosophy. But these are frequently too short to be able to provide, by argument and the assessment of evidence, an analysis of the implications of the conception in question for an understanding of the *Scienza Nuova*, taken as the synthesis of various subject matters which it is undoubtedly intended to be. Whatever the individual merits of these often conflicting interpretations, there is little doubt that their main over-all effect has been to increase, rather than to diminish, the confusion which exists with regard to the character of Vico's philosophical enterprise.

On the other hand, there has also been a very much smaller number of studies which have engaged with this central problem and which have done so at sufficient length and with sufficient comprehensiveness as to make it possible to evaluate them critically in the light of their implications for the relationship between the philosophical basis of the *Scienza Nuova* as a whole and its component parts. To a greater or lesser extent, it must be said, these studies approach the work in a different way from that developed here. In particular, they lay much greater stress than I have upon the importance of Vico's debt to the juridical and rhetorical traditions which arose from the work of his humanist predecessors and much less upon his claim to have produced a 'science', in the sense in which I have interpreted that here. It is, indeed, frequently thought that the approach which I have taken, in which Vico is treated as trying to provide the philosophical foundations of a 'science', in some fairly rigorous sense of the word, is incompatible with thinking of what he has produced as a humanist conception of the philosophical foundations of history. I am far from persuaded that this is so and I have, therefore, in the present edition, included an extra chapter, analysing Vico's conception of the principles which govern the development of law. My aim there is to show that there is no incompatibility in thinking that Vico wished to produce and apply an account of the philosophical foundations of a rigorous science of history and that he also wished to allow that the techniques of rhetorical argument, both in everyday life and also in such specialised areas as law, could play a constitutive role in the historical development of man. Since the account of the principles which determine the development of law has implications for other related concepts, notably those of providence, of the barbarism of reflection and of the cyclical theory of history, I have taken advantage of the opportunity thus offered to extend the analysis of these beyond the account offered in the first edition of this book. None of this additional discussion, however, leads me to believe that there is an incompatibility between the *philosophical* conception of a rigorous science of man's historical development, which is the ultimate aim that I ascribe to Vico, and acknowledgement of an important place for rhetoric as an essential component in the processes whereby, according to that science, historical development takes place.

Whether or not this is correct, however, I remain unpersuaded that one can make much sense of many parts of the *Scienza Nuova* unless considerable weight is placed upon his explicit claim to have produced a science. The word 'science', of course, can have various meanings, especially as used in the Latin and Italian of Vico's day. On the one hand, it could be used to indicate knowledge in little more than an everyday sense. On the other, it could signify a coherent and structured body of knowledge, presupposing a variety of principles operating at different, related levels of enquiry, supplied with its own methods for applying these principles to its subject matter, and deriving claims to certainty from the consistency and comprehensiveness of the results which, in virtue of these features, it can produce. This would be the sort of meaning which it would have had, for example, for Descartes, although his specific account of the source and nature of these principles and of our mode of access to them was very different from Vico's. The *Scienza Nuova*, I believe, is intended to provide both the philosophical principles for, and also to be an exemplification of, a science of this sort, and unless it is understood in this sense many parts of it will remain wholly opaque or eccentrically irrelevant. Consequently, I have added a further chapter, discussing three recent works in which it is not considered to be a science of this sort, and have tried to demonstrate the difficulties which are engendered if alternative conceptions of a science are adopted.

Apart, therefore, from the inclusion of additional material, the main justification for issuing a second edition of this monograph is two-fold. Firstly, it is still the only work which is devoted almost exclusively to an interpretation of the *Scienza Nuova*, developed by means of a considerable amount of textual analysis, on the basis of which it seeks to establish the philosophical grounds for the coherence which Vico claimed for the whole work. Thus, irrespective of whether or not the reader agrees with its conclusions, or even its general line of argument, it provides a reasonably comprehensive guide to the main theoretical problems to which the text gives rise and with which alternative interpretations should be expected to contend. Secondly, it accepts and tries to explain Vico's claim to have produced a science, in some fairly rigorous sense. It is thus to be distinguished from more recent interpretations which present him as essentially an exponent, albeit a most distinguished one, of modes of thought which could arise only within the humanist tradition. For reasons to be given later, this seems to me to be, at best, a half-truth which, when given too much prominence, is liable to issue in partial and misleading interpretations of the *Scienza Nuova*.

I have already, in an earlier article, 'Vico's Science' (*History and Theory*, vol. 10, no. 1, pp. 49–83), analysed Vico's conception of a science. I am grateful to the editors of *History and Theory*, Wesleyan University, for permission to re-use some of the material contained in that article, particularly in chapter 16. Since writing it, however, my view of Vico's theory of knowledge has been modified in one important respect, a modification which took place in the course of thinking about the interpretation put forward by Sir Isaiah Berlin. The interpretation which I offer in chapters 15 and 16 is by no means identical with that suggested by Berlin. I there present several reasons why I am not able to accept his view exactly in the way in which he has formulated it, and these are developed further in the concluding chapter of this new edition. Nevertheless, I have benefited both by a study of what he has written and by a series of stimulating conversations which I have had with him on the subject, for all of which I wish to express my gratitude to him. I welcome also the opportunity to express my great debt to my friend the late Professor W. H. Walsh, who read the entire first edition in manuscript and made innumerable suggestions, without which it would be more unsatisfactory than it now is. Amongst others who have helped me, I thank Dr G. E. Davie and Dr Giorgio Tagliacozzo, both of whom have encouraged me with much kindness. I wish also to thank my wife, who gave me considerable help in preparing the translations from *De Antiquissima* which appear in chapter 7, and Miss Margaret Paterson, who typed out the manuscript from my handwritten copy.

By permission of Cornell University Press, I have quoted extensively from the splendid translation of the third (1744) *Scienza Nuova*, by T. G. Bergin and M. H. Fisch (*The New Science of Giambattista Vico*, copyright © by Cornell University Press, revised and published, Ithaca, 1968). The numbered references to the *Scienza Nuova* refer to the system of numbered paragraphs used in this translation and in the edition of the *Scienza Nuova* given in *Giambattista Vico: Opere* edited by F. Nicolini, Riccardo Ricciardi, Milan 1953. For translations from Vico's earlier works given in the additional two chapters, I have used my own *Vico: Selected Writings*, details of which are given in the Bibliography.

Birmingham 1988   L.P.

1

The structure of the 'Scienza Nuova'

One of the main reasons for the failure of Vico's *Scienza Nuova* to establish itself as a widely read philosophical work is the sheer obscurity of the text. One source of this obscurity lies in the fact that in his great work Vico tried to do two things without always explicitly distinguishing them from each other: to reconstruct the histories of some of the principal ancient nations known to him; and to give some account of the main philosophical and theoretical presuppositions involved in this reconstruction. Vico was, nevertheless, fully aware of the distinction between these two tasks and this is clearly enough reflected in the structure of the text. A short account of the latter is therefore a useful way to begin this discussion of the *Scienza Nuova*, since it will serve to give both a preliminary idea of the contents and also some first idea of what Vico took himself to be doing and how he hoped to do it.

The *Scienza Nuova* consists of an Introduction, five Books, and a Conclusion. The Introduction takes the form of some comments upon an allegorical picture which constitutes the frontispiece. These comments are so condensed that it is to be doubted that it can ever have succeeded, as was evidently intended, in giving a clear idea of the contents of the work to a new reader.

Book I is sub-titled *Establishment of Principles*, and commences with a Chronological Table. Here Vico sets out in seven different columns the leading events and dates of Hebrew, Chaldean, Scythian, Phoenician, Egyptian, Greek and Roman history. In effect he offers the schematic outlines of seven separate histories.

The Chronological Table is followed by Section I, which consists of a series of notes and comments upon the proposed scheme. These show that Vico realised that the account he was offering differed from some of the leading interpretations of the day, both in detail and in principle. In matters of detail what he is concerned to dispute are questions related to the dating and interpretation of specific events. Behind this, however, there lies a fundamental conceptual issue. For certain of Vico's opponents while exhibiting differences among themselves on particular historical points, shared one common assumption: that the growth of civilised practices in the world was a consequence of the fact that the various nations of the world had had a single historical origin. The accounts offered were thus all varieties of the transmission theory of civilisation, involving explanations which were exclusively causal in kind.

The historical scheme which Vico put forward as an alternative to these accounts involves the entirely different assumption that the parallel growths of civilised practices in different historical nations were a consequence not of some common historical origin but of a common essential nature. On this view, the nature of a nation is such that if the various historical nations were left to develop without external interference, they would necessarily develop certain common characteristics in their social, economic and cultural conditions at correspondent points of their histories.

Vico recognised that it was a consequence of this different conception that certain things which on the transmission theory were explained in one way would have to receive an entirely different kind of explanation. The rest of his notes in this section indicate briefly some points which are claimed to invalidate his opponents' common thesis and support his own alternative. These points are, however, almost exclusively historiographical in character, i.e. they are concerned with the question how well or how badly the two kinds of theory are supported by the available historical evidence.

In Section II, entitled 'Elements', the discussion moves to a different level. In conclusion to the historical notes, and as a prelude to the introduction of the 'Elements', Vico makes a remark of considerable significance:

It can be seen from our discussion in these Notes that all that has come down to us from the ancient gentile nations for the times covered by this Table is most uncertain. So that in all this we have entered as it were into a no man's land where the rule of law obtains that 'the first occupant acquires title' (*occupanti conceduntur*). We trust therefore that we shall offend no man's right if we reason differently and at times in direct opposition to the opinions which have been held up to now concerning the principles of the humanity of the nations. By so doing we shall reduce them to scientific principles, by which the facts of history may be assigned to their first origins, on which they rest and by which they are reconciled. For until now they seem to have no common foundation or continuous sequence or coherence among themselves.[1]

The point to be noted here is Vico's claim that his reasoning will differ from those of other historians by its utilisation of a 'scientific' account of the 'principles of the humanity of nations'. These scientific principles will make possible the resolution of certain difficulties concerning the origins of ancient nations and, equally importantly, will allow the facts to be set forth in continuous and mutually coherent sequences. In short, the claim is that a certain set of scientific principles is going to make possible a kind of historical account superior to those of contemporary historians.

This quotation reveals that Vico had grasped the distinction between historical interpretations and the various kinds of principles which support historical interpretations. His account of these principles is now set out in Section II, which opens with another remark of significance:

In order to give form to the materials hereinbefore set in order in the Chronological Table, we now propose the following axioms, both philosophical and philological, including a few reasonable and proper postulates and some clarified definitions. And just as the blood does in our animate bodies, so will these elements course through our Science and animate it in all its reasonings about the common nature of nations.[2]

The Elements, of which there are various kinds, are thus claimed to be responsible for giving the historical accounts their 'form'. This again shows clearly Vico's grasp of the difference between the content of a given historical account and the philosophical presuppositions responsible for making it the kind of account it is.

Section II consists of one hundred and fourteen Elements, in which Vico sets out the main general presuppositions involved in his account and tries to show that they must be involved in any

---

[1] The third *Scienza Nuova* (hereafter *S.N.*) 118. [2] *S.N.* 119.

acceptable account. These fall roughly into three classes.[1] First, there is a group of philosophical principles, of which the most important constitute a theory of knowledge and a theory about the social and historical nature of the causes of human activities, i.e. a metaphysical theory. Next comes a group of sociological or, more properly, historico-sociological, theories. Finally there is a group of theories and recommendations for the reform of historiographical method. Apart from these there are also a number of places in which Vico repeats and expands the historical accounts and points which belong, properly speaking, to the previous section.

Vico does not himself explicitly distinguish his Elements into these three groups. He does, however, divide them into two groups, the first twenty-two (plus Element CVI)[2] which are said to be 'general' and to provide the foundation for the whole science and the other ninety-one which are 'particular' and provide 'more specific bases for the various matters it treats of'.[3] It will be shown that what Vico here calls 'general' are the elements concerned with the philosophical or non-empirical aspects of his work. They thus cover the first and third groups of the above classification. The 'particular' Elements are those concerned with its empirical aspects and thus cover both its historico-sociological theories and its historical claims.

Sections III and IV, which complete Book I, are concerned partly with elaborating further the various things which it will be necessary to do if historical accounts are to be constructed in the way Vico suggests and partly with a more detailed enquiry into the verification conditions for such accounts. Sections II–IV thus constitute the main part of Vico's theoretical account of the nature of his task and the way in which he proposes to solve the problems it poses. They will accordingly form the central area of discussion of the present study.

Book II, sub-titled *Poetic Wisdom*, is an account of the main features of what Vico calls the 'poetic' mode of life, i.e. the first stage of social life through which, according to Vico's thesis concerning their common nature, the history of all (independent) nations must pass. It constitutes, in fact, a part of their common nature. It is called

---

[1] In presenting the contents of the Elements in this way I shall assume distinctions which, in the rest of this analysis, it will be my task to justify.
[2] *S.N.* 314–15.　　　　　　　　　[3] *S.N.* 164.

'poetic' because its institutions are the product of men whose response to their environment is dictated by their largely imaginative and non-rational mentality.

The account Vico gives is long and often perplexing. This is partly because he attempts simultaneously to do two things: to analyse the internal features of such a society (e.g. by showing how the existence of a professional caste of priests is a necessary consequence of a certain understanding of religion in a certain institutional context), and to show that all, or nearly all, known nations have exhibited such a phase in their history. The book has therefore both sociological and historical aspects: sociological in that it tries to show that given certain conditions of society and culture certain others must follow; and historical in that it seeks to establish, on the basis of historical evidence, that in the past these conditions have been instantiated.

The apparent conflation of these two tasks in one account, which occurs in this book more than anywhere else in the *Scienza Nuova*, has led to considerable perplexity over whether what Vico is producing is sociological or historical in character.[1] It will be argued later, however, that Vico's 'scientific' approach to history required that the establishment of historical accounts be based upon the interpretation of evidence in accordance with determinate historico-sociological theories, while the establishment of the latter depends upon their successful involvement in such interpretations. Vico's simultaneous pursuit of the two kinds of enquiry is not an indication of the conflation of two different kinds of thing but of his understanding of the mutual relevance of two equally necessary kinds of enquiry for his science. Once this claim is accepted the question of what Vico is doing in different parts of Book II largely resolves itself.

Book III, *Discovery of the True Homer*, contains a detailed discussion of Vico's claim that the Homeric writings were not the creation of a single author but were the inventions of the rhapsodes, living in different parts of Greece and at different times in Greek history, calling upon beliefs common to themselves and their audience for the contents of their tales. This material is included in the *Scienza Nuova* primarily as a demonstration of the proper use of a body of historical

---

[1] B. Croce, *The Philosophy of Giambattista Vico*, trans. by R. G. Collingwood (London 1913), chapter III.

evidence, a use made possible only by Vico's whole conception of a science.

Book IV, *The Course the Nations Run*, consists in a very schematised account of the main phases of the 'ideal eternal history', i.e. of the stages of birth, development and ultimate decline through which the histories of all nations must pass if left to develop freely. It thus represents Vico's historico-sociological theories in the most abstract way possible, though even here not without some reference to certain historical facts claimed as instantiations of them. The emphasis is, nevertheless, on the theories themselves rather than on the facts.

Book V, *The Recourse of Human Institutions which the Nations Take When They Rise Again*, consists of a series of relatively brief indications about how later history, e.g. the Dark Ages and early feudal times in Europe, should be interpreted in the light of these same theories. Here, however, the emphasis is on the illumination which the historical events themselves receive when thus treated rather than on the theories involved in such treatment.

From this brief account of the structure of the *Scienza Nuova* it would appear that Vico's work is largely concerned with the questions how to understand and establish the truth in human history. It will be argued in what follows that this is the correct way in which to approach Vico's thought and that many difficulties of interpretation can be resolved if Vico's preoccupation with these problems is kept well to the fore of attention. Starting from a set of purely historical problems, Vico shows that any answer to them involves philosophical theories about the nature of knowledge and of human affairs, and determinate historico-sociological theories about the conditions which determine the occurrence of the various possible kinds of human institutions. Setting out his theories in both these areas he defends them by reference to their different functions in a science whose object is to make possible the most illuminating and best verified interpretations of historical evidence, i.e. interpretations which satisfy criteria laid down in Vico's epistemological theory. On this view, history and sociology can be proper objects of knowledge only when conceived in such a way as to bring mutual support to each other, while the task of metaphysics is to explicate the basic categories which will allow this to be done.

2

Critique of current historiography

Vico's initial task in the *Scienza Nuova* is that of supporting what is, in effect, a series of particular, if wide-ranging, historical theses. One of the main historiographical problems of the seventeenth and early eighteenth centuries was that of explaining certain institutional and cultural similarities which appeared to obtain both among the ancient nations of the civilised world and the more primitive nations of the contemporary world. The existence of such similarities was supported by appeal to an ever-increasing amount of evidence, drawn from historical documents and from tales brought back by the explorers and missionaries who were in touch with contemporary primitives. A certain number of historians had attempted to explain these similarities by reference to some historical origin which these nations had in common. Historical dispute therefore tended to be about the details of such an account, centering upon such issues as which country had first developed the institutions of civilised life and by what historical route they had travelled to the other nations which shared them. Vico's position in this debate involved a radical conceptual departure for, while not disputing that there were facts here to be explained, he wanted to offer an explanation of an entirely different kind, resting upon the concept of a common historical nature and not that of a common historical origin. Thus on his view the similarities in institution and culture to be found in the histories of different nations were a consequence of some more fundamental identity of nature.

In the 'Elements' Vico does not attack his opponents on historical grounds. This is done elsewhere, in the notes on the Chronological Table, and throughout Book II, where his positive account of the institutions proper to the poetic mode of life is given concurrently with a critique of the historical absurdities which, he alleges, follow from the kind of view his opponents wish to adopt. Instead of such an historical dispute, in the 'Elements' he produces an account of the inadequate philosophical conceptions and methodological procedures upon which these interpretations are founded.

He begins, in the first group of four Elements, with an account of the inadequacies of his opponents' methodological procedures. Instead of formulating a proper method for the critical interpretation of historical evidence most historians have simply relied on something akin to their native common sense to guide them in their accounts. But, Vico claims, the ways in which human thought characteristically and naturally operates cannot provide an acceptable basis for the interpretation of historical evidence and they must be corrected by the application of a sound critical method.

The first of these natural but unsatisfactory ways in which human thought operates is stated in Element I: 'Because of the indefinite nature of the human mind, wherever it is lost in ignorance man makes himself the measure of all things.'[1] This, it is said, explains how it is that rumours become increasingly distorted the further they are removed in time and place from the events they purport to relate.[2] Vico's point is that in each retelling of the original event it is reinterpreted and embellished along the lines indicated by the general principle. The effect of this is to render traditional accounts of events, which are in some cases the historian's primary source of data, *per se* untrustworthy. They cannot, as some historians have thought, be accepted as though they were the products of some tradition of objective reporting.

A second general characteristic of human thinking is stated in Element II: 'Whenever men can form no idea of distant and unknown things they judge them by what is familar and at hand.'[3] This tendency leads to two kinds of error to which historians themselves are naturally prone. First there is the 'conceit of nations', i.e. an inclination to adopt one's national point of view and to write history in the light of this. Vico believed that this tendency explained the disagreements among his opponents about which country should be credited with the original creation of civilised life. An historian prone

---

[1] *S.N.* 120. [2] *S.N.* 121. [3] *S.N.* 122.

to this error would naturally believe that his own nation 'before all other nations invented the comforts of human life and that its remembered history goes back to the very beginning of the world'.[1] In effect he would lack an impartial or objective viewpoint.

The second error is the 'conceit of scholars', the tendency to believe that all contemporary knowledge has always been known. Vico claims that this belief had led historians to attribute to former ages the possession of knowledge which could only obtain in their own age. It therefore explains how historians have come to believe in 'the matchless wisdom of the ancients...It further condemns as impertinent all the mystic meanings with which the Egyptian hieroglyphs are endowed by the scholars and the philosophical allegories which they have read into the Greek fables.'[2]

What Vico is here drawing attention to is the sheer unhistorical character of many accounts of the past. They are lacking in any sense of what Sir Isaiah Berlin has called 'historical perspective', i.e. any recognition that at different times in the past men's mental and intellectual abilities have varied widely and that the sorts of knowledge that could be formulated and used in one age could not be formulated and used in another.

The manner in which Vico understood these rather general complaints is best seen from the way he applies them when trying to refute his opponents' views on particular historical points. In general he appeals to the conceit of nations rather less than to the conceit of scholars. This is because the former is used mainly in the *Scienza Nuova* to explain examples of faulty chronology. For example, Vico uses it to dispute the datings of historical events, and the interpretations of world history to which these datings were central, to be found in the works of Marsham, Spencer and van Heurn. These historians had accepted at its face value the Alexandrian academicians' claim that the first civilisation was Egyptian and that ancient history was to be seen as the spreading of civilised practices from Egypt to the rest of the world.[3] They had failed to realise that these Egyptian writers themselves suffered from the conceit of nations and so ought to be treated with caution and in the light of a properly developed critical method.[4] In a similar way Justin (*Historiarum Philippicarum Libri*

[1] *S.N.* 125. [2] *S.N.* 128.
[3] *S.N.* 44–7. [4] *S.N.* 46, 126.

XLIV 1.1.3) had accepted a Scythian (Russian) tradition that their civilisation predated that of Egypt and had made this claim central to his account of ancient history.[1] Of ancient historians Vico finds only Flavius Josephus in his *Against Appion* free from this error.[2]

The fact that the principle is applied by Vico mainly in discussions of chronological matters should not be taken to imply that its importance is confined solely to such questions. Vico applied the principle primarily in this area because in the early eighteenth century little progress had been made in establishing an objective chronology for the events of ancient history. Devoid of any help whatsoever from the physical sciences historians had to rely entirely on literary remains and ancient traditions for the construction of their chronological schemes.

The general point involved in Vico's principle is, however, of much greater importance and wider application than this. The historians he castigates, Marsham, Spencer, Justin, had failed to realise that their sources, the great literary remains of the past, were not the products of impartial, objective observers, whose reports conformed to scientific norms of accuracy. They were the products of men or, in the case of traditions, of generations of men, to whom it was the most natural thing in the world to adopt a partial and prejudiced viewpoint and incorporate this unblushingly into their accounts of the past.

It is not Vico's intention to suggest that the presence of such a viewpoint is something which renders these accounts and traditions useless as historical evidence. It necessitates, however, that if they are to be of use to the historian they must be subjected to a rigorous scientific criticism which, by elucidating the viewpoint from which they have been written, will open the way to the ultimate recovery of the truths they embody.[3]

In making this point Vico was not thinking of viewpoints reflecting the personal or idiosyncratic prejudices of their authors. He intended it to apply to the general conceptual scheme and system of knowledge and beliefs which a writer or teller of tales holds by virtue of belonging to a given historical society. The conceptual scheme used and the things known and believed by, for example, a group of

---

[1] *S.N.* 48. [2] *S.N.* 126.

[3] This is the function of what Vico calls his 'metaphysical art of criticism' (*S.N.* 348) which is discussed below, pp. 99–103.

raconteurs such as the rhapsodes, are not the products of the individual rhapsodes themselves but of the society in which they existed and for whom they created their tales. It is not therefore simply the case that traditional sources of historical evidence reflect the personal prejudices of the individual or individuals most instrumental in producing them, though, of course, they may also do this. Much more importantly, they reflect the system of beliefs, values and assumptions, both factual and normative, and the general conceptual scheme within which these can obtain, of the society to which their creators belonged.

This point can best be brought out by a brief consideration of some of Vico's examples of the second source of error, the 'conceit of scholars'. His application of this principle differs from that of the 'conceit of nations' in that, where the latter is largely used to explain certain characteristics of firsthand historical evidence itself, the former is used to explain certain kinds of mistake committed by the historian when interpreting such evidence. The mistake in question is that of interpreting historical and literary evidence on the assumption that it is the product of ways of thought proper to, and possible only for, societies much later than those which actually produce it. It is thus, in effect, a sort of conceptual anachronism which the historian is bound to make if he approaches the interpretation of his material on the assumption that what to him would seem a sensible or rational course of action, or a persuasive or plausible way of looking at a certain problem, would have seemed the same to historical agents themselves. It is the assumption that the criteria of rationality proper to one's own historical society are proper to all possible societies.

Vico attributes this error to a whole tradition of writers, from Plato to Francis Bacon, who had interpreted the Greek fables as symbolic representations of certain esoteric, philosophical doctrines, thus committing themselves to what he calls 'the matchless wisdom of the ancients'. He does not wish to deny that these fables reflect a certain wisdom or set of beliefs, but it is a wisdom of a practical and social kind, reflecting the beliefs of a fairly primitive people. It neither does nor could include philosophical doctrines of the kind which were possible in the sophisticated conceptual circumstances of the ages in which Plato and Bacon wrote. These would have been literally inconceivable in the ages in which the Greek fables were produced.[1] Vico goes on to argue that precisely the same mistake had been made by those writers who had tried to solve the problem of the interpretation of the hieroglyphs by arguing that they were a language for the concealed transmission of certain religious and philosophical truths.[2]

The above examples are taken from an area of enquiry particularly liable to be affected by this error, that of the history of intellectual ideas. This represents, however, only a part of a more general and, according to Vico, more important area affected by the principle, that of the history of institutions and of the communal and social aims in the light of which alone this can be made intelligible. What Vico claims here is that many historical accounts of past institutions have been based upon thoroughly anachronistic assumptions about the aims and purposes of the social groups that have created and maintained them. Once the anachronistic nature of the accounts of these aims has been established, not only must these accounts themselves be rejected but so also must any accounts of the activities of particular individuals where these presuppose the defective institutional accounts.

Vico quotes as an example of this kind of error, some interpretations of parts of early Roman history in which it was claimed that 'the Roman people from the time of Romulus had been composed of citizens both noble and plebeian, that the Roman kingdom had been monarchical and that the liberty initiated by [Junius] Brutus had been a popular liberty'.[3] This account of the nature of the change brought about by Brutus rested upon an interpretation of documents in which the key words, 'people', 'kingdom' and 'liberty', were undefined. Vico's claim is that in interpreting these words philosophers and historians had fallen into the 'conceit of scholars', by taking 'the word people in the sense of recent times and applying it to the earliest times'. They had thus interpreted Brutus's actions as bringing liberty to the whole people, patricians and plebeians alike, whereas on Vico's account they involved only the restoration to the patricians of certain rights which had been usurped by the Tarquin tyrants.[4] Nor

[1] S.N. 384, 412.
[2] S.N. 384, 435–7. For an account of these writers see Nicolini, *Commento Storico alla Seconda Scienza Nuova*, vol. I, pp. 170–4.
[3] S.N. 105. [4] S.N. 105, 108, 666.

was this an isolated mistake. These false assumptions about the constitution of the Roman 'people', the monarchical nature of a Roman 'king' and the kind of changes which would be described by the Romans as leading to greater 'liberty' were built into a whole view of Roman history, involving equally false accounts of the significance of the Publilian and Petelian laws. Thus, by attributing to the Romans conceptions proper to a later age, these historians had given false accounts of the history of Roman ideas, of the nature of Roman institutions and of the very activities of historical agents and groups of agents.

Vico's first group of elements therefore makes two claims: that no traditional account is *per se* trustworthy; and that the natural way in which we interpret history, as though we were interpreting phenomena and activities within our own historical society, is inadequate. Vico has implied the need for a proper approach to historical knowledge by producing general arguments to throw doubt on the reports contained in traditional accounts and on the subsequent reworking of these by historians when the latter are relying upon little more than their natural common-sense to guide them in their task.

Since one of Vico's stated objectives is to establish historical knowledge which is properly founded and free from any suspicion of the above flaws, it is important to have a clear idea of the general nature of his complaints. This can be put in two points. His first objection is to the *arbitrary* character of the assumptions upon which much current historiography is based. This is what lies behind his criticism of the unjustified chauvinistic or nationalistic assumptions made by the various historians in their debate about the origins of Western civilisation. It must be noted that Vico is not suggesting that the utilisation of assumptions is alone enough to invalidate the accounts in question for he invariably exposes their deficiencies on the basis of his own historical arguments which involve a different set of assumptions. The point is, however, that the latter are *not* arbitrary. They can, as we shall see, be justified by considerations of an appropriate nature. Vico is not therefore objecting to the fact that his opponents have made assumptions in their approach to history, nor even to the fact that these are of a chauvinistic kind. The real point of his objection is that they are arbitrary.

Vico's second objection is to the historically naïve manner in which these writers have approached the past. They have shown no awareness of the fact that men's minds are historically conditioned and have attributed to past ages conceptions possible only in later historical times. As a result the histories they have produced have lacked either continuity or coherence[1] for the assumption that certain ideas and institutions have been present throughout history has made it impossible for them to offer satisfactory explanations of those historical times in which the institutions and ideas really were created or given a new development.

In the 'Elements' Vico does not explicitly state the lesson to be drawn from these points. In a later passage, however, after giving an abbreviated account of the above position, he concludes that 'for purposes of this enquiry, we must reckon as if there were no books in the world'.[2] His point is not, of course, that all books should be disregarded, but that nothing should be accepted on the basis of previous scholarship. In other words the whole of historical knowledge must be rebuilt upon a foundation which will enable it to free itself from the errors with which it has so far been tainted. This, however, raises two problems with which the rest of the general elements are concerned: what is a sound epistemological foundation and what is the correct way to conceive the subject matter of history?

[1] *S.N.* 118.   [2] *S.N.* 330.

3

Human nature and social change

Vico offers accounts of four different kinds in the *Scienza Nuova*. There is first a series of determinate historical theses, of which the interpretation of Roman history given in Book II is the most fully developed. Beyond this there is a set of empirical theories about the determinate historico-sociological laws which determine the events involved in the historical accounts and upon knowledge of which our knowledge of the events depends. This set of theories, brought together in the 'ideal eternal history', is expressed largely in the second (i.e. 'more specific') set of elements and in Book IV. Beyond this again there are Vico's metaphysical theories proper, in which he offers an account of the general nature of historical fact and of the concepts necessary to understand it. Finally there are his epistemological and methodological theories, which state the conditions that must be satisfied if we are to have knowledge of historical fact and the methods whereby such knowledge may be reached.

This four-fold classification departs in several ways from classifications propounded by other Vichian commentators. Its most crucial divergence, however, is from the claim, common to both the idealist and Catholic interpretations of Vico, that the determinate laws of history, and hence ultimately the determinate historical facts themselves, are metaphysically determined. In these interpretations there is therefore no such distinction as that suggested above between Vico's metaphysical and empirical theories.[1] I shall indicate my reasons for

[1] In what follows I shall characterise Vico's position in terms of the distinction between metaphysical and historico-sociological theory, even though he does not himself explicitly draw the distinction. I shall argue later that he does draw a distinction correspondent to it and that, at all times, such a distinction is implicit in his work. The word 'philosophical' will be used to refer to his *a priori* theories in general, i.e. to his metaphysical and epistemological theories together.

dissatisfaction with accounts which fail to draw this distinction after I have presented my own case for it.

It is useful to commence with a discussion of Vico's metaphysical theory rather than with his epistemological theory because the latter presupposes the former and should therefore be considered in the light of it. This can be easily seen from the best known statement of Vico's basic epistemological principle in which he asserts that 'the world of civil society has certainly been made by men, and that its principles are therefore to be recovered within the modifications of our own human mind'.[1] Here it is at least a necessary condition of our coming to knowledge of the world of civil society, i.e. the historical world, that we should recover the principles upon which it has been made from within the 'modifications of our own human mind'. To ascertain what sort of modifications Vico is thinking of here we must know upon what sort of principles the human world has been made. It is evident therefore that the correct interpretation of the epistemological claim depends upon that of the metaphysical theory which is mentioned in it.

A further reason why it is convenient to start with Vico's metaphysics is that in the 'Elements', after having devoted the first four axioms to his critique of the basis of current historiographical practice, Vico himself commences with this. By adopting Vico's own order it becomes possible to combine an account of the general character of his theory with a discussion of certain specific considerations with which in his own presentation it is connected.

Before proceeding it is necessary to explain why I have chosen to describe the theories with which this and the next three chapters are concerned as 'metaphysical', since Vico does not himself describe them in this way. In Element XXII he refers to them as a set of 'general' propositions which will provide the 'basis' of his science throughout. I call them 'metaphysical', however, for they state the most ultimate assumptions about the nature of things upon which all else in the *Scienza Nuova* depends. They are necessary, therefore, in the sense that none of the various kinds of explanation to be found in the *Scienza Nuova* can be accepted without them. They are not, however, conceptually necessary, since they can be denied without self-contradiction. Despite this, however, Vico does not offer inde-

[1] *S.N.* 331.

pendent arguments to support or justify them. They are justified by what they make possible. Their acceptability therefore depends upon that of the *Scienza Nuova* in general.

One reason why it is difficult to understand the general metaphysical claim that 'the world of civil society has certainly been made by men'[1] is that Vico gives the terms 'men' and 'making' a special technical sense which depends upon the theories of human nature and historical change that he develops in Elements v–viii, xi–xii and xiv–xv. An elucidation of these elements is therefore necessary if we are to understand the meaning of the general claim. Before undertaking this, however, one further general point must be made. In the *Scienza Nuova* Vico often connects the claim that men have made the world of historical events with another rather more obscure claim, that providence has also played a part in shaping human affairs. Indeed, he claims that it is one of the main functions of his work that it should be a 'demonstration so to speak, of what providence has wrought in human history'.[2] References to the concept of providence therefore abound in the *Scienza Nuova* and they are frequently found in the same passages in which Vico discusses the way in which the historical world is a human product. In the interests of clarity, however, these references will largely be ignored in the present chapter and the topic of providence considered independently in chapter 5.

SOCIAL MAN

Vico introduces his account of human nature and social change by some brief remarks about philosophy in general and the shortcomings of certain older philosophies. If philosophy is to be of practical use it 'must raise and direct weak and fallen man, not rend his nature or abandon him in his corruption'.[3] In the light of this account of the purpose of philosophy, he proceeds to reject certain theories of the Stoics and Epicureans on the grounds that neither have recognised the part played by providence in human affairs. The Stoics have substituted for it the concept of fate, the Epicureans that of chance. Both, moreover, are 'monastic or solitary' philosophers.

[1] *S.N.* 331, 349, 374, 1180. [2] *S.N.* 342.
[3] *S.N.* 129.

The first of these criticisms is directed against rival theories of social and historical causation. Discussion of it may therefore be briefly deferred until Vico's account of this is reached. The second, however, is connected to his account of human nature, in relation to which it must be understood.

Vico's statement of his theory of human nature begins with a claim about the nature of legislation:

Legislation considers man as he is in order to turn him to good uses in human society. Out of ferocity, avarice and ambition, the three vices which run through the human race, it creates the military, merchant and governing classes, and thus the strengths, riches and wisdom of the commonwealths. Out of these three great vices, which could certainly destroy all mankind on the face of the earth, it makes civil happiness.[1]

This introduces a theme which runs throughout the *Scienza Nuova*: the difference between the character of the motives which move men to action and that of the consequences of their actions. The former is wholly destructive, the latter wholly constructive. Vico resolves this paradoxical situation by drawing attention to the importance of the institutional context within which men's actions are performed. Thus, because men live in a society in which there is legislation, i.e. because they live in a legally-structured society, the ferocity, avarice and ambition which inspire them to action, and which could result in their destruction, lead them to become soldiers, merchants and governors and so to contribute to the public good.

It is thus implied that if philosophy is to help man better himself, to 'raise weak and fallen man', it must take cognisance of the importance of the legally-structured social context in which alone man can avoid the consequences of his own vicious nature. Part of the point of Vico's complaint against the Stoics and Epicureans is therefore that, although they had correctly understood the aim of philosophy and had offered rules of conduct purporting to help man improve himself, the recommendations of these philosophers were bound to fail for lack of a sound metaphysical basis, in this case revealed in their failure to acknowledge the dependence of human goods upon an institutional context. The description of these philosophers as 'monastic or

[1] *S.N.* 132.

solitary' is intended to draw attention to this fundamental omission in their work.[1]

The wording of the suggestion that 'legislation considers man as he is in order to turn him to good uses in society' is unfortunate, in that it seems to suggest that legislation is an extra-human agency compelling man to live in society against his nature and thus, that it is contingent that man should live in this way. The next Element, however, makes it clear that this is not Vico's view:

Things do not endure out of their natural state.

In view of the fact that the human race, as far back as the memory of the world goes, has lived and still lives conformably in society, this axiom alone decides the great dispute still waged by the best philosophers and moral theologians against Carneades the sceptic and Epicurus – a dispute which not even Grotius could set at rest – namely, whether law exists by nature or whether man is naturally sociable, which comes to the same thing.[2]

---

[1] These suggestions were by no means new. Indeed, in making them Vico is placing himself firmly in one of the main streams of Italian philosophy, in which ontological primacy has been given to the active and social side of human nature and consciousness as against its theoretical and contemplative side. A large number of Renaissance humanists, including Petrarch, Coluccio Salutati, Leonardo Bruni, Lorenzo Valla and Leon Battista Alberti, had subscribed to some or other version of belief in a necessary relationship between man's humanity and his social and legal environment. In 1451, for example, in words strongly reminiscent of Vico's, Andrea Benzi had asked, 'If the laws were abolished would not every community, every house, every family decay? Would this not result in the destruction of the whole human race?' Even the neo-Platonist Ficino accepted that society provided man with the conditions necessary for the development of those virtues by which he came to imitate properties of God himself. These claims were often accompanied by polemical attacks upon the sterility and inadequacy of monastic and solitary disciplines as a means whereby man could achieve his true end, the development of practical virtue and wisdom. Vico's remarks about the Stoic and Epicurean philosophers are a clear echo of this theme, as is also his claim that philosophy must contribute to fallen man's moral improvement. A further point of contact between Vico and his Renaissance forerunners is to be found in his insistence, shared, for example, with Petrarch, some of whose works he is known to have studied, that knowledge of the natural world is unobtainable whereas that of the human world is not. But the humanists failed to provide the philosophical theories necessary to support these claims so that they failed to survive Descartes's attack upon the purely contingent as a proper object of knowledge (see below, p. 76). Vico's great contribution in this debate is to have tried to provide the framework of philosophical theory necessary to substantiate the epistemological respectability of the human sciences. His work can thus be regarded as an attempt to re-establish many of the humanists' claims but with the greater rigour required in the post-Cartesian world. For the many variations of the above ideas to be found in the works of the various humanists, see Eugenio Garin, *Italian Humanism*, translated by Peter Munz (Oxford 1965), pp. 1–77 especially. The quotation from Benzi is taken from p. 34 of this work.   [2] *S.N.* 134–5.

The identification of the questions whether law exists by nature and whether man is naturally sociable (i.e. is sociable by nature) implies a necessary connection between the concepts of society and law. For Vico society is a legally-structured form of association. There can thus be no question of society being a product of law nor, indeed, of either being other than a necessary consequence of the nature of man.

The latter point can be reinforced by a brief reference to the theories of Carneades and Grotius to which Vico alludes. Carneades had held the view that men imposed laws upon themselves for reasons of expediency, thus implying that it was contingent and not necessary that they should live in society. In *The Law of War and Peace* Grotius, disputing this, had claimed that 'among the traits characteristic of man is an impelling desire for society, that is for the social life – not of any and every sort, but peaceful and organised according to the measure of his intelligence, with those of his own kind'.[1] In claiming that Grotius had failed to settle the dispute, Vico's point would seem to be that the notion of an 'impelling desire' could not support the claim that society was necessary to man since men can have impelling desires for that which is not necessary to them.

In the passage quoted above, Vico presents an argument which appeals both to metaphysical and empirical considerations to support the conclusion that society is necessary to man. The metaphysical principle, that 'things do not settle or endure out of their natural order' (i.e. out of a state that follows from their nature), determines what conclusions are to be drawn from certain facts. The fact that men have always lived in society is thus claimed to establish that such a life is necessary for man. In effect Vico is presenting an *a posteriori* argument to establish something about human nature.

The suggestion is therefore that it follows from the nature of man that he should live in a legally-structured society. This precludes not only the possibility that legislation forces man to live in society against his nature but also Grotius's view that society exists because man has a natural desire for it. In a passage in the Introduction, Vico writes in respect of the property of being social:

In providing for this property God has so ordained and disposed human institutions that men, having fallen from complete justice by original sin, and

[1] *The Law of War and Peace*, translated by F. W. Kelsey (Indianapolis 1925), Prolegomena 6.

while intending almost always to do something quite different and often quite contrary – so that for private utility they would live alone like wild beasts – have been led by the same utility and along the aforesaid different and contrary paths to live like men in justice and to keep themselves in society and thus to preserve their social nature. It will be shown in the present work that this is true of the civil nature of man and thus that law exists in nature.[1]

Society is thus not the product of a desire for social living, for men would, if they could, 'live alone like wild beasts'. Moreover, since 'law exists in nature' it cannot be something that forces man to act against his nature. What in fact legislation forces man to act against is the unconditioned exercise of his individual self-will and the arbitrary satisfaction of his own vicious desires. How it does so remains, of course, to be seen.

In asserting that man is by nature social Vico is locating the ground of society at a more basic level than Grotius. For the latter society cannot be an ultimate concept because it can be explained by something else – human desire informed by human reason. For Vico, however, it can neither be, nor can it be required to be, explained. Man's sociability is fundamental, a principle to be used in explanation but not itself susceptible of explanation. That there are irreduceable social aspects to human history is something therefore to be taken for granted in Vico's Science.

SOCIAL CHANGE

If man's social nature does not require explanation the same is not true of the way in which the different modes of social organisation come into existence, are modified and finally destroyed. It is necessary therefore to see how Vico's account of man's social nature is connected to his account of the nature of social change. This is presented in the form of two associated theories, a theory of common sense and a theory of natural law, in Elements XI and XII:

Human choice, by its nature most uncertain, is made certain and determined by the common sense of men with respect to human needs or utilities, which are the two sources of the natural law of the gentes.

Common sense is judgment without reflection, shared by an entire class, an entire people, an entire nation, or the entire human race.[2]

---

[1] *S.N.* 2.   [2] *S.N.* 141–2.

Vico begins here with two fundamental claims about human choice: uncertain by its own nature, it is made certain by the common sense of men. These claims are best considered in relation to Vico's criticism of Stoic and Epicurean theories of causation, for in them he is trying to express a conception of social causation which constitutes a compromise between these two extremes.

The claim that human choice is uncertain by its nature must be understood in relation to Vico's complaint that the Stoics had erred by introducing the concept of fate into human affairs. Vico's point here is best indicated by the fact that in his mind Spinoza is associated with the Stoics in perpetrating this error.[1] The fate which Vico is concerned to deny is therefore a metaphysical fate of the sort that Spinoza posited. For in the last analysis for Spinoza everything, including every determinate occurrence, follows from the nature of a necessary being, *Deus sive Natura*. This is true both of the actions of men and of the changes in society. It is therefore simply an illusion that man has free-will or that society is in any sense his free creation. Men's actions, although paralleled by mental events, are in no sense explained by them, so that for the explanation both of men's individual actions and of general social change one must look to a necessity resident in the necessary being itself, i.e. to an absolute, unconditioned, metaphysical necessity. Vico's assertion that human choice is *by its nature* uncertain[2] is to be understood therefore not as a denial that human choice is conditioned in some or other way but as a denial that it is metaphysically determined. Human history is thus not to be thought of as the product of some transcendent cosmic necessity.

At the other extreme from metaphysical determinism lies the theory Vico attributes to the Epicureans, i.e. that all that happens is the outcome of pure chance. Applied to the problems with which Vico is concerned this would amount to the claim that the forms of social life are the chance outcome of men's individual activities. It is thus a theory of pure contingency. Vico dismisses this sort of theory on the ground that it is 'refuted by the facts',[3] a study of which reveals that the same sequences and systems of institutions have arisen in all the

---

[1] 'The Stoics, who (in this respect the Spinozists of their day) made God an infinite mind, subject to fate, in an infinite body', *S.N.* 335. See also *S.N.* 1108–9.
[2] *S.N.* 141.   [3] *S.N.* 1109.

nations of the past. In effect, therefore, what he is claiming is that similarities between systems of institutions must indicate a common cause for these institutions and thus rule out the theory of pure contingency.

From these criticisms it is clear that what Vico seeks is an intermediate position reconciling what is true in these views, while jettisoning what is false. The objection to Spinozism reveals his recognition of the necessity to allow for some contingency in human affairs, but the objection to Epicureanism shows that this must not be allowed to deteriorate into a theory of pure chance. The latter objection shows, in fact, that he wants to recognise, as had Spinoza, the law-governed nature of some aspects of the human world but, unlike Spinoza, to stop short of making this all-pervasive. Since the universal character of Spinoza's determinism stems from the metaphysical necessity basic to his system, it is clear that Vico would not allow that human affairs had this sort of necessity.

These considerations are reflected in Vico's account of human choice. The claim that it is 'uncertain by its own nature' is tantamount to a denial that it is determined by some metaphysical necessity. The claim that it is 'made certain and determined by the common sense of man' implies that it is nevertheless conditioned in some way and so represents a denial of any theory of pure chance. Vico has thus denied metaphysical determinism to allow for contingent determination by common sense.

In his theory of common sense Vico makes the following four claims. Common sense is 'judgment without reflection'. It is shared by 'an entire class, an entire people, an entire nation, or the entire human race'. It is concerned with 'human needs or utilities' which are themselves the 'two sources of the natural law of the gentes', and is thus itself the source of these. And it determines human choice.

Although Vico is here presenting a metaphysical theory, i.e. a theory about the nature of the things which determine human activity, it would be useful to consider these points first in connection with two long passages in which he summarises a part of his historico-sociological theory. Since this presupposes the metaphysical theory in question it is possible to gain from it some initial idea of the way in which the latter is to be taken. In the first of these Vico writes:

It is true that men have themselves made this world of nations (and we took this as the first incontestable principle of our Science...) but this world has without doubt issued from a mind often diverse, at times quite contrary and always superior to the particular ends men had proposed to themselves; which narrow ends, made means to serve wider ends, it has always employed to preserve the human race upon this earth. Men mean to gratify their bestial lust and abandon their offspring and they inaugurate the chastity of marriage from which the families arise. The fathers mean to exercise without restraint their paternal power over their clients and they subject them to the civil powers from which the cities arise. The reigning orders of nobles mean to abuse their lordly power over the plebeians and they are obliged to submit to the laws which establish popular liberty...That which did all this was mind, for men did it with intelligence; it was not fate, for they did it with choice; not chance, for the results of their so acting are perpetually the same.[1]

Here Vico sets out a part of his theory about the sequence of social and institutional stages through which, he maintains, under certain conditions, the history of all nations must pass.[2] In itself this is an historico-sociological theory for it refers to a series of determinate historical and social stages of development. But it presupposes Vico's metaphysical theory of causation insofar as he claims that, whenever men act in the ways he describes, the consequences of their actions must also be as he describes them. Moreover, it is clear that Vico thinks of himself here as presenting an application of his theory of common sense since his final assertion that the cause of this sequence is 'mind, for men did it with intelligence', is associated with a denial of the concepts of fate and chance.

A striking feature of the passage is the way in which Vico draws attention to the gap between the reasons for, and the institutional consequences of, men's actions. At a primitive stage men act to satisfy their lust but their actions result in the creation of the institution of marriage. Later the members of the aristocracy want to oppress the plebeians but they succeed instead in creating popular liberty. It might thus seem that human institutions were the unintended and hence chance consequences of human choice. Yet while they are unintended from the point of view of man's initial reasons for undertaking action, Vico's final assertion that men did all this 'with intelligence' shows that it is not the case that at no point do men

---

[1] *S.N.* 1108.

[2] Vico calls this theory the 'ideal eternal history'. This expression will henceforth be adopted.

acquiesce in their creation. There are in fact two kinds of reason or intelligence involved in this conception of causation. There is the reason by which men propose to themselves their particular ends, lust, power and so on, and also some other reason which uses courses of conduct begun for such ends 'as means to its own wider ends'. Moreover, this second kind of intelligence, though contrasted with the intelligence at work in instigating men's particular actions, is not itself superhuman, for Vico insists that, in the end, *men* did all this 'with intelligence'.

Vico is therefore denying that social change rests upon some far-sighted appreciation men have of the benefits of such change, while asserting at the same time, that social institutions nevertheless do rest upon some sort of human intelligence. Further light is thrown upon this obscure claim in the following passage in which Vico again comments upon the gap between individual intention and social change:

But men, because of their corrupted nature, are under the tyranny of self-love, which compels them to make private utility their chief gain. Seeking everything useful for themselves, and nothing for their companions, they cannot bring their passions under control to direct them towards justice. We thereby establish the fact that man in the bestial state desires only his own welfare; having taken wife and begotten children, he desires his own welfare along with that of his family; having entered upon civil life he desires his own welfare along with that of his city; when its rule is extended over several peoples he desires his own welfare along with that of his nation; when the nations are united by wars, treaties of peace, alliances and commerce, he desires his own welfare along with that of the entire human race. In all these circumstances he desires principally his own welfare. Therefore it is only by divine providence that he can be held within these institutions to practice justice as a member of the family, of the city, and finally of mankind. Unable to attain all the utilities he wishes, he is constrained to seek those which are his due; and this is called just. That which regulates all human justice is therefore divine justice which is administered by divine providence to preserve human society.[1]

This passage involves some of the same claims as that quoted above. There is the same sequence of phases of institutional development, going from a purely bestial state, through family life (i.e. some sort of tribal organisation based upon ties of kinship) to civil and national life. There is also the same insistence that the growth of these further systems of institutions is not to be explained by some far-sighted

[1] *S.N.* 341.

25

appreciation of the benefits they bring. Man's nature is 'corrupted' and he acts only for self-love and for 'his own utility'. The claim of Element v, that man is 'weak and fallen' and in a state of 'corruption' is plainly taken for granted in both passages.

But the relationship between man's particular ends and those 'wider ends' referred to in the earlier passage is made much more explicit. Man may never cease to act for what he takes to be his own particular ends, but what he takes these to be depends upon the various institutional rôles he occupies. Thus when he is a father (i.e. the quasi-monarchical leader of a primitive tribe or 'family') he identifies his interests with those of his kin; when he is a citizen he identifies them with those of his city; and when a national with those of his nation.

Certain points stand out here. Vico is insistent that the expansion in man's desires is not the consequence of some developing spirit of altruism for 'in all these circumstances man desires principally his own welfare'. The true explanation for this expansion is that man's decisions are determined by his system of institutions – 'unable to attain all the utilities he wishes he is *constrained by these institutions* to seek those which are his due'.[1] Thus the character of man's institutions determines his social activity. It is because of the way in which man's conception of his self interest is determined by his institutions that his actions, undertaken for what seems to him his own 'particular ends', should serve to promote other 'wider ends'. Thus the 'mind' referred to in the earlier passage as the possessor of these wider ends is not some transcendent, non-human mind but the intelligence of human agents under the determining influence of human institutions.

It is noticeable that the relationship between men's particular or individual ends and these wider, socially-conditioned ends is not described in the same way in the two passages. In the first passage it is not suggested that men's ends are ever simultaneously both particular and socially conditioned, whereas in the second passage it is clear that the same end can have this double character. Thus in the first passage the nobles are described as intending to exercise their power tyrannically over the plebeians but succeeding only in submitting themselves to the laws upon which popular liberty is based.

[1] My italics.

But in the second passage the explanation for the creation of these laws is that man 'having entered upon civil life, desires his own welfare along with that of his city'. There is thus an apparent discrepancy between the first passage, which explains the creation of popular liberty as the unintended consequence of actions undertaken for different reasons, and the second, which implies that its creation is based upon a realisation of certain benefits it offers.

The difficulty here is more apparent than real and the way to its resolution is indicated by the claim, in the second passage, that man, 'unable to attain all those utilities he wishes, is constrained by these institutions to seek those which are his due'. This makes it clear that the particular ends towards which man's activities may initially be directed constitute a larger class than the wider ends which are fulfilled by social change. It is thus possible for those changes which fulfil wider ends to be both a fulfilment of some particular ends and a denial of others. Vico is therefore claiming that among the many reasons for which an individual may initially undertake a specific course of activity, only some will be fulfilled in any new institutional change and these will be those in which, by virtue of their common social conditioning, his interests are identical with those of others.

It must be noted also that institutions determine the direction of human activity by means of their effect upon man's beliefs about what is just or what is due to him. These beliefs determine what new sets of social relationships are acceptable and, hence, can endure. In effect, therefore, Vico is suggesting that any (new) set of institutional arrangements must always involve underlying agreement about the justice of the practices they make possible and that the determinate content of this depends upon the previous institutions of the system.

COMMON SENSE

To explicate the above theory more fully and to understand its significance within Vico's thought, it is necessary to return to the account of common sense given in Elements XI and XII, where it was said 'to make certain and determine' human choice, itself by nature 'uncertain'. It is evident that what Vico is offering in place of Epicurean and Spinozistic theories of causation is a theory of social conditioning. He is not, of course, asserting that human beings can desire only those things which are a product of their social conditioning. The fact that the class of things that men may desire and have desired is wider than that which their institutions lead them to want makes this clear. The 'human choices' which are determined by common sense are only those on which social practices rest. What Vico is claiming therefore is that social decision is determined by common sense.

Vico's use of the term 'common sense' is most significant here, for it indicates the strong connection between the theory he is advocating and the question of the metaphysical categories necessary for a correct approach to the understanding of history. In the seventeenth and early eighteenth centuries a number of such theories had sprung up as thinkers tried to explain the similarities they found in the myths of the various ancient nations and between these and the various religious rites and practices which the missionaries had found in the non-Christian worlds, especially in China and the East. One way of explaining these similarities adopted by thinkers such as Hyde, Cudworth and Lecomte, had been to posit some body of belief common to all nations past and present. Grotius had held a weaker version of this theory, claiming that the only beliefs common to all nations were those which sprang from man's natural capacity to grasp rational or *a priori* truths. The piecemeal but steady advance of historical scholarship in the later seventeenth century had, as its implications become clearer, thrown considerable doubt upon the plausibility of such views. As a consequence of the work of the philologists, and particularly that of Jean Le Clerc, many thinkers had begun to recognise the extent to which the beliefs of a nation were dependent upon the historical and social conditions in which they were formed. Recognition of this fact tended, in fact, though Le Clerc himself did not go this far, to be taken as implying that there were no beliefs at all common to all historical societies.

It had been left to Bayle, however, to draw out the philosophical consequences of this view. The French thinker had pointed out that one conclusion that could be drawn from insistence upon the purely historical character of human belief was that the beliefs of one historical society would be unknowable to the inhabitants of later societies not sharing the same historical conditions. The thesis of historical conditioning led to that of the autonomy of historical systems of belief and thus to the ultimate unknowability of the historical past, i.e. to historical pyrrhonism.

In the *Scienza Nuova* Vico takes issue with Bayle over only the apparently limited issue of the possibility of a purely atheistic society.[1] But this disagreement is of the utmost importance for it is the consequence of a more fundamental disagreement over the question whether there are any beliefs at all common to all societies. For while Vico's grasp of the fact of historical conditioning would not allow him to agree with those who held that all beliefs were common to all societies, he accepted the presupposition of Bayle's argument, that if there were none at all that were common to all societies historians would be denied any possibility of understanding the past. What is really at issue in the dispute over the possibility of a purely atheistic society is the question whether there can be a society such that no historical knowledge of it whatever is possible.

Vico's position on the question of common sense is therefore an attempt to find a metaphysical theory that would enable him to allow for the knowability of the human past without denying its historical and conditioned character. It is unfortunate, however, that in the statement of his theory of common sense in Elements xi and xii he confines his references to those aspects of past systems of belief that develop only at particular stages of institutional organisation and which thus, though common to all nations *at some time* in their history, are not common to all nations at all times.

This can be seen from the claim that common sense is 'shared by an entire class,' an entire people, an entire nation or the entire human race'. Common sense is here the possession of peoples whose institutions are at varying levels of integration. It is, of course, possible for various kinds of common sense to co-exist, as, for example, the common sense proper to a class within a nation and that proper to the nation within which the class exists, and, indeed, it is difficult to see how this could fail to be the case. Nevertheless, it is not Vico's intention to suggest that the common sense proper to 'the entire human race' (i.e. to the most general of the above classifica-

[1] *S.N.* 334, 1110. For an extremely illuminating account of Vico's relationship to Bayle and Le Clerc set in the context of the general state of historical scholarship in the seventeenth and early eighteenth centuries, see *Vico e Bayle: Premesse Per un Confronto*, by Gianfranco Cantelli (Guida Editori, Napoli 1971).

tions) represents a system of beliefs common to all peoples at all times, for what is offered here is an account of the philosophical distinctions underlying his historico-sociological claims. This is evident from the fact that the above Elements give a purely formal account of those changing systems of organisation involved in the 'ideal eternal history'. Thus in the passage quoted earlier, Vico asserts:

man in the bestial state desires only his own welfare; having taken wife and begotten children, he desires his own welfare along with that of his family; having entered upon civil life, he desires his own welfare along with that of his city; when its rule is extended over several peoples, he desires his own welfare along with that of the nation; when the nations are united by wars, treaties of peace, alliances, and commerce, he desires his own welfare along with that of the entire human race.

The suggestion here is that man's desires are conditioned by the various systems of institutions in which he lives, which themselves develop according to a definite historico-sociological sequence. There is no suggestion that any class is ever-present in the sequence, hence that any of these systems of common sense belief could be common to all historical societies at all times. Moreover, the desires proper to the 'whole human race' are explicitly said to arise 'when the nations are united by wars, treaties of peace, alliances and commerce', i.e. at a certain stage only in the historico-sociological sequence. It is clear therefore that in this passage, and in Elements XI and XII in which he sets out the philosophical distinctions involved, Vico is dealing only with those aspects of common sense which change in history. He is, in effect, setting out the concepts by means of which he intends to allow for the fact of historical conditioning.

To discover the common sense that belongs to all nations at all times and through which Vico hopes to demonstrate the possibility of historical knowledge, it is necessary to turn to three other propositions which he frequently describes as the three 'first principles of his science'. The principles in question are the institutions of religion, marriage and burial of the dead, regarded by Vico as so important that a separate chapter of Book I is devoted to them. Their character is clearly brought out in the following passage:

Now since the world of nations has been made by men, let us see in which institutions all men agree and always have agreed. For these institutions will be able to give us the universal and eternal principles (such as every science must have) on which all nations were founded and still preserve themselves.

We observe that all nations, barbarous as well as civilised, though separately founded because remote from each other in time and space, keep these three human customs: all have some religion, all contract solemn marriages, all bury their dead. And in no nation, however savage and crude, are any human actions performed with more elaborate ceremonies and more sacred solemnity than the rites of religion, marriage and burial. For, by the axiom that 'uniform ideas, born among peoples unknown to each other, must have a common ground of truth', it must have been dictated to all nations that from these three institutions humanity began among them all, so that the world should not again become a bestial wilderness. For this reason we have taken these three eternal and universal customs as three first principles of this Science.[1]

Two points are of special importance here: the claims that the specified institutions give 'the universal and eternal principles upon which all nations were founded and still preserve themselves' and that they must be maintained 'so that the world should not again become a bestial wilderness'. These show that the institutions in question are common to all nations at all times in their history and that this is so because they are necessary conditions of civilised life.

The common sense that belongs to all nations at all times is therefore composed of the beliefs that correspond to, and are necessary for the maintenance of, these institutions. These are the beliefs that there is a provident divinity, that human passions ought to be moderated and that the human soul is immortal.[2]

It might seem an objection to the claim that Vico is here presenting a metaphysical theory that he should seek to support it by an appeal to evidence, for this might be taken to imply that it is an empirical discovery within his Science. To show that this is not the correct way to understand the status of the theory of common sense it will be convenient to consider briefly how Vico supports it.

In general he does this in two ways: by claiming that there is no empirical evidence of any exceptions to his theory and by presenting arguments to show why there could not be any exceptions to it.

To understand the significance of Vico's claim that there are no empirical exceptions to his three principles it is necessary to recall his general view that 'things do not settle or endure out of their natural

---

[1] *S.N.* 332–3.　　　　　　　　　　[2] *S.N.* 130.

state'.[1] This, in effect, asserts a connection between certain empirical features of the world and certain metaphysical features, thus allowing empirical evidence to be used in *a posteriori* arguments on behalf of metaphysical truths. Thus understood the present claim is that since there have never been any societies in which these three kinds of institutions and their attendant beliefs have failed to obtain it must follow from the nature of society that they should obtain.

The status Vico wishes to assign to these propositions comes out more clearly from two arguments he presents in support of the second and third principles. On behalf of the claim that marriage is an institution necessary to any human society he adduces the following argument. Let us suppose that marriage were not to arise but that people were to continue to procreate, then parents

since they are held together by no necessary bond of law will proceed to cast off their natural children. Since their parents may separate at any time, the children, abandoned by both, must lie exposed to be devoured by dogs. If humanity, public or private does not bring them up, they will have to grow up with no one to teach them religion, language or any other human custom. So that, as for them, they are bound to cause this world of nations, enriched and adorned by so many fine arts of humanity, to revert to the great ancient forest through which in their nefarious feral wanderings once roamed the foul beasts of Orpheus, amongst whom bestial venery was practised by sons with mothers and by fathers with daughters.[2]

The general run of this argument is fairly clear. The progress of civilisation requires that the achievements of one generation should be handed on to the next by the transmission of certain human habits through public or private teaching. If there were no such institution as marriage (i.e. legalised marriage, involving a 'necessary bond of law' and, hence, legal duties and obligations) these conditions would not be satisfied, for without the enforceability of duty that marriage brings people would simply abandon their offspring to die or to decline into bestiality. In effect, the prolongation and development of civilisation depends upon there being institutions to compel people to do what they otherwise would not.

The argument assumes that unmarried parents would not do all that the institution of marriage obliges them to do simply out of some natural love they might have for their children. It could therefore be

[1] *S.N.* 134–5. [2] *S.N.* 336.

defeated simply by denying the assumption. It is important to note that Vico here presents no argument in support of the assumption. It is perhaps for this reason that it has been suggested that 'proofs like those of the universalisability of marriage and burial depend upon analyses of the concepts involved: they show that all human societies observe those customs because a society that did not would not be "human" but "feral"'.[1] However, it is clear that Vico cannot be appealing to an analysis of the concepts involved since there is no purely conceptual contradiction in the idea of a society which lacked the institution of marriage. The real reason why Vico presents no argument against the possibility that unmarried parents might look after and educate their children is that it has already been ruled out by the view, presented in the 'Elements', that man is 'weak and fallen' and subject to the vices of 'ferocity, avarice and ambition'.[2] This account of human nature, not in itself necessary since to deny it implies no contradiction, has the status of being necessary or unchallengeable within the system of concepts by means of which Vico is seeking to explain human history.

This can be confirmed by a brief mention of the argument by which Vico defends his third principle, the institution of burial based upon belief in the immortality of the soul:

Finally [to realise] what a great principle of humanity burial is, imagine a feral state in which human bodies remain unburied on the surface of the earth as food for crows and dogs. Certainly this bestial custom will be accompanied by uncultivated fields and uninhabited cities. Men will go about like swine eating the acorns found amidst the putrefaction of their dead.[3]

The claim here is that failure to bury the dead would bring disease and inhibit social advance. It is not, however, suggested that an advanced society without burial is a conceptual impossibility for Vico's argument depends upon certain general assumptions, such as that the human body is mortal, that it putrifies when left unburied, that contact with putrified matter is a cause of disease and that diseased persons are unable to concern themselves with the creation of socially desireable practices. All this being assumed true, civilised life, it is claimed, would simply disappear if the institution of

---

[1] *Philosophy of History*, by Alan and Barbara Donagan (New York 1965), p. 8.
[2] *S.N.* 129, 132–3.   [3] *S.N.* 337.

burial were not to be adopted. The conclusion of the argument is thus a straightforward deductive consequence of the general assumptions Vico has made about the nature of things. Consequently it shares with them the status of being unchallengeable within his Science.

From these considerations two points emerge. First, Vico's account of the status of his first principles is connected to certain assumptions he makes about the generic nature of historical agents, which form part of a set of conditions claimed to be necessary to all human societies. Second, since the assumptions about the generic nature of historical agents are unchallengeable within the system of concepts Vico is formulating, a similar status must be shared by the three sociological principles he deduces from them. Thus the principles of religion, marriage and burial of the dead are all unchallengeable, and hence not empirically falsifiable, within Vico's Science.

What is common to the history of all nations at all times is therefore a set of sociological conditions and a set of characteristics of mankind necessary for their operation. The common sense that is common to all nations at all times consists of those beliefs that lead men to maintain the institutions in question, i.e. the beliefs that there is a provident divinity, that the passions ought to be controlled and moderated (or that one ought to pursue a virtuous life),[1] and that the human soul is immortal. It will be noted that these beliefs are stated very generally, to allow for the fact that the conception of a provident divinity can vary widely in different historical societies, from the polytheism of Homeric man to the monotheism of fully human man, and that similar historical differences can obtain in relation to men's conceptions of what is virtuous and in what the immortality of the human soul consists. But in the end, Vico's claim is that it is a necessary condition of any historical society, i.e. any society that can have a history, that its institutions involve these three beliefs of common sense. His dismissal of Bayle's thesis that a society of atheists is possible[2] rests upon this claim.

There are thus two kinds of common sense in Vico's Science. There is what for convenience's sake I shall call 'absolute' common sense, i.e. the three beliefs mentioned above, which are necessary to any

[1] *S.N.* 504.
[2] 'Bayle affirms in his treatise on comets that people can live in justice without the light of God', *S.N.* 334.

possible historical society, given man's nature as it is, and which are therefore common to all nations at all times in their history. There is, further, what may be called 'relative' common sense, i.e. those beliefs that belong to a nation or to some sub-section of a nation, at some determinate period in its history, which are therefore also common to all nations at some time in their histories. By means of this double conception of common sense Vico hopes to establish the generic identity of the historian with his subject, i.e. of man as historian with man as historical agent, without at the same time denying the historical and social differences that may obtain between them.

One further point must be made about common sense: its description as 'judgment without reflection'. This is a further consequence of Vico's desire to find a conception of human nature that would allow for its capacity to change in history. This is most easily shown by reference again to the debate which took place both before and during Vico's life concerning the significance of the myths of the past. Prior to Le Clerc's critical enquiries, the most widely held view had been that the myths were allegories which embodied certain religious and philosophical truths at all times accessible to human reason and hence susceptible of historical rediscovery by other rational beings. Le Clerc's investigations had, however, emphasised the unhistorical character of the various versions of this theory and had emphasised the need to replace such interpretations by others that connected the myths with the various historical circumstances in which they had been created. He, himself, took this methodological rule so literally that he often tried to present the myths as accounts of actual historical events. Although Vico did not accept Le Clerc's specific interpretations of myth, he did accept the main general presupposition upon which these were based: that interpretations of myth must take into account the historical conditions in which they were created.[1] He thus opposed both the allegorical interpretations them-

---

[1] The extent to which Vico was directly influenced by Le Clerc is problematic. Vico sent Le Clerc copies of the *De Uno*, *De Constantia*, and the first *Scienza Nuova* (1725), the first two of which were favourably reviewed. But there are no direct references to Le Clerc in these works or in the second *Scienza Nuova*, even in matters, such as the interpretations of myth, where Vico would be expected to be interested in Le Clerc's work. Vico's references tend to be to figures such as Casaubon, van Heurn, Wits, Selden, Grotius and Huet, all of whom wrote well before the period 1680–1710 in which Le Clerc's investigations were carried out and

selves and the conception of human nature as necessarily rational upon which they rested.

The description of common sense as 'judgment without reflection' therefore indicates a desire to find a conception of human nature that would allow for the less rational character of man's history in its early stages as well as its more rational character in its later stages. The 'reflection' Vico is concerned to deny is rational reflection of the sort that, for example, Grotius had believed held men together in society, which made it impossible to recognise any less than rational phase of human history. In asserting the *unreflective* character of the beliefs of common sense Vico is denying that their content is determined by any rational apprehension of eternal truths. What determines common sense beliefs is not some *a priori* grasp of the truth of those beliefs but the social conditioning to which the institutions of a system expose people.

Vico did not intend, of course, to deny that man could develop those capacities later called 'rational' nor that when he did so they might not be operative in determining his activities. Indeed, he claims that at a later stage of the 'ideal eternal history' this is bound to occur. But the necessity for it at that stage is a consequence of the determinate content of common sense as it is then conditioned and not of the very idea of a common sense. In other words it is historically but not metaphysically necessary. The concept of common sense thus entails that for all individuals of the same social kind, i.e. conditioned by the same institutions, there must be an identity of social attitudes and beliefs but not that all social beliefs are rational.

were under public discussion. This circumstance has been used to support the view that Vico was not up-to-date in his learning. In his *Vico e Bayle: Premesse Per Un Confronto*, Cantelli has disputed this conclusion, pointing out that many other writers of the period preferred to present their views as discussions of the great figures of the past rather than by direct reference to their own contemporaries. Moreover, Cantelli goes on to point to a most impressive list of points on which there is a very close correspondence between the views of Le Clerc and Vico, including, amongst other things, their common objections to Selden, Mossius, Huet, Marsham and Spencer, their insistence upon the non-allegorical significance of myth, their denial of the ancient wisdom of the legislators, their reduction of many fables to profane history, their beliefs in the isolation of the Hebrews and of all other nations at the start of their histories, in the barbarism of first peoples and in the methodological principle that in interpreting history one must not attribute to former peoples one's own religious and philosophical concepts. In view of this it seems impossible not to accept Cantelli's conclusion that Vico was well acquainted with the state of recent philological and historical research and, in particular, with the work of Le Clerc.

NATURAL LAW

The connection between common sense and historical and social change is stated in the claims that common sense is about 'human needs and utilities' and that such judgements are 'the two sources of the natural law of the gentes'. In the general Elements human needs and utilities are mentioned as though they were the only objects of common sense and thus as though it was a metaphysical truth that common sense is about them. This is not, however, what Vico means to suggest for in a later Element he writes: 'Men first feel necessity, then look for utility, next attend to comfort still later amuse themselves with pleasure, thence grow dissolute in luxury and finally grow mad and waste their substance.'[1]

Here necessity and utility form only the first items in a sequence that is intended to assert the changing determinants of the content of natural law throughout the entire history of any nation, i.e. throughout the entire 'ideal eternal history'. It is thus clearly not an *a priori* or eternal truth that common sense is about human needs and utilities but rather an historico-sociological truth, for there can be, and there are, historico-sociological conditions under which it has a different content.

To understand the expression 'natural law of the gentes' it is necessary to draw a distinction between two kinds of law. On one side there is enacted law, the formal product of properly constituted legal mechanisms. On the other there are the conceptions of what is socially right and just, which affect the way in which people feel about their lives, their institutions and their society at a much more fundamental level. The second of these, but not the first, can be a source of movements which aim to change institutions and modes of life. And it is to this, which may or may not be satisfied by a given set of institutional practices at any one time, that Vico means to refer by the phrase 'natural law of the gentes'.[2]

The fundamental character of natural law is well brought out in a series of remarks Vico makes about the difference between natural law and enacted law. These occur towards the end of the 'Elements' in a

[1] *S.N.* 241.
[2] For an historical account of Vico's derivation of the expression, see T. G. Bergin and M. H. Fisch, *The New Science of Giambattista Vico* (New York 1968), pp. XXVII–XXX.

passage in which he re-addresses himself to the question whether man is by nature sociable, i.e. whether it is necessary or contingent that man should exist in society. He quotes first with approval the remark of Dio Chrysostom that 'custom is like a king and law like a tyrant; which we must understand as referring to reasonable custom and to law not animated by natural reason'. He then adds:

This axiom decides by implication the great dispute 'whether law resides in nature or in the opinion of men', which comes to the same thing as that propounded in the corollary of Axiom VIII, 'whether man is naturally sociable'. In the first place, the natural law of the gentes was instituted by custom (which Dio says commands us by pleasure like a king) and not by law (which Dio says commands us by force like a tyrant). For it began in human customs springing from the common nature of nations (which is the adequate subject of our Science) and it preserves human society. Moreover there is nothing more natural (for there is nothing more pleasant) than observing human customs. For all these reasons, human nature, in which such customs have had their origin, is sociable.

The natural law of the gentes came forth with the customs (*è uscito coi costumi*)[1] of the nations, conforming one with another in virtue of a common human sense, without any reflection and without one nation following the example of another.[2]

By linking natural law with human custom and insisting that both spring from the nature of nations, i.e. from the sociable aspect of human nature, Vico makes it clear that it is necessary that men should have natural law. The two are harnessed by common sense, i.e. by the beliefs that men develop in their various institutional rôles.

In asserting that the natural law of the gentes is based upon common sense judgements about human needs and utilities, Vico is claiming that communal conceptions of what is right and just arise from the necessities and utilities people feel in their institutional and social capacities. He does not, however, mean to imply that because human judgement is involved these conceptions are in any sense arbitrary. They are, on the contrary, the necessary consequences of the beliefs, attitudes and modes of thought that are attached to any given institutional rôle. They are objective therefore in the sense of being seen as necessary by all who share such a rôle. For all others, however, they will have no compulsion at all.

[1] I have altered Bergin and Fisch's translation of this phrase from 'is coeval with' to 'comes forth with' to capture the sense of both being a product of common sense.
[2] *S.N.* 308–11.

The latter point provides one of the main reasons for Vico's dissatisfaction with the static conceptions of natural law he found in the works of Grotius, Selden and Pufendorf. Though Vico admired these thinkers for their recognition of the importance of normative belief in any system of social relationships, he was nevertheless strongly opposed, on historical grounds, to their attempts to show that one system of natural law had been, and must be, common to all societies. He located one source of their mistake in the assumption that a law that is objective given one system of social institutions (i.e. their own) must be objective given any system whatsoever.[1] For this assumption fails to allow for the intimate connection between the historically conditioned character of institutions and the content of natural law.

In its place Vico offers an historical conception of natural justice as one of the determining conditions of social change. The institutional context in which, at any given period in history, man finds himself conditions future social change by conditioning the conceptions of natural justice upon which such change must rest. The concept of natural justice is thus a social concept, i.e. one whose content is to be explained by the social organisation of the times in which it arises. It is also, however, an historical concept for it is conditioned by the historical circumstances in which it arises and is itself a determining condition of any further historical change. That is why Vico writes of fallen man that 'unable to attain all the utilities he wishes, he is constrained by these institutions to seek those which are his due and this is called just'.[2] This is not, of course, to say that when historical agents try to change some or other aspect of their society they know from the start the form this change will finally take. They may, and most likely will, act from any of a number of selfish reasons that appeal to them. But when it comes to the question what new social institutions will result from these activities, this depends not upon personal and idiosyncratic ambitions but upon what seems just to everybody in the light of the necessities they feel in their various institutional rôles.

---

[1] 'For they [Grotius, Selden and Pufendorf] believed that natural equity in its perfect form had been understood by the gentile nations from their first beginnings; they did not reflect that it took some two thousand years for philosophers to appear in any of them', *S.N.* 329. See also *S.N.* 313, 318, 394, 972, 974.

[2] *S.N.* 341.

Accordingly there is a double relationship between institutions and natural law. A given institutional system makes possible a way of life that seemed just to its creators. It also provides the basis of whatever new conception of justice will be embodied in its historical successor. Why it should have a successor, however, is not something that can be explained, nor does Vico try to do so, without recourse to the activities of individual man acting for his own ends. It is individual man's vicious and corrupt nature that creates his dissatisfaction with any given institutional system and drives him on to change it. It is, on the other hand, the socialised aspect of man's nature that determines what forms institutional change will take.

Vico is thus quite justified in denying both fate and chance. Chance is ruled out for he has produced a theory in which history is determined. But fate equally is ruled out for it is only the general pattern of historical change *if there is change* that is determined. But for the history of any actual society to exhibit such a pattern will require also the exercise of their free will by the individuals of that society.

CONCLUSION

Vico's theory can be summarised in the following way. Human institutions undergo constant change and are a product of human choice. Individual actions, inspired by self-centred motives, are the efficient causes of this change. Its character, however, is determined immediately, by a system of rights, duties and obligations, and mediately, by the institutional needs and utilities man feels, upon which this system itself rests. The notion of a common sense serves to stress the fact that when men share an institutional or social situation they will feel the same social needs and seek and accept the same solutions as one another. It thus emphasises the fact that the beliefs, presuppositions and attitudes which determine men's social activity are social phenomena.

It is a most important feature of this account that institutions not only give rise to (judgements of) new needs and utilities but also satisfy former needs and utilities. Institutions, in other words, necessarily satisfy social aims. They thus always have a *rationale* in the sense that they can be understood only by a grasp of those needs for the satisfaction of which they exist.

By insisting upon the necessary character of these relationships Vico is drawing attention to the fact that they are a consequence of the nature of things – in their case, the nature of man himself. He has therefore produced the basis of a programme for the explanation of things which, in fact, justifies the manner in which he himself sets about this in the more purely historical parts of the *Scienza Nuova*. The adoption of certain social practices is not to be explained by reference solely to efficient causes, in the manner adopted by the advocates of the transmission theory of the origins of civilisation. They must be shown to satisfy certain necessities of human nature. Thus, for example, when Vico has demonstrated the various anomalies involved in attempts to explain the similarities in the myths of ancient nations as a consequence of their causal transmission from one nation to another, he does not offer another account of this type. Instead, myths 'had their beginnings in the public needs or utilities of the peoples'.[1] Their interpretation must therefore proceed in the light of some or other claims about what these needs and utilities were.

It will be seen, moreover, that in producing the theory here explicated, Vico has solved the problem of historical scepticism raised by Bayle, in a manner consistent with the principle of historical relativity. Man is not cut off from his own past because the historian shares the same metaphysical nature as the historical agent. It is legitimate for the historian to apply to history explanations which are formally of the same kind as those applicable to his own society and to make certain assumptions about the most basic content of the nature of all human beings. This does not, however, do violence to the principle of historical relativity since it implies only that the historian and his subject must have some general metaphysical features in common and does not preclude the possibility of very considerable differences in the kinds of society in which they live, or the life-styles and sets of beliefs they adopt. It is clear therefore that in offering such a theory Vico is in no way guilty of making suggestions that would result in the production of unhistorical accounts of the past.

[1] *S.N.* 51.

4

Human nature and historical change

Vico's theory of social change implies a theory of historical change. Social changes are determined immediately by man's conception of what is right and mediately by the needs and utilities men are constrained to feel in the institutional contexts in which they play out their lives. These contexts have, however, themselves been created to satisfy former needs and utilities, thus implying the dependence of the character of the institutions of one historical period upon that of its predecessor. Vico is therefore posed with the problem of giving an account of the nature of this dependence. His principal formal statement of it is made in Elements xiv and xv:

> The nature of institutions is nothing but their coming into being at certain times and with certain guises. Whenever the time and guise are thus and so, such and not otherwise are the institutions that come into being.
>
> The inseparable properties of institutions must be due to the modification or guise with which they are born. By these properties we may therefore verify that the nature or birth was thus and not otherwise.[1]

These axioms express a very strong relationship between the conditions under which institutions arise (i.e. their times and modifications or guises) and their natures. Times and modifications are presented first as the sufficient conditions of institutions for whenever they have a certain character (are 'thus and so') this is shared by the institutions. Yet institutions are also sufficient conditions of times and modifications for, from the properties of the former, we may verify those of the latter. But if p is a sufficient condition of q, q is a necessary condition of p, and if q is a sufficient condition of p, p is a

[1] *S.N.* 147–8.

42

necessary condition of q. It follows therefore that times and modifications are both sufficient and necessary conditions of institutions and institutions sufficient and necessary conditions of times and modifications.

The reference made here to modifications or guises raises a difficult issue of interpretation. If these are taken to be identical with the judgements of common sense, Vico will be doing no more than reiterating the point already established, that institutions necessarily satisfy human needs and utilities. He will not thus be offering an account of some further principle concerning the conditions which govern the development of common sense itself.

The idealist interpreters of Vico have rejected this sort of account, offering in its place an interpretation in which they lay stress upon the connection between the concept of a modification and that of a metaphysic of the human mind which is also prominent in the *Scienza Nuova*. But by identifying the latter with the Hegelian concept of Reason, and thus claiming that it is deducible *a priori*, they have used it to ascribe to Vico a metaphysical determinism of the sort discussed and rejected as inappropriate in the last chapter.

To show that Vico is here presenting a principle which is neither a mere restatement of the relationship between common sense and human institutions, nor a pre-statement of the Hegelian notion of Objective Reason, it is necessary to turn to other references to the modifications in question. These are most usually made in connection with Vico's basic epistemological claim that since 'the world of civil society has certainly been made by men...its principles are therefore to be found within the modifications of our own human mind'.[1] In statements such as this, however, Vico merely mentions the modifications without giving examples of them. What is required is a passage in which Vico gives examples of the modifications, intending his examples to be understood as a direct application of the metaphysical principle under consideration. The most striking passage of this sort occurs in Book II in connection with Vico's account of the religious beliefs of the first, primitive, men:

From these first men, stupid, insensate and horrible beasts, all the philosophers and philologians should have begun their investigations of the ancient gentiles...And they should have begun with metaphysics, which seeks its

---

[1] *S.N.* 331.

proofs not in the external world but within the modifications of the mind of him who meditates it. For since this world has certainly been made by men, it is within these modifications that its principles should have been sought. And human nature, so far as it is like that of animals, carries with it this property, that the senses are its sole way of knowing things.

Hence poetic wisdom, the first wisdom of the gentile world, must have begun with a metaphysics not rational and abstract like that of learned men now, but felt and imagined as that of these first men must have been, who, without power of ratiocination, were all robust sense and vigorous imagination.[1]

Vico then goes on to show how primitive man, because he was a creature of the senses and the imagination and not of the intellect, believed only what was apprehended by the senses or produced by his own imagination. Given certain associative and natural principles which determine the working of the imagination, Vico demonstrates how, as a consequence of his imaginative nature, primitive man's religion,[2] language,[3] and other institutions took on a certain character. These institutions, of course, fulfil certain needs. Nevertheless, both their character and that of the needs they fulfil are conditioned by these fundamental, albeit general, characteristics of the minds of these first men, characteristics which pervade and colour their every activity, belief and creation. It is clear from the above extract that these are the modifications to which Vico is referring.[4]

Part of what Vico is asserting in Elements XIV and XV is thus that certain fundamental, general characteristics of the human mind are among the determining conditions of human institutions. Since they give a certain character to *all* the institutions of a given kind of man, they are not individuating conditions of institutions, i.e. they are responsible not for the differences between the institutions of any

---

[1] *S.N.* 374–5.   [2] *S.N.* 377.   [3] *S.N.* 375.

[4] In the light of this example it is useful to draw attention to the word *guisa* which Vico gives as a synonym for *modificazione*. One of the meanings of *guisa* is 'mode' in the sense in which this is distinguished from 'substance'. The substance–mode distinction has often been employed to indicate the relationship between mind and its various different ways of functioning, as, for example, by Descartes in the *Principles of Philosophy*, Part I, Principles XI and XXXII. Malebranche, on the other hand, used the terms 'modification' and 'mode' interchangeably and regarded the understanding, the imagination and the senses as merely three different modes or modifications of thinking substance. It has been suggested by A. Corsano (*G. B. Vico* (Bari 1956), pp. 220–1) that Vico's use of *modificazione* may derive from that of Malebranche. To take *guisa* in this sense of 'mode' would be consistent with the interpretation offered above.

given kind of man, but for the differences between the whole of these and the whole of those of some other kind of man. Common sense thus explains why, within a given society, there should be institutions for, say, safeguarding the laws or determining the political succession, but the modifications of the human mind explain a certain unity of character which pervades all the institutions of a given society. This is not therefore to deny that institutions satisfy the felt needs of social man. It is to add to this the claim that these needs are themselves conditioned not merely by characteristics peculiar to the specific institutional context in which they arose, but also by certain general mental characteristics common to the whole society of which these institutions are a part.

The second condition mentioned in the elements is the 'time' at which an institution arises. Vico uses the concept of time to indicate a certain stage in the order of development of the modifications of the human mind by which institutions and common sense themselves are ultimately affected. The modifications mentioned in the example quoted above represent the basic mental characteristics of the poetic age or time, so called because at that stage in the development of the human mind men cannot fail to attribute sentience and life to all they perceive and this, in turn, must be reflected in all their normative beliefs and institutions. But at another 'time', i.e. at another stage of development, men's capacities will assume a quasi-logical character, which in turn will also be reflected in their common sense, in their institutions and so on.

By including the time at which an institution is born as one of the determining conditions of its character Vico is offering his account of the historical category by means of which the error he calls the 'conceit of scholars', i.e. the error of conceptual anachronism, is to be avoided. For what he is doing is, in effect, to introduce into his metaphysical framework, a category which will allow for the notion of conceptual development in history. The error involved in the 'conceit of scholars' springs, on Vico's view, from the mistaken assumption that the ideas and institutions of all historical ages are the products of a human nature whose character is fixed and constant throughout history. Vico's own claim, that the 'times' of the 'modification' of mind is a fundamental condition of the character of ideas and institutions, allows, on the contrary, that human nature itself may develop in history and that such development will be responsible for the difference in ideas and institutions at different periods of history.

This can perhaps best be made clear by reference to Vico's account of the history of natural law and his criticism of certain alternative theories. Vico's attitude to the classical natural law theorists was ambivalent.[1] On the one hand he admired them for their recognition of the socially cohesive function of natural law, even though, as we have seen, his own theory differed from those of the natural law theorists by making men's conception of their natural rights rest upon something yet more basic, i.e. their common historically and socially conditioned natures. Despite his admiration for this aspect of their theories, however, Vico also criticises them for their failure to allow for the historically different social and conceptual conditions which affect the content of natural law at different times. What he charges them with is having analysed the content of natural law in one particular age, i.e. in their own relatively sophisticated and enlightened age, and then assuming the adequacy of this analysis for natural law throughout history. In their analyses of the concept as it obtained in their own age they had laid great weight upon the central rôle of the notion of natural equity. To explain man's capacity to understand this they had therefore found it necessary to endow him with a faculty of reason by which he could grasp eternal truths. They had thus offered a rationalist account both of man's nature and of the content of natural law. From here, however, they had gone on to assume that man had always had such a rational capacity and that natural law had always rested upon an appreciation of necessary truths. They had accordingly been led to interpret the institutions and customs of former ages in the light of this assumption. In effect, therefore, they had committed the error of the 'conceit of scholars' in respect of the history of law.

Vico refers to this conception of natural law as the 'natural law of the philosophers' and describes it as the belief that 'natural equity in its perfect form had been understood by the gentile nations from their

---

[1] The authors most often quoted are Selden, Pufendorf and Grotius, described, at one point, with no intended irony, as the 'three princes of the natural law of the gentes' (*S.N.* 329). Of these three, however, Grotius is singled out as having made the most significant contribution to our understanding of society and in the *Autobiography* Vico refers to him as one of the four authors to whom he owes the greatest intellectual debt.

first beginnings'.[1] It should be noticed that in explaining the content of natural law in accordance with a certain model of the human mind this theory conforms to Vico's claim that institutions are conditioned by the modifications of the human mind. His rejection of the theory does not therefore involve disagreement on this point. It rests, instead, upon the claim that in assuming that natural law at all times stemmed from the same modifications of men's mind, the theory could not allow for the fact that the modifications themselves took on a different character at different 'times'. This had led Grotius, Selden and Pufendorf into giving false accounts of the natural law of past nations for 'they did not reflect that it took some two thousand years for philosophers to appear in any of them',[2] i.e. they had failed to realise that no nation had produced people with the intellectual capacity necessary to understand truths of the sort posited for two thousand years of its history.

Vico is thus claiming that the capacity to reason abstractly is itself an historical product, a modification which the human mind undergoes at some but not at all 'times' in its history. If, as Vico himself accepts, natural law is a necessary feature of any society and if its character is always dependent upon some modification of men's minds, it is nevertheless determined in some ages by other modes of thought than those assumed by the natural law theorists.

Vico's conception of the relation between institutions, modifications and times can be most easily demonstrated by reference to the summary he gives in Book IV of the sequence of stages through which the human mind modifies itself, and the corresponding changes which take place in natural law. This account involves a tripartite division, put forward as a doctrine of 'three natures':

The first nature, by a powerful deceit of imagination, which is most robust in the weakest at reasoning, was a poetic or creative nature which we may be allowed to call divine, as it ascribed to physical things the being of substances animated by gods...

The second was heroic nature, believed by the heroes themselves to be of divine origin; for, since they believed that the gods made and did everything, they held themselves to be the sons of Jove, as having been generated under his auspices. Being thus of a human species, they justly regarded their heroism as including the natural nobility in virtue of which they were princes of the human race.

[1] *S.N.* 329.   [2] *Ibid.*

The third was human nature, intelligent and hence modest, benign and reasonable, recognising for laws, conscience, reason, and duty.[1]

From this sequence of natures spring three kinds of customs or institutional practices[2] and from these in turn the following three kinds of natural law:

The first law was divine, for men believed themselves and all their institutions to depend upon the gods, since they thought everything was a god or made or done by a god.
The second was heroic law, the law of force but controlled by religion, which alone can keep force within bounds where there are no human laws or none strong enough to curb it...
The third is the human law dictated by fully developed human reason.[3]

In this summary it can be seen that the character of natural law at any stage of development is determined by the prevalent features of human nature at that stage. Moreover the sequence of changes through which natural law develops is determined by the sequence through which human nature develops. The idea of a system of natural law based upon 'fully developed reason' belongs to the final stage of the sequence and is not, as the natural law theorists had claimed, a universal feature of society in all its phases of development.

Vico's disagreement with the natural law theorists here reflects his belief that it is not enough to explain human institutions by reference to the modifications of the human mind. The attempt by these theorists to do precisely this is responsible for the historically unacceptable nature of their accounts of early institutions. To produce historically acceptable accounts, to avoid the 'conceit of scholars', it is necessary to recognise that the modifications are themselves historically conditioned, i.e. that there is a necessary relationship between 'times' and 'modifications'. Man's nature thus undergoes a process of historical development in the course of which its dominant modes of functioning alter, bringing correspondent changes to the whole character of his activities, customs and institutions.

[1] *S.N.* 916–18.   [2] *S.N.* 919–21.
[3] *S.N.* 922–4.

In effect therefore Vico is adding to his account of the nature of social change a further historical dimension. Institutions change in accordance with human thought but thought itself, and hence the institutions which depend upon it, changes as human nature itself undergoes a process of development. Thus, ultimately, developments in institutions and in human nature are mutually conditioning aspects of a single historical process.

To see how they affect each other it is sufficient to recall Vico's summary of the historical and social conditions under which the content of common sense and natural law changes in history and to note again the reciprocal relationship which exists between the institutional context and men's social aims. Early man seeks only what is useful for himself but, given his crude religious institutions and the beliefs which are involved in these, the only way he can satisfy his desires in the light of the necessities his religion imposes on him is by the creation of the institution of marriage. Life in this new institutional context creates a new human emotion, love for one's family, so that henceforth man identifies his own welfare with that of his family. Attempts to promote his family interests lead to the development of various institutions to do with ownership, the protection of ownership and of different kinds of ownership, ultimately providing the basis for a new kind of human feeling, civic pride and so on.[1] Throughout this sequence human institutions and human nature have a reciprocal effect upon each other. A system of institutions provides the conditions which bring about an alteration in human consciousness while the latter in turn leads to a change in the system of institutions. These changes constitute, moreover, a process of development. For when, in any given age, man's ever-present natural dissatisfaction causes him to try to alter the institutional context in which he lives, the desires and expectations whose fulfilment he wants to make possible will be a development of those possible in the previous historical age. The changes at which heroic man aims differ from those of poetic man precisely because heroic man's aims involve the satisfaction of desires which can obtain only subsequent to the institutions created by poetic man. Thus the institutions of any given age rest upon aspects of human conscious-

---

[1] The account given here is a gloss on *S.N.* 341 quoted and discussed above, pp. 25–7.

ness made possible only by the institutions it has inherited from its predecessor.[1]

It will be seen from this account of the relation of human institutions to human nature that Vico is not merely reiterating his view of the relationship of human institutions to common sense. He is, in a manner which could be thought reminiscent of Hegel, drawing attention to the importance of the idea of development in history. It must be noted, however, that there is nothing in his claims to suggest that he is presenting an early account of the Hegelian doctrine of Reason. For a cardinal feature of the latter is that, theoretically at least, the *content* of Reason is deducible *a priori*. But the account Vico gives in the general Elements, i.e. in his philosophical theory, contains no claims whatever about the content of the modifications beyond the fact that they are historically and socially conditioned. It is thus a necessary truth within Vico's science that explanations of human history should involve reference to the historical development of human nature. It is not, however, necessary in the same sense that human nature should develop in any given way.

[1] For a detailed account of the reciprocal influence of the content of human consciousness and human institutions upon each other see below, pp. 113–17, 123–7.

5

Providence

The difficulty of finding a consistent interpretation of Vico's claim that human history is the work of man is much increased by his simultaneous and frequent insistence that it is also the work of providence. There has been almost no agreement amongst past commentators as to how to reconcile those two claims. The divergent accounts given by Vico's Catholic and idealist commentators have, indeed, constituted one of the most striking differences between their interpretations. The source of the difficulty unquestionably lies in the obscurities and ambiguities in what Vico has to say about providence. These are such, in fact, as to have led recently to the suggestion that they represent a conscious attempt by Vico to cloak the unorthodox and heretical nature of the religious implications of his general theories.[1] This is perhaps too extreme a view to take but any decision with regard to it must, in any case, be subsequent to an analysis of the function of the concept of providence in Vico's work.

The *Scienza Nuova* contains many references to providence. A large part of these are to historical facts which are claimed as instances of its working. Others, however, involve theoretical claims about the nature of providence itself. References of the latter kind are most characteristically made in connection with Vico's rejection of Stoic and Epicurean theories of causation. The concept is therefore perhaps best approached in this connection, i.e. in the light of Vico's claim that his use of it will enable him to avoid both the meta-

---

[1] ' *La Scienza Nuova*: Orthodoxy and the Art of Writing', by Frederick Vaughan. In *Forum Italicum*, vol. II – no. 4 (December 1968), pp. 332–58. See also the same author's *The Political Philosophy of Giambattista Vico* (The Hague 1972).

physical determinism of the Stoics and the indeterminism of the Epicureans.[1]

It will be seen that the account of causation ascribed to Vico in the foregoing chapter is compatible with this claim. Courses of action are undertaken freely by men in the pursuit of their own self-centred interests. Were men not to seek these ends there would be no developments in social and institutional history. Yet, despite the heterogeneity of the ends which move individuals to action, the histories of different nations reveal the same sequences of institutions and practices. This is a consequence immediately of the normative beliefs about social justice which classes of men share and, ultimately, of the needs and utilities they cannot but feel when in certain institutional contexts. The pattern of institutional development, i.e. of history, is thus determined, but in a manner that allows for, and indeed requires, that men should exercise their free will in certain areas of activity. Social change thus requires both free action and causally determining conditions, the one provided by man's activity as individual, the other by the limitations imposed on him by his social nature.

The difficulty facing this account is that, while Vico is insistent that men create their own institutions, he is equally adamant that providence determines them. Indeed, he writes:

Our new Science must therefore be a demonstration of what providence has wrought in history, for it must be a history of the institutions by which, without human discernment or counsel, and often against the designs of men, providence has ordered this great city of the human race. For though this world has been created in time and particular, the institutions established therein by providence are universal and eternal.[2]

The difficulty therefore is that of understanding how human institutions can be creations of man, springing from his social nature, and yet require the operation of some other force.

To avoid confusion it is necessary to distinguish between three different ways in which Vico uses the term 'providence'. These

---

[1] 'Hence Epicurus who believes in chance, is refuted by the facts, along with his followers Hobbes and Machiavelli; and so are Zeno and Spinoza, who believe in fate. The evidence clearly confirms the contrary position of the political philosophers, whose prince is the divine Plato, who shows that providence directs human institutions', S.N. 1109. See also S.N. 129–30, and 341–2.

[2] S.N. 342. See also 348, 385, 1108–9.

constitute what may conveniently be called the historical, immanental and transcendent concepts of providence.

The historical concept of providence belongs properly to the history of ideas. It is the belief, held in the various historical societies, that God is in contact with man, that he can and does intervene in human affairs and that, consequently, certain kinds of religious and social behaviour are prescriptive within society.[1] This belief, as we have seen, also forms one of the three first principles of Vico's science, i.e. one of the three necessary conditions of any society. Its history will therefore be a part of a history of the common sense of any nation.

Vico claims further that the fact that men should have the concept of providence is itself the work of providence in some other sense.[2] There has, however, been considerable disagreement amongst commentators over whether there is one or two further senses of providence to be taken into account here. The idealist tradition, stemming from Croce, has put all the emphasis upon the immanental interpretation. This is achieved by a straightforward identification of providence with some immanent rational spirit, governed by nothing other than its own nature, which determines man's history despite his conscious aims. Croce freely acknowledged the Hegelian nature of this interpretation in his claim that 'no less than Hegel, Vico had the concept of reason which he called Divine Providence'.[3]

This interpretation is consistent with some parts of what Vico says, e.g. that 'providence directs divine institutions'[4] and that 'this world has issued from a mind often diverse, at times quite contrary to and always superior to the particular ends that men had proposed to themselves; which narrow ends, made means to serve wider ends, it has always employed to preserve the human race upon this earth'.[5] On the other hand it does not agree with the claims that 'this world has certainly been made by men'[6] and that they have made it 'by

---

[1] S.N. 342, 374–80.
[2] 'Divine providence initiated the process by which the fierce and violent were brought from the outlaw state to humanity and nations were instituted among them. It did so by awakening in them a confused idea of divinity, which they in their ignorance attributed to that to which it did not belong', S.N. 178.
[3] B. Croce, *Saggio Sullo Hegel* (Bari 1913), p. 51. See also *The Philosophy of Giambittista Vico*, chap. x.
[4] S.N. 1109.   [5] S.N. 1108.
[6] S.N. 331.

choice'.[1] For if Vico's providence is essentially Hegel's Reason the course of history is determined *a priori* and human choice is not relevant to its explanation. It would be strange if Vico, sensitive and hostile, as we have seen, to the metaphysical determinism he saw in Spinoza and the Stoics, should be advocating what is, in the end, a determinism of a very similar kind.

The idealist account has been opposed by the Catholic interpreters who have argued that the implied identification of God with an immanent rational principle in human affairs is inconsistent with Vico's constantly and sincerely reiterated expressions of orthodox religious belief. This thesis has been developed most recently by Bellofiore[2] who argues that Vico's concept of providence is a straightforward adoption of the Thomist conception of God, in which it follows from the nature of God, as an infinite and absolute Being, that he must be both transcendent and immanent at once. 'It is necessary that God, the Infinite and Absolute, *precisely because he is Infinite and Absolute* (which here more or less means *transcendent*) is present in, pervades and works in finite being'.[3] Interpreted in the light of this conception, Vico is represented as asserting that the providence which informs human history and directs its progress from barbarism to reason is an aspect of an Infinite Being, whose ends transcend, but whose operations are internal to, history itself. Providence, in its immanent aspect, operates primarily through the nature of things, a nature which determines that their operations should be in accordance with God's ends. Bellofiore identifies this largely with man's social nature and particularly with the part which the historical idea of providence plays, in Vico's scheme, in directing the course of human affairs.

This account certainly does more justice to those of Vico's remarks about providence in which two aspects seem to be distinguished. It also rescues Vico from an outright identification of Reason with God, an identification which, one cannot doubt, would have been abhorrent to him. Nevertheless, the difference between the two views is nominal rather than real. For even if, as on Bellofiore's view, man's social nature is to be identified only with an aspect of God, i.e.

[1] *S.N.* 1108.
[2] L. Bellofiore, *La Dottrina della Providenza in G. B. Vico*, chapters VIII–X (Padua 1962).   [3] *Ibid.* 149.

immanent providence, it remains the case that, in a sense, man is a part of God, part, moreover, of a God who, being infinite must also be necessary. It is difficult therefore to see how this account can fail to entail that, despite his own claims, Vico's view is fundamentally Spinozistic. There would be no room on this view for any free choice whatsoever in human history.

Apart from the question how Vico thought of God's relation to man's history, these discussions throw almost no light at all on the important question *how* providence is supposed to influence man's history. We have, on the one hand, individual and fallen man, acting with thought only for his own gain and, on the other, an orderly sequence of social forms unfolding in accordance with a plan of which its agents are largely ignorant. This is the doctrine of the heterogeneity of ends. To say, as for example does Bellofiore, that God's ends are here brought about because he gives man a (social) nature whereby they will be brought about, involving a 'collaboration' between God and man,[1] is to draw attention to the nature of the difficulty, rather than contribute to its solution.

As a preliminary to developing an alternative to these views, it will be convenient to show that the difficulty presented by the theory of the heterogeneity of ends is not so acute in Vico as it might seem. What makes it appear so mysterious is largely the way in which Vico expresses his more general claims about it. These point up the fact that though man does not act for the improvement of the institutional context his actions result in its improvement, thus fulfilling the aims of providence. This, however, is only mysterious if one takes Vico to be suggesting that, because man's actions are not *initiated* by a desire to improve the organisation of society, he is unable to recognise some possible change as an improvement upon the existent arrangements in respect of his needs and to accept it for this reason. If the account given in the foregoing chapter is correct, however, this is not what Vico is saying. The impulse to action may depend upon a desire solely for one's own improvement. But any institutional changes that result from this are determined by normative social beliefs which force man to accept social arrangements which are 'just' to all. Men's actions are not undertaken for the sake of common sense, but any new institutional arrangements which they occasion are made in the light of

---

[1] *Ibid.* 199–200.

common sense. There is thus nothing mysterious at all about this aspect of the theory of the heterogeneity of ends, or about the process by which institutional change is determined. In claiming that 'this world without doubt has issued from a mind often diverse, at times quite contrary, and always superior to the particular ends that men had proposed to themselves...ends, made means to serve wider ends...'[1] Vico is not saying that because a social structure is not to be explained by some aim proper to an individual as such it is to be explained by some superhuman agency. On the contrary he is saying that, because it is not to be explained by aims proper to individuals as such it is to be explained by judgements common to people who share the same system of institutionalised beliefs. Hence he can still confidently assert that 'that which did all this was mind, for men did it with intelligence'.[2]

The above account still, however, fails to deal with Vico's other, more extreme claim. For he does not only claim that the social structure is explained by common sense rather than individual aims. He claims also that in so doing it fulfils an overriding aim of providence: that of preserving human society.[3] Were Vico merely suggesting that it was a consequence of the operation of providence that society was preserved there would be no difficulty in accepting its identification with common sense. It is with the suggestion that providence is purposive in a *long-term* sense which cannot be attributed to common sense that the difficulty reappears.

This difficulty can be met in the following way. Vico's claim concerning providence's overriding aim only constitutes an objection to the foregoing account if providence in this sense is taken to constitute an internal aspect of Vico's account of social change in the way in which common sense is, i.e. if Vico is claiming that a knowledge of providence's overriding aim is as necessary for our understanding of human affairs as a knowledge of common sense. It can be shown, however, that Vico does not hold any such view.

This can be demonstrated by consideration of an argument which appears in Element VII. In the axiom itself Vico gives an account of the social function of legislation: 'out of ferocity, avarice and ambition it

---

[1] *S.N.* 1108. [2] *Ibid.*
[3] *Ibid.*

creates the military, merchant and governing classes...Out of these three great vices, which would certainly destroy all mankind on the face of the earth, it makes civil happiness.' He then adds:

> This axiom proves that there is divine providence and further that it is a divine legislative mind. For out of the passions of men each bent on his private advantage, for the sake of which they would live like wild beasts in the wilderness, it has made the civil institutions by which they may live in human society.[1]

The argument may be summarised in the following way:

(1) Men are naturally vicious and if their behaviour were controlled only by their individual natures they would destroy themselves.

(2) By acting within a framework of legislation, however, they form civil orders in which their individual vices naturally contribute to a happy social life.

(3) These facts prove that there are forces which work for man's good other than his own individual nature, i.e. that there is divine providence.

(4) This, in turn, proves the existence of a 'divine, legislative mind'.

Vico here presents a version of the argument from design. The move to note is the inference from (3) to (4), in which the existence of a certain social element, i.e. legislation or, as it is here called, 'divine providence', is alleged to be evidence of a 'divine legislative mind'. The argument thus distinguishes between two senses of providence, in one of which it is identified with certain features of the social structure, and is therefore immanent, and in the other of which it is a 'mind' and is transcendent. This is the sense of providence to which Vico attributes the overriding aim of preserving human life on earth. It will be seen, however, that since the claim that providence is a mind (and thus has its own purposes) is an inference from Vico's demonstration that order in social affairs is effected by legislation, the concept of transcendent providence cannot enter into Vico's account of the nature of society in the way the concept of immanent providence can. But the concept of immanent providence, since it is identified with the social function of legislation, appears to be

---

[1] *S.N.* 133.

nothing more than another way of talking about man's social nature itself.[1]

The rôle of the concept of providence in the *Scienza Nuova* may thus be summarised in the following way. There *is* a distinction in Vico between a transcendent and immanent providence. The concept of a transcendent providence is not, however, basic to his Science as such, since the claim that there is a transcendent providence is an inference from the conclusions established by the Science. One could reject the inference without in any way casting doubt upon the adequacy of the Science itself. The concept of an immanent providence, on the contrary does constitute a fundamental category of the Science. But, if the foregoing account is to be accepted, this is to be identified with common sense itself, not, however, as a quasi-Hegelian metaphysical category but simply as involving man's inability to reach social decisions without doing so in a social capacity and thus in his full relations with others.

It might be useful to summarise the differences between this account and those considered above. The distinction which Bellofiore maintains between a transcendent and an immanent providence is accepted but the logical connection he asserts between them is denied. The operations of immanent providence are not therefore the necessary consequences of the nature of a transcendent and necessary God. Vico is thus saved from the charge of metaphysical determinism to which this view would ultimately commit him. It is accepted, however, that immanent providence *is* a fundamental category in the *Scienza Nuova* and that its workings are largely to be identified with those of common sense. But the common sense referred to here is the sequence of communal decisions men reach in the light of their normative beliefs as effected by their historical, social and institutional situations. It is not an *a priori* sequence, governed by some kind of metaphysical necessity, as the idealists would claim.

This account of the concept of providence is based upon an analysis of Vico's most fundamental metaphysical doctrines. It has the consequence that some of Vico's explicit remarks about providence cannot be taken at their face value. This is unfortunate yet it is probably unavoidable, for these remarks involve claims so different in

[1] Vico produces a shorter version of the argument from design later. See *S.N.* 1107.

kind that it is difficult to see how they can all constitute instances of a single, self-consistent principle. Sometimes they are very general in character as, for example, when Vico asserts that his Science must provide 'a demonstration of what providence has wrought in history'[1] for 'providence directs human institutions'.[2] At other times they are more specific: providence is responsible for awakening in man the confused idea of divinity which is a necessary condition of any social progress whatsoever;[3] it has led society through a sequence of different kinds of theological beliefs until finally it was ready to receive a revealed (Christian) theology;[4] it caused early man to seek to classify things before attempting to explain them,[5] and 'by means of religion...to unite with certain women in constant and life-long companionship; hence the institution of marriage'.[6] At stages such as these Vico rarely fails to point out how the influence of providence is to be seen in the course of history.

To support the above analysis examination of one characteristic example must suffice. In Book II Chapter v, Vico offers an account of the many ways in which providence has worked to bring about commonwealths and, at the same time, the natural law of the gentes. In the course of this he writes:

Let us consider and meditate on the simplicity and naturalness with which providence orders the institutions of men...Then let us ask ourselves if, among all human possibilities, so many and such diverse institutions could in any other way have had simpler or more natural beginnings among those very men who are said by Epicurus to have been born of chance and by Zeno to have been creatures of necessity. Yet chance did not divert them nor fate force them out of this natural order. For at the point where the commonwealths were to spring forth, the matters were all prepared and ready to receive the form, and there issued from them the format of the commonwealths, composed of mind and body. The prepared matters were these men's own religions, their own languages, their own lands, their own nuptials, their own names (clans or houses), their own arms, and hence their own dominions, their own magistrates, and finally their own laws. And because all these were their own they were completely free and therefore constitutive of true commonwealths.[7]

---

[1] *S.N.* 342.
[3] *S.N.* 177–8.
[5] *S.N.* 498.
[7] *S.N.* 630.

[2] *S.N.* 1108.
[4] *S.N.* 366.
[6] *S.N.* 629.

In this passage Vico reiterates his rejection of the theories of Epicurus and Zeno. The 'simplicity and naturalness' with which providence, rather than chance or fate, orders human affairs, is claimed to be seen in the way in which the growth of states with the structure of a commonwealth is a natural consequence of a social situation in which all the elements of which commonwealths are composed are already existent. In these circumstances, men *freely* bring about the creation of commonwealths because these materials are themselves men's creations.

What is to be noticed here is that the action of providence is, indeed, so natural that one cannot detect in what it consists, over and above the various institutions said by Vico both to constitute all the materials required for the formation of commonwealths and also to be men's own creations. Taken in its relation to the theory of common sense, Vico's explanation really amounts to saying that commonwealths arise because when a certain institutional context exists men can see that a certain political structure is best suited to fulfil its needs. Nothing is *added* to this already satisfactory explanation by the pronouncement that we thus see providence directing human affairs. Such a claim is both gratuitous and empty.

According to this account, Vico's remarks about the rôle of providence in its immanent and transcendent senses represent an attempt to present what is basically a naturalistic theory in a religious light. It would be interesting to know whether this attempt was the consequence of a certain confusion on Vico's part with regard to the ultimately naturalistic character of his own theories or whether, as Vaughan has suggested, it is a deliberate attempt by Vico to obscure what he well knew to be their naturalistic character. It is probably impossible, however, to come to a definitive decision between these alternatives. For, although Vaughan presents a certain amount of circumstantial evidence on behalf of his thesis, the question in the end turns upon the inconsistencies in what Vico says about providence, and here it seems difficult to find enough evidence to decide conclusively between his own conscious and unconscious misrepresentation of his view. With regard, for example, to his use of the argument from design to argue for a transcendent God, one clearly could not use the fact that this argument is invalid as evidence of Vico's insincerity in using the argument, since the argument has found many sincere supporters despite its lack of cogency. Similarly, one cannot use the fact that his identification of the causal process at work in institutional change with immanent providence is empty as evidence that Vico realised that it was so.

In the end, therefore, it is not possible to present definitive reasons for or against Vaughan's account and it may well be that the explanation for Vico's constant reiteration of the Christian nature of his thought is not so much that he knew that it was naturalistic and wanted to obscure this fact as that his enthusiasm for Christianity led him to overlay his philosophy with a set of fairly empty claims.

It is, fortunately, not necessary to decide between these possibilities, since neither interpretation has any consequences for the analysis of the rôle of providence in Vico's philosophy.[1] The interpretations which do have such consequences are the idealist and Catholic accounts considered above, which are concerned not with the nature of Vico's beliefs but with the nature of his doctrines, and what I have tried to show is that while it would not be impossible to accept that Vico's personal beliefs were Christian it is impossible to construe his doctrines to be in accordance with the orthodox theology of the time. It would, indeed, be very strange if Vico had been able to develop such a novel theory of institutional change without departing radically from the orthodox religious philosophy of his time. The fact that his pronouncements about the influence of providence in human affairs are empty, simply serves to underline this point.

---

[1] I do not mean by this to imply that Vaughan does not offer an account of the meaning of the concept of providence in Vico's philosophy, for he goes on to offer a different version of the naturalistic account suggested here. I mean simply that the question of Vico's awareness of the full implications of his doctrines is less important than the analysis of those doctrines themselves.

6

The character of Vico's metaphysics

It will be convenient to commence this discussion of the fundamental categories Vico proposes for the study of history by reconsidering a characteristic statement of his theories. Perhaps the best known of such statements is his claim that 'men have themselves made the world of nations...but this world has undoubtedly issued from a mind often diverse, at times quite contrary and always superior to the particular ends that men had proposed to themselves'.[1]

The men who have made this world are, at one and the same time, both private individuals, with their own personal hopes, fears and ambitions, and social persons occupying social rôles within a system of social relationships. In one sense men are free, for their actions are usually inspired by ends proper to themselves as individuals. In another sense, however, they are not free. For when men pursue their private ends they cannot avoid changing the social structure in various ways. These ways depend, however, not upon the private ends men had in mind, but upon the beliefs and attitudes which are proper to the occupants of social rôles in their historically conditioned states. Men's social actions therefore always take place within limitations of mental horizon and normative aim which are historically and socially imposed. Individual man, in other words, cannot escape from the fact that generically he is an historical and social being.

Since any person is both a particular individual and yet possesses a generic nature, his freedom as an individual exists within limitations which his generic nature imposes upon him. These limitations are the historical and social conditions of life within which, at any given time,

---

[1] *S.N.* 1108.

he finds himself. From the point of view of those interested in human freedom, there are limitations *within* which an individual has freedom. But from the point of view of those who wish to understand human history, they are the determining conditions which, by affecting man's social activity, bring about and explain historical change. Historical change is therefore brought about by two kinds of condition, social and historical, which are both equally necessary. Vico is thus offering a theory of historico-sociological change.

The world of nations is also made by men in the sense that it is made only by men. Vico's references to the part providence plays in directing human affairs are either references to the importance which a particular kind of religious belief has had in producing historical change – an importance fully explained by the historically conditioned nature of the men whose belief it was – or they emphasise his claim that institutions condition men to reach decisions which, individually, they never sought. Since this last fact is a consequence of man's generic nature, there is nothing to be explained by adding that in seeing this process at work we see providence direct human affairs.

Finally, in claiming that the character of human history is fully explained by reference to men's historical and social nature, i.e. that historical changes are fully determined by the historical and sociological conditions in which men must exist, Vico is implying that there are historico-sociological laws. Those laws will be statements of the specific historico-sociological conditions which determine the character of any specific kind of historical phenomenon. Since this claim is a consequence of Vico's metaphysical account of the relation of human nature to human history, it is itself metaphysical and, as such, assumed *a priori* in Vico's science. Nevertheless, it does not follow, as has been suggested in the idealist interpretation of Vico, that the content of these laws is metaphysically necessary and hence can be determined *a priori*.[1]

In evaluating these assertions we must ask first why Vico thought that historiography could transcend its previous unsatisfactory state and become scientific in character if it involved use of the proposed categories while it could not do so if it continued to regard history as

---

[1] The claim that these laws are empirical will be more fully supported later by a consideration of Vico's account of the 'proofs' for his science. See below, pp. 145–53.

the outcome of the doings of individuals as such. Two claims are especially relevant to understanding this.

First, Vico thought, for reasons which are not entirely clear but which may ultimately be theological in origin, that individual man had free will and that his choice of action as an individual always consequently involved an arbitrary element.[1] This being the case there could be no science for such activities, for there could be no knowledge of their causes.

This, it should be noted, only goes to show that were human history dependent upon individual activities there could be no scientific history. But it does not show that human history is not the outcome of individual activities.

Vico's belief in the latter point is explained by his second claim: that the sorts of cause he adduces are sufficient to determine the character of historical change and that the kind of explanation he wishes to rule out, i.e. explanation by recourse to individual action, is irrelevant. It remains therefore to ask how plausible is the suggestion that historical development is determined by historical and sociological conditions of a non-personal kind.

The first thing to note here is that Vico is refering only to institutional history. He is certainly not claiming that to the explanation of no events whatsoever are personal and individual factors relevant. This is made quite clear by his constant references to the viciousness of human nature and to the selfish reasons which almost invariably initiate men's actions. His suggestion is not that there are no matters whatsoever in the past to the explanation of which individual features are relevant, but that institutional history is not among them.

A possible objection to Vico's position would be that the kinds of causes he adduces in his preferred explanations are abstractions from the kinds which would operate in his rejected explanations, i.e. that to talk of social purposes is to talk of purposes held by individual men and to talk of social pressures is to talk of pressures exerted by individual men.

Vico might meet this objection in the following way. It is true that

---

[1] In Element XI where Vico contrasts the two kinds of action open to man, i.e. action as an individual and action as a social agent, the latter is 'made certain and determined' by common sense whereas the former is 'by its nature most uncertain'.

there is a sense in which social purposes are held by individual men. But they are held by individual men in their various social rôles and capacities and not by individual men as such. Thus although, for example, Henry VIII intended to alter the relationship between the Church and the State in England, this is an intention he would only have had by virtue of a number of institutional conditions. These would include that he occupy a particular political position, giving him the capacity to initiate changes that might lead to the fulfilment of his intention, that the status of the crown be such that the king should be able to command enough support to carry through the changes of his policy involved, that where this was not so the desire for economic advantage should be strong enough to lead men to support the king, and, finally, that the status of the Church of Rome should be so diminished in men's minds that respect for it should no longer operate as a bulwark against the proposed changes. An explanation of the changing relationships between Church and State in the reign of Henry VIII would therefore involve things of these kinds, Henry's private intentions in the matter being largely irrelevant. Insofar, however, as his intentions, being those of a person occupying a uniquely important political office, were taken into account, it would be his intentions considered in the light of their possible institutional significance. For the degree of support or opposition his intentions aroused would depend upon whether people thought that they were justified in the light of the position of the monarchy at that time or what might be the institutional consequences of allowing them as legitimate to occupiers of the throne. Thus it would be Henry VIII in his full constitutional position that an historian would deal with if he turned to Henry VIII at all in explaining these matters.

This might not, however, be sufficient to meet the objection. For though it might be admitted that to understand the historical significance of an individual involves taking him in his various institutional rôles, it would still be contended that there is an ineliminable difference between considering him as the individual he is in these relationships and as a sort of anonymous occupier of rôles involving these relationships. Surely, it will be argued, it makes all the difference to the way the occupier of a certain institution will act in face of certain, say, social demands, that he is intelligent rather than stupid, optimistic rather than pessimistic, cautious rather than bold.

For example, is it not true that if there had been no such person as Hitler, with his particular qualities of character, there would have been no Second World War? Or had there been no such person as Churchill, with his particular qualities of character, would Germany not have won that war?

In making suggestions such as these it is not being proposed that Hitler was the sole cause of the war. It is recognised that Hitler would only bring about the war *given* certain already existent general conditions, such as the economic and social situation in Germany, the spirit of international hostility and mutual suspicion which was an aftermath of the First World War, the ideological fear of Russian Communism which acted as a check upon the willingness of some countries to declare war upon Germany, and so on. But, the objection goes, these conditions were not themselves enough to bring about the war. What was equally necessary was that there be somebody in a position to bring about those events which actually initiated the war and only a person of Hitler's unique blend of fanaticism, megalomania, utter ruthlessness, and so on, could have done this. So without such an individual as Hitler there would have been no war. But, the objection finally states, it is simply an historical accident that such a person should exist at the time, and that he should be in the one position in which he could have exercised such an influence upon events. For if the appearance of such a man with the personal qualities of character of Hitler in Germany in the first half of the twentieth century was determined, it was certainly not determined by such factors as those adduced by Vico in his theory, which have all to do with the general structure of a society and the general modes of thought and belief prevailing in it. In this way, therefore, it is argued that, although the context in which historical events occur is important in helping to explain their character, it is never possible wholly to do away with the decisions of individuals and these are in part, at least, dependent upon the character of individuals. Vico's account of the causes of historical change is therefore inadequate.

Before considering this objection a further point must be made. We must be careful not to think that the objection is plausible only in relation to certain kinds of history such as political and cultural history. It is certainly true, of course, that individuals figure much more prominently in political and cultural history, which often involve biographical accounts of certain historical persons, whereas social and economic history deal with anonymous entities such as the medieval burgher or the Elizabethan gentleman. However, it would not follow from this fact that the objection only went to show that Vico's theory was inapplicable to political and cultural history but allowed that it was (possibly) applicable to social and economic history. For the objection is stating a connection between individual character as such and events in general, not just events of a particular kind. Thus, if accepted, it would entail the consequence that social and economic change should also be the outcome of human actions to the explanation of which individual human characteristics were necessary. The medieval burgher and the Elizabethan gentleman would thus be understood as abstractions, as a convenient way of talking about the relations between individual persons. Explanations of events to which they were relevant would have to allow for the importance of individual human characteristics and the ultimate contingency of the latter. Thus, by insisting that all historical events whatsoever are affected by the qualities of character of individual persons and that it is just a matter of historical chance what these are, the objection is asserting that no history is determined in the manner Vico alleges.

There are two points to be made in face of this objection. First it must be noted that Vico himself would have accepted a certain part of it. He would certainly not have denied that the qualities of mind of individuals were important. For example, he was himself a great admirer of Augustus and he believed that had it not been for certain qualities of character which Augustus had, the decline of Rome would have taken place more quickly than it did.[1] Nevertheless, the decline of Rome was only temporarily arrested by Augustus. After his death it came about just the same because it was made inevitable by conditions operating at too fundamental a level to be affected by the activities of any one man. On this view, therefore, the success or the failure of the plans and ventures of the great figures of history are explained by the extent to which they are in harness with the underlying and quite inevitable general changes. The great individual, like the rest of us, has some small amount of manoeuvre left to him, but whether his exercise of it has a relatively permanent or

[1] *S.N.* 1102–6.

merely temporary effect in history depends entirely upon whether what he does is in conformity or in conflict with the inevitable pattern of change.

Secondly, however, in allowing for the importance of qualities of character in human history Vico would not have thought of himself as making an exception to his general account. For in the objection as above stated, they only constitute an exception because they are claimed not to be fully determined by the individual's social and historical background. In defence of this claim it might be asked in what way, for example, the social and historical environment in which Hitler was brought up, which would be responsible for his megalomania, differed from that in which thousands of his non-megalomaniac contemporaries were brought up? If we cannot produce such an element in the social and historical environment we cannot claim that Hitler's character was fully determined by social and historical conditions. And if we cannot say that his character was fully determined by such conditions we cannot claim that those events which turned upon his activities were.

What this objection overlooks, however, is that it is misleading to talk as if the actions of any one individual are effective simply because they are his actions alone. Any ruler, for example, no matter how absolutist or dictatorial, must have support for his policies. When he decides upon a policy or tries to put it into operation he has to carry with him a certain amount of support. Hitler did not act in isolation nor in the face of the wishes of everybody in Germany. His policies were either supported or tolerated by enough of the German people to be practicable. Again, Churchill was effective as a leader in the war because what he said and did struck a chord in the attitude of the British people. In a different people, or at a different time, the response might have been very different and Churchill consequently would have had little of his present fame. So, if we say that Hitler was a megalomaniac and that only a megalomaniac could have done what he did, we have to recognise that his megalomania (if that is what it was) was not a purely idiosyncratic feature but something which could develop in some fairly large section of the German people in the social and historical situation in which they were. Likewise, if we say that only a patriot could do what Churchill did, we have to recognise that he shared in a sentiment which was held by a large part of the British people, a sentiment which could only be held, in that form, in the kind of historical and social circumstances in which Britain was.

Historical and social factors thus account for certain of the qualities of mind which classes of individual possess and in so doing provide the basis of various historical policies and activities. This is not to deny that people can have qualities of mind which are not of this kind, some that are perhaps purely idiosyncratic. But it is to assert that where historical events turn upon qualities of mind they are always qualities of the historical and social sort. For only qualities of this sort can command the kind of support that historical events require.[1]

Finally, however, it may be objected that even if this is so it merely reflects a determination to use the word 'history' in such a way that only institutional events are to be allowed to be called 'historical'. In other words it would be an analytic truth that historical events are institutional in character. But, it may be asked, what justification would there be for such a usage? Indeed, does not the existence of biographical histories show that it is false that all history is institutional and hence that it cannot be accepted as an analytic truth?

---

[1] The view here attributed to Vico is not merely something implicit in his general theory of historical change but is also stated explicitly by him in the more detailed section of the 'Elements', devoted to the historico-sociological laws on which the 'ideal eternal history' is based. In the relevant section he writes: 'The order of ideas must follow the order of institutions' (S.N. 238). 'This was the order of human institutions: first the forests, after that the huts, then the villages, next the cities and finally the academies' (S.N. 239). 'Men first feel necessity, then look for utility, next attend to comfort, still later amuse themselves with pleasure, thence grow dissolute in luxury, and finally go mad and waste their substance' (S.N. 241). 'The nature of peoples is first crude, then severe, then benign, then delicate, finally dissolute' (S.N. 242). 'In the human race first appear the huge and grotesque, like the cyclopes; then the proud and magnanimous like Achilles; then the valorous and just like Aristides and Scipio Africanus; nearer to us figures with great semblances of virtue accompanied by great vices, who among the vulgar win a name for true glory, like Alexander and Caesar; still later the melancholy and reflective, like Tiberius; finally the dissolute and shameless madmen, like Caligula, Nero, and Domitian' (S.N. 243). In these passages Vico shows how an historical sequence of institutions determines a sequence of human natures and human attitudes and how the latter are reflected in the characters of the great figures of the times. The latter are thus the possessors of human characteristics the basis of which lies in the nature of the historical and social environment. It is true that Vico's actual examples are implausible, the temporal gap between some of the figures mentioned, such as that between Tiberius and Caligula, being only a few years and too short to reflect fundamental historical changes of character. Nevertheless the example shows quite clearly that Vico explicitly embraced the principle that historico-sociological conditions determine the qualities of character of all men, including the great historical figures.

There are two levels at which Vico could reply to this objection. First, with regard to the claim that the existence of biographical history shows that it is false that history is essentially institutional, he could point out that our understanding of biographical history takes place against, and presupposes a knowledge of, the habits of mind, manners, communal practices and institutions of the time. It is impossible to understand a biographical history of, say, King James II of Great Britain, without understanding the character of the religious and military training he received and it is impossible to understand this without taking into account the historical and sociological circumstances in which the institutions of religion and the army had developed in England in the seventeenth century. Thus only if one understood the latter could one fully understand why a person in James's position should take the decisions he did or why they should have had the consequences they had. Biographical history therefore presupposes institutional history. Even if it is true that in biographical history one's interests are turned towards the understanding of a particular individual, it remains the case that this understanding cannot be reached without a more fundamental understanding of the institutions of the times.

In a sense, however, acceptable though it may be at this level, this answer begs the more fundamental point behind the objection. For in effect it responds to the claim that the existence of biographical history shows that it cannot be an analytic truth that history is institutional by asserting that biographical history itself presupposes, and therefore has an essential connection with, institutional history. But this leaves unanswered the question whether it is an analytic truth that history is essentially institutional.

It is not possible at this point to deal adequately with this objection. The issue which it raises is fundamentally that of the status of Vico's claim, i.e. whether it is a claim about the meaning of a word or about the nature of a certain class of phenomena. It is clear, of course, if the foregoing account of Vico's theories is accepted, that he thinks he is making a claim about the nature of certain things and to the extent that it is a reflection of his intentions, it would be permissible to call his theories 'metaphysical'. But what the objection is raising is not the question 'What kind of theory does Vico think he is offering?' but 'What kind of theory is Vico offering?' In other words it is casting doubt upon Vico's capacity to defend the claim that what he is offering is a metaphysical theory.

At this level, therefore, a proper consideration of the objection would have to take into account whatsoever reasons Vico could adduce to show that the theories and concepts he has formulated are adequate to an understanding of the nature of a certain class of things. For only thus could he defend himself against charge that he is merely advocating a certain usage of the word 'history'. But to investigate these reasons would require a discussion of the 'proofs' he considers relevant to his Science and, indeed, of the whole question of the ultimate justification of his work. It must therefore be left until Vico's conception of such notions as 'science' and 'knowledge' have been clarified.

7

The problem of knowledge

SCIENZA AND COSCIENZA

There is an intimate link between Vico's theory of knowledge and his metaphysical theories, as is revealed in the following characteristic statement:

The world of civil society has certainly been made by men, and...its principles are therefore to be found within the modifications of our own human mind. Whoever reflects on this cannot but marvel that the philosophers should have bent all their energies to the study of the world of nature, which, since God made it, He alone knows; and that they should have neglected the study of the world of nations, or civil world, which, since men made it, men could come to know.[1]

This passage suggests that the relationship is one of presupposition, for the possibility of knowledge of the human world depends upon the fact that this world is a human creation. Knowledge of the natural world, on the contrary, is denied because that world is a divine and not a human creation. The theory of knowledge presented here therefore presupposes the theories of historical and sociological causation formulated in Vico's metaphysics and must, consequently, be considered in connection with them.

The account which Vico gives of his theory of knowledge in the 'Elements' is incomplete. It will nevertheless be convenient to commence with this for it contains the only detailed statement of several indispensable aspects of his theory, without which one's interpretations of more general statements, such as those quoted above, are liable to serious error.

Vico begins with a series of parallel distinctions between know-

---

[1] *S.N.* 331. Cf. 349 and 374, where the wording is almost identical.

ledge and consciousness, the true and the certain, and philosophy and philology. The first two pairs of terms are mentioned in Element IX: 'Men who do not know what is true of things (*il vero*) take care to hold fast to what is certain (*il certo*), so that if they cannot satisfy their intellects by knowledge (*scienza*), their wills at least may rest on consciousness (*coscienza*).'[1]

Thus knowledge (or science) and consciousness are related to the true and the certain respectively. It is implied that consciousness is a lower epistemological state than knowledge for the suggestion is that it is accepted as a basis for action only where knowledge is unobtainable.

It is necessary first to establish the meanings of *il vero* and *il certo* which are here left undefined. An important definition is, however, offered in Element XXII, in which Vico states that it is 'a property of every science (*scienza*), noted by Aristotle, that science has to do with what is universal and eternal'.[2] The true, which is the object of knowledge, is therefore the universal and eternal.

Vico has thus defined *il vero* in terms of its logical and not its psychological characteristics. Since *il certo* is related to consciousness as is *il vero* to knowledge, it would seem that it must also be understood in terms of its logical characteristics. This would rule out any such definition of *il certo* as 'that of which one is psychologically certain'.

The obvious logical contrast to 'what is universal and eternal' is 'what is particular and contingent'. A clue that this is the way to take *il certo* is provided by a remark Vico makes about the Latin *certum*. In Element CXI he writes: 'In Latin *certum* means particularised, or, as the schools say, individuated.'[3] It would be consistent with Vico's habit of giving to Italian words meanings derived from his own interpretation of their Latin origins that *il certo* should mean the particular or the individuated.

This suggestion is confirmed by the further contrast Vico introduces between philosophy and philology. In Element X he writes:

[1] *S.N.* 137. This proposition, like many others in the *Scienza Nuova*, fulfils a double function. First it states a connection between two epistemological states and two subject matters and, in so doing, reveals that Vico's problem is that of showing how one of these epistemological states can be related to both kinds of subject matter. In its second function it states a law about the historical development of the human mind. For the moment it will be considered solely in its first capacity.
[2] *S.N.* 163.   [3] *S.N.* 321.

Philosophy contemplates reason, whence comes knowledge of the true; philology observes that of which human choice is author, whence comes consciousness of the certain.

This axiom by its second part includes among the philologians all the grammarians, historians, critics, who have occupied themselves with the study of the languages and deeds of peoples: both at home as in their customs and laws, and abroad, as in their wars, peaces, alliances, travels and commerce.[1]

The terms 'philology' and 'philologian' are here being used rather as the terms 'history' and 'historian' would now be used. Philology arrives at consciousness of the certain by investigating those things made by human choice and these include peoples' languages, deeds, customs, laws, wars, peaces, alliances, travels and commerce, that is to say, their particular, free creations. *Il certo* is therefore the particular and contingent.

The contrast is thus between philosophy which produces knowledge of the universal and eternal by contemplating reason, and history which produces consciousness of particular, contingent facts. Consciousness is a lower epistemological state than knowledge and may, for the moment, be thought of as belief or psychological conviction.

With these definitions stated Vico next makes it clear that he disagrees with the way in which both of these disciplines have hitherto been conceived:

This same axiom shows how the philosophers failed by half in not giving certainty to their reasonings by appeal to the authority of the philologians, and likewise how the latter failed by half in not giving their authority the sanction of truth by appeal to the reasonings of the philosophers. If they had done this they would have been more useful to their commonwealths and they would have anticipated us in conceiving this science.[2]

In these remarks Vico both explicitly criticises the way in which philosophy and history have previously been conducted and also implies a view about how they should be conducted. To some extent the critical part of his remarks can be understood as a reiteration of some of the points he has already made. The charge against the historians, for example, is that they have failed to establish the truth of their findings by appeal to philosophical reasoning. This is largely a restatement of the complaint that historians have failed to free themselves from assumptions of an arbitrary or an unhistorical

---

[1] *S.N.* 138–9.   [2] *S.N.* 140.

nature. They have, in effect, failed to base their work upon an adequate conception of its subject matter or to pursue their enquiries in an objective or scientific way. Vico's philosophical account of the historical and sociological character of the human world has indicated the correct way in which to conceive the subject matter of history. The question of how historical method should be modified so that its products can be a proper branch of knowledge has not, however, so far been answered. Again, the charge against the philosophers, that they have failed to make any appeal to historical findings, can be understood in part as a reference to the claim that the natural law theorists had failed to allow for the historically conditioned nature of human creations. But here also Vico has in mind a further claim: that philosophers have failed to give an acceptable account of the nature of knowledge. It will be seen that there is a close connection between the two problems which Vico has so far not considered, for an enquiry into the question how historical method should be reformed to meet the requirements of knowledge proper or science presupposes some account of what these requirements are. Vico's own methodological recommendations are therefore preceded by a statement of his theory of knowledge and the latter by his critical reference to former theories of knowledge. It will be most convenient to approach the elucidation of Vico's own theory by considering his criticisms of former theories of knowledge. These are, however, taken for granted in the *Scienza Nuova* and can best be understood by reference to the development of his thought in some of his earlier works.

THE DEVELOPMENT OF VICO'S THEORY OF KNOWLEDGE

In the development of Vico's theory of knowledge prior to the *Scienza Nuova* two distinct but complementary tendencies can be traced. On the one side there is Vico's gradually increasing criticism of Cartesian rationalism and the theory of clear and distinct ideas which brought him in the end to a total rejection of these doctrines. On the other side, proceeding more or less step by step in pace with this, there is his gradual development of the theory that we can know only what we can make, which resulted, in its final form, in the epistemological doctrines of the *Scienza Nuova*.

The demand for certainty which had inspired Descartes in his search for a theory of knowledge had led him and his followers to the conclusion that knowledge was obtainable only with regard to the propositions of metaphysics, mathematics and those aspects of the natural world which could be given a mathematical basis and upon which the science of physics depended. The criterion of 'clear and distinct' ideas offered, however, no guidance in matters of probability which, on this basis, could not be distinguished from the downright false. Consequently the whole of historical and practical learning was judged to lie outside the field of knowledge. Vico, who in his first writings accepted these aspects of Cartesianism,[1] later recalled them in these words: 'All my life I had delighted in the use of reason more than memory and the more I knew in philology the more ignorant I saw myself to be. Descartes and Malebranche were not far wrong, it seemed, when they said it was alien to the philosopher to work long and hard at philology.'[2]

Vico's dissatisfaction with some aspects of Cartesianism first appears in his *De Nostri Temporis Studiorum Ratione*,[3] published in 1709. In this work Vico was prepared to allow the capacity of the Cartesian criterion of truth to guarantee such metaphysical propositions as the *Cogito*[4] and mathematical propositions. The first indication of his disenchantment with the theory is to be seen, however, in his unwillingness to allow its capacity to guarantee our knowledge of truths of physics, on the ground that the nature of the subject-matter of physics is not suited to the deductive methods characteristic of the Cartesian approach.[5]

---

[1] Yvon Belaval has cast doubt upon the extent and depth of Vico's reading of Descartes's own works as against those of other rationalists, notably Malebranche and Spinoza. This does not, however, affect the account given below, in which it is Vico's 'Descartes' rather than an historically accurate Descartes that is important. See 'Vico and Anti-Cartesianism', in *Giambattista Vico, An International Symposium*, eds. Tagliacozzo and White (Johns Hopkins Press, Baltimore 1968).

[2] From the chapter 'Nova Scientia Tentatur' of Vico's *Universal Law* (1721), quoted and translated by M. H. Fisch and T. G. Bergin, *The Autobiography of Giambattista Vico* (Great Seal Books, Ithaca, New York 1963), p. 37.

[3] Translated under the title *On The Study Methods of Our Time*, by Elio Gianturco (The Library of Liberal Arts, Bobbs-Merrill, U.S.A. 1965). All quotations from this work are taken from this translation.

[4] 'Modern philosophical critique supplies us with a fundamental verity of which we can be certain even when assailed by doubt', *On the Study Methods of Our Time*, p. 9.

[5] 'Let us not deceive ourselves and others. In the geometrical field, these deductive methods, these sorites, are excellent ways and means of demonstrating mathema-

These first intimations of a more critical attitude towards Cartesianism are accompanied also by the first indications of the alternative theory of knowledge by which Vico was eventually to replace it. This is to be seen in his reason for denying the demonstrability of the propositions of physics while allowing that of geometrical propositions:

The method by which they [propositions of physics] are reached is that of geometry but physical truths so elicited are not demonstrated so reliably as geometrical axioms. We are able to demonstrate geometrical propositions because we create them; were it possible for us to supply demonstrations of propositions of physics, we would be capable of creating them *ex nihilo* as well.[1]

Thus geometrical propositions are demonstrable because we create them, the propositions of physics indemonstrable because we do not create their subject-matter. Were we able to create their subject-matter the propositions of physics would also be demonstrable.[2]

The precise aspects of Cartesianism against which Vico was here reacting are important for their later bearing upon the interpretation of the *Scienza Nuova*. It must be noted therefore that Vico does not here present himself as being against deduction as such. His claim is that it is a necessary but not a sufficient condition of knowledge. Its application in geometry but not in physics is sufficient to guarantee knowledge only because in the former, but not in the latter, we create the propositions themselves, i.e. we create all the elements upon which a successful deduction depends, including not only its deductive structure but its very premisses as well.

It should further be noted that in *De Nostri Temporis Studiorum Ratione*, where he is concerned with the methods by which knowledge is reached and confirmed and not with its content, Vico does not offer an independent theory of truth. He seems content to accept that the truth is what we know when we know. In his next major work, however, *De Antiquissima Italorum Sapientia*, published a year later in 1710, his objections to Cartesianism are further extended and his

tical truths. But whenever the subject matter is unsuited to deductive treatment, the geometrical procedure may be a faulty and captious way of reasoning...As a consequence the principles of physics which are put forward as truths on the strength of the geometrical method are not really truths but wear a semblance of probability', *ibid*. pp. 22–3.   [1] *Ibid*. p. 23.
[2] For convenience I shall refer to this theory as the creative theory of knowledge.

theory of knowledge is expanded by being brought into relationship with a causal theory of truth.

In this work Vico still maintains the creative theory of knowledge: 'human truths are those of which we ourselves create the elements'.[1] But the case against the Cartesian theory of clear and distinct ideas rests not so much upon a disagreement about the nature of knowledge, though there is such disagreement, as upon disagreement about the nature of truth. This can be seen in Vico's reasons for rejecting for the first time the claim that the *Cogito* is a bulwark against scepticism. The *Cogito* is disallowed as an item of knowledge on the ground that, although one is certain that one thinks and that one exists, this certainty is nothing but a simple consciousness or apprehension of the facts in question, available as such to anybody and not confined to those capable of philosophical reflection.[2] It is not knowledge, however, for when we have knowledge we possess the form, genus or cause of things and the consciousness of thinking upon which Descartes's claim rests is a sign but not a cause of mind.[3]

The notion of cause is here used in a very extended, Spinozistic, sense, to include not only the full logical ground of the effect but also its efficient cause. This is made clear from the very close connection Vico sees between knowing the cause of something and actually creating that thing. For 'science is the knowledge of the genus or mode by which a thing is made, by means of which the mind, at the same time that it knows the mode, because it arranges the elements, makes the thing'.[4] What is true is convertible with what is made

---

[1] *Giambattista Vico, Opere*, vol I, edited by G. Gentile and F. Nicolini (Bari 1914), p. 141. The translations, which I have deliberately kept as literal as possible, were prepared with my wife's assistance.

[2] 'But the sceptic does not doubt that he thinks; indeed, he professes himself as sure of it as if he were [literally] seeing it...Nor does he doubt that he exists...However, he maintains that his certainty is not knowledge but consciousness, a common cognition found even in the unlearned...not a rare and exquisite truth such as to require for its discovery a meditation by such a great philosopher [as Descartes]. For to know means to possess the genus or form by which the thing is made: but consciousness is of those things of which we are not able to demonstrate the genus or form', *Opere*, vol. I, p. 139.

[3] 'For to know...means knowing the causes from which a thing originates...And, indeed, thinking is not the cause but simply the sign of my being a mind. And precisely because the sign is not the cause the prudent sceptic will not deny the certainty of the signs but rather will deny that of the causes', *ibid.* p. 140. Vico uses the terms 'cause', 'form' and 'genus' more or less interchangeably in this work.

[4] *Ibid.* p. 132. See also n. 3 below.

'when the object recognised as true owes its very being to the mind that knows it'.[1]

The identification of knowing the cause of a thing with making that thing provides Vico with a reason for claiming that mathematics is the highest branch of human knowledge. For the human mind contains in itself and can order and compose all the elements necessary for such knowledge, i.e. the rules and conventions upon which mathematical knowledge depends.[2]

The position is different, however, with regard to knowledge of physical and human things. For here Vico holds a neo-Platonic theory of essences or forms which subsist as a unity in God's but not in man's mind. Consequently they are knowable to God but not to man.[3] Man is in contact with them only insofar as they are immersed in corporeal matter and the degree to which they are so makes knowledge of their causes increasingly inaccessible to him. Mechanics is consequently less certain than arithmetic, physics less certain than mechanics and human activity less certain than both.[4] In this way Vico is able to construct a scale on which the various kinds of knowledge can be assigned a status relative to one another. It is important to note, however, that this scale is not a consequence

[1] *Ibid.* 137.

[2] 'Arithmetic and geometry, which are commonly thought not to prove by causes, [are the sciences which] do prove by them. And they demonstrate by causes because the human mind contains, and hence can order and arrange, the elements of the truths; and from these ordered and composed things arise the truths which they demonstrate, so that the demonstration is identical with the operation (*operatio*) and the true with the made', *ibid.* pp. 149–50.

[3] 'Being, unity, figure, motion, body, intellect, will are one thing in God, in whom they constitute an indissoluble unity, and another thing in man, in whom they are divided', *ibid.* p. 134.

'God knows all things because he contains the elements from which he arranges them in himself. Man, however, strives to know these things by dividing them. Therefore human knowledge is seen to involve a certain dissecting of the works of nature', *ibid.* p. 133. 'We are not able to prove physics by causes because the elements of natural things exist outside us', *ibid.* p. 150.

[4] '[The different kinds of] knowledge will be less certain according as, in their different ways, they are immersed in corporeal matter. Mechanics is less certain than geometry and arithmetic because it considers movement but with the aid of machines; physics is less certain than mechanics because where mechanics studies the external movement of peripheries, physics studies the internal movements of centres; morality (*moralis*) is less certain than physics because while the latter studies movement within the body this is an element of nature and so is certain, morality studies the movement of minds which are very deep and which come from desires which are infinite', *ibid.* p. 136.

merely of his theory of knowledge, but of this taken in conjunction with his theory of truth and his metaphysical theory, i.e. his theory of the nature of the various things involved in the different branches of knowledge.

Finally, even with regard to the empirical sciences, which man cannot fully know, Vico proposes an appropriate method which again involves a reference to making, though of a somewhat different kind. Physical theories are to be accepted insofar as they allow us to make things which conform to them, discoveries in the field of nature to be confirmed by experiments in which we create imitations of natural conditions.[1] The suggestion is of a combination of theoretical reasoning with empirical verification, a method Vico attributes with approval to Pythagoras, Plato and Galileo.[2]

The salient points of the theories of knowledge and truth in the above account may be summarised in the following way. Men can have knowledge only where they have in some sense made the thing recognised as true. In so doing they satisfy the demand for an account of the 'cause' or 'form' of the thing known, i.e. for a complete explanation of the kind given by a mathematician when he derives a proposition from the basic definitions, rules and axioms of his system. Consciousness of particular facts, even of the particular facts of one's own mental life, can give us certainty but not knowledge of those facts, for consciousness alone fails to provide an account of their causes.

Vico has thus connected the creative theory of knowledge with a causal theory of truth. The connection between them lies in the claim that where a branch of science is such that its basic elements consist in nothing other than rules and conventions of our own making, we can

---

[1] 'In physics those theories (*ea meditata*) are proven which allow us [successfully] to operate something similar to them: and the clearest and most commonly accepted reasonings about natural things are those supported by experiments in which we create imitations of nature', *ibid.* p. 137.

[2] 'Let us conclude finally that it is not the geometric method that should be used in physics, but demonstration itself. The greatest geometers have contemplated the principles of physics in the light of those of mathematics, e.g. among the ancients, Pythagoras and Plato, and amongst modern thinkers, Galileo. Thus it is right to explain the effects of nature by means of such experiments as are proper to geometrical works', *ibid.* p. 184. The linking of Pythagoras and Plato in this connection suggests that Vico may have in mind the passage in the *Republic* 531, in which the Pythagorean conception of a mathematically based science of harmonics is placed upon a higher scientific level than enquiries which study harmonic relations on a purely audible basis.

justifiably claim to know the causes of the things with which the science is concerned. These two theories, taken in connection with certain metaphysical theories about the nature of the subject-matters of the various sciences, have further allowed Vico to produce a scale of knowledge, for the metaphysical theories have enabled him to decide, with respect to any given branch of science, whether or not its basic elements are purely conventional.

It would be difficult to accept these claims just as they stand, involving, as they do, an unargued and highly problematic relationship between 'knowing the causes of' and 'knowing by virtue of causing'. For it is far from obvious that the condition that knowledge involves knowledge of the causes of something is satisfied by the fact that we ourselves are responsible for the creation of the causes of that thing. Yet Vico so clearly thinks that this condition is thus satisfied that he does not argue the point at all. Discussion of this claim, however, may be deferred until the doctrines of the *Scienza Nuova* are reached since its theories of knowledge and truth will there be shown to be connected in a similar but modified way.

It is more important for the moment to note the nature of the difference between consciousness and knowledge. This is not a difference in degree of verification, for Vico is prepared to allow that our consciousness that we are thinking is the best support we can have for our certainty that we are thinking. It is, rather a difference between two kinds of knowledge. In one we understand something when we have a full causal explanation of it, so that in knowing that it is true we know why it is true. In the other we have certainty but we lack any causal knowledge.

A number of important relationships may be discerned between the doctrines of the *De Antiquissima* and those of the *Scienza Nuova*. First, it is clear that the kind of taxonomic scheme which arises from the theories contained in the two works is entirely different. In the *De Antiquissima* mathematics is the highest kind of knowledge accessible to man. It is followed by knowledge of mechanics, physics, and human activity in that order. In the *Scienza Nuova*, however, the highest kind of knowledge is that of the world of human affairs which 'since men had made it, men could come to know'.[1] Mathematics is still thought to satisfy most of the conditions of knowledge, yet is

[1] *S.N.* 331.

regarded as inferior to knowledge of human affairs because it deals with abstractions rather than with realities.[1] The natural world, however, is now regarded as altogether unknowable. It is that which 'since God made it, He alone knows'.[2]

It is clear also that this change in the taxonomic scheme of the two works is not a consequence of a change in Vico's view about the nature of knowledge as such, for the distinction between, and definitions of, *scienza* and *coscienza* are common to both. *Coscienza* is that certainty that belongs to simple, psychological apprehension of the particular and, as such, does not constitute knowledge. In the *De Antiquissima*, *scienza* involves a making of something in which its full logical cause is adduced. It thus involves that knowledge of the universal and eternal which in the *Scienza Nuova* is said to be a property of every science.[3]

The degree of identity which obtains here must, however, not be exaggerated. A full theory of knowledge states both the conditions which must be satisfied for the attainment of knowledge and the methods whereby such conditions can be satisfied in the various fields of knowledge. The agreement which has been shown to obtain between the epistemological doctrines of the two works extends only to the first part of this, i.e. to agreement about the nature of knowledge itself, and not to any further methodological matters.

There is, moreover, a major change in the metaphysical doctrines of the two works. In the *De Antiquissima* the causes of both physical and human phenomena are neo-Platonic essences or forms. These subsist in the mind of God but not that of man. Knowledge of them is therefore available to God but not to man. As the exposition of the metaphysical theories of the *Scienza Nuova* has shown, however, the latter work contains an entirely different account of the causes of human institutions. A distinction has been drawn between formal and empirical causes. Vico's account of the formal causes of human institutions is given in his theories of man's social nature, common sense, natural law, and so on; the empirical causes of human institutions are the determinate historical and sociological conditions which, given man's ever-present dissatisfaction, determine the outcome of

---

[1] 'Now, as geometry, when it constructs the world of quantity out of its elements, or contemplates that world, is creating it for itself, just so does our Science [create for itself the world of nations] but with a reality greater by just so much as the institutions having to do with human affairs are more real than points, lines, surfaces and figures are', *S.N.* 349.

[2] *S.N.* 331. [3] *S.N.* 163.

his unrest. There is thus a shift in Vico's metaphysics of human development from transcendent formal and efficient causes subsisting in God's mind to immanent formal causes which constitute man's nature and empirical historical and sociological causes which determine his institutional history.[1] The knowledge of the universal and eternal in which *scienza* consists will not therefore be knowledge of transcendent neo-Platonic forms but of causes of these other two types. In contrast to both of these kinds the causes of physical things remain transcendent and, as such, unknowable to man.

The fundamental reason why, therefore, Vico was able to claim in the *Scienza Nuova* a knowledge of human affairs he had denied in the *De Antiquissima* is that in the period between the two works his conception of the nature of the causes of human affairs had entirely altered. Correctly conceived and described, and with the development of a methodology appropriate to them, these affairs, which had formerly fallen into one part of the *scienza–coscienza* dichotomy, would now be shown to fall into the other.

Before leaving the *De Antiquissima* one further point must be made, although its full relevance will not become clear until the final consideration of Vico's theory of knowledge is reached. Vico denies that one can have *scienza* of one's own thoughts merely by apprehending them because in apprehending them one is not making them. For *scienza* one would have to know the mind which is their cause. It follows that, if this claim is maintained in the *Scienza Nuova*, the knowledge of human affairs which it makes possible will not be the same sort of thing as that apprehension which historical agents themselves had of those affairs, for the latter will only constitute a species of *coscienza*. *Scienza* will, in fact, have to involve an explanation of the nature of the apprehending and active capacities of historical agents, i.e. precisely the sort of thing for which Vico's theory of man's historico-sociological nature has laid the groundwork. The knowledge which the new science is to make available

---

[1] This claim will be supported on independent grounds, see below, p. 174 ff. There is, however, an interesting difference between Vico's references to the properties of science in the two works. In the *De Antiquissima* he approvingly attributes to Plato the view that 'science has for its object the eternal and immutable' (*Opere*, vol. I, p. 151). In the *Scienza Nuova*, however, it is to Aristotle that he turns for support for his claim that 'science has to do with what is universal and eternal' (*S.N.* 163). This difference in attribution may well reflect the shift in Vico's thought from transcendent to immanent causes.

could never, therefore, be just an account of the historical or social situation as appreciated by historical agents themselves. It would also have to involve an account of those historico-sociological conditions under which such appreciations arise, i.e. an account of the historical and sociological conditions under which common sense itself receives its content.

THE UNION OF PHILOSOPHY AND PHILOLOGY

It is clear that by the time of the *Scienza Nuova* Vico had come to feel a deep dissatisfaction with various aspects of the Cartesian theory of knowledge. To some extent this was based upon an awareness of its inadequacy to guarantee the truth of the limited number of propositions to which, on its own terms, it was applicable. Beyond this, however, it also reflected his view that the limits it set upon human knowledge were far too narrow and excluded the very things we were best fitted to understand, knowledge of our own human affairs.

In the light of this it is possible to consider what Vico means when he says that had the philosophers and historians not failed to take each other's disciplines into account 'they would have anticipated us in conceiving this science'. The implication is that in Vico's science philosophy will do what it has previously failed to do, i.e. give certainty to its reasonings 'by appeal to the authority of the philologians' while the latter will do what they have likewise previously failed to do, i.e. 'give their authority the sanction of truth by appeal to the reasoning of the philosophers'.[1] In other words philosophical theory is to be given particular application by reference to history while history is to become a science by being pursued in accordance with sound philosophical theory.

These claims may be put in the following way. Hitherto philosophers have been too much taken up with the necessity to confine knowledge to what is beyond all possible doubt and have consequently made no contribution to our understanding of the concrete facts of human life with which history is concerned. The 'clear and distinct ideas' of Cartesian thought, although postulated in a laudable attempt to establish knowledge, have simply no bearing upon particular fact. Historians have been concerned with such fact but, in

[1] *S.N.* 140.

their turn, they have pursued their investigations on the basis of arbitrary, inadequate and unsystematic, metaphysical and epistemological assumptions. Consequently their work lacks the consistency and objectivity necessary for knowledge.

The new science is to correct the mistakes of both these approaches by bringing philosophy and history into a mutual relationship, the product of which will be *knowledge of fact*. The peculiar, and crucial, difficulty which faces Vico here is that he does not want to abandon either the claim that 'knowledge is of the universal and eternal' or that history deals with that created by human choice, i.e. the particular. For the former claim rules out the possibility that knowledge can be of that which is purely contingent, as it might have been for the Epicureans, while the latter rules out the possibility that the facts be the consequence of some eternal and necessary being, as they were for Spinoza, thus losing all contingency.

The development which enabled Vico to surmount this difficulty was his realisation that knowledge of the universal and eternal was not, as in their various ways Plato and Descartes had thought, confined to knowledge of what was conceptually true, but could include knowledge of the empirical laws which determine the actual behaviour of things. In the *De Antiquissima* Vico had thought that even efficient causes were aspects of forms which subsisted in God's mind and of which we consequently could have no knowledge. In the *Scienza Nuova*, however, he had come to realise that although man's nature was such that it necessitated that certain aspects of human behaviour be causally determined it necessitated only the form and not the content of these causes. The latter remained a purely empirical matter. The way was thus opened for his coming to knowledge of human affairs, by establishing what these causes were and revealing their operation in concrete facts.

It is important to note that the theory which Vico has put forward in the earlier elements, i.e. the account of man's historical and sociological nature, entails that there will be historico-sociological laws but does not entail what these laws will be. What Vico offers in his metaphysical theories is a general philosophical theory of man, involving an account of those concepts required to understand the claim that man makes his own world. This theory is *a priori* but it does not of itself involve the statement of any determinate law. It offers instead an account of these concepts which would have to appear in the statements of such a law if we were to understand the latter through our knowledge of human nature. These, of course, are concepts such as the modifications of the human mind, common sense, human needs and utilities, natural law and so on. But in offering such an *a priori* theory of man's historical and social nature, even a theory which entails that there will be historico-sociological laws, Vico is not committed to a theory of *a priori* laws.

The suggestion therefore is that in the *Scienza Nuova* Vico distinguishes two kinds of causation which he had conflated in his earlier thought. These are metaphysical causes which determine the formal characteristics of phenomena in the human world, and empirical causes which determine what actually occurs. The first of these has already been discussed, the second remains to be established.

The idea that human history is, in a certain sense, determined, is very prominent in the *Scienza Nuova*. Vico claims that:

The course of the institutions of the nations had to be, must now be and will have to be such as our science demonstrates, even if infinite worlds were born from time to time through eternity, which is certainly not the case. Our science therefore comes to describe an ideal eternal history traversed in time by the history of every nation in its rise, development, maturity, decline and fall. Indeed, we make bold to affirm that he who meditates this science narrates to himself this ideal eternal history so far as he himself makes it for himself by that proof 'it had, has and will have to be'.[1]

Furthermore, for anybody who attends to Vico's comparisons between different histories 'there will unfold before us, not the particular history in time of the laws and deeds of the Romans and Greeks, but (by virtue of the identity of the intelligible *substance* in the diversity of their modes of development), the ideal history of the eternal laws which are instanced by the deeds of all nations'.[2]

It is clear therefore that the same irreversible sequence of events occurs in the history of all nations and that it does so because the deeds of nations are instances of laws. The claim that the laws in question are empirical and not metaphysical is, however, much more questionable and, indeed, cannot be established without a consideration of Vico's methodological recommendations.

[1] *S.N.* 348–9.   [2] *S.N.* 1096.

8

The problem of methodology

THE INDUCTIVE THESIS

It would be simple enough to demonstrate the empirical character of the laws upon which the 'ideal eternal history' depends were one able to appeal to one of the traditional interpretations in which the *Scienza Nuova* is regarded in large part as an attempt to formulate an inductively established sociology.[1] Unfortunately, this interpretation fails to do justice to the subtlety and sophistication with which Vico attempted to meet the methodological problems confronting him, and, indeed, fails to base itself upon any adequate understanding of the nature of these problems. This can best be shown by indicating the outline of, and evidence for, such an account and then showing how it fails to meet Vico's particular problems.

One reason why Vico's methodological recommendations have been thought to be inductive in character is that in the *Scienza Nuova* he lays great stress upon the fact that his account of the laws which govern human history has widespread empirical support. In Element XIII, one of the most fundamental yet most obscure of all, he writes:

Uniform ideas originating among entire people unknown to each other must have a common ground of truth.

This axiom is a great principle which establishes the common sense of the human race as the criterion taught to the nations by divine providence to define what is certain in the natural law of the gentes. And the nations reach this certainty by understanding the underlying identity which, despite variations of detail, obtain among them all in respect of this law. Thence

---

[1] This was the view of the late-nineteenth-century positivist interpreters of Vico. See Siciliani, *Rinnovamento della Filosofia Positiva in Italia* (Florence 1871).

issues the mental dictionary for assigning origins to all the diverse articulated languages. It is by means of this dictionary that the ideal eternal history is conceived, which gives us the histories in time of all nations.[1]

The 'ideas' referred to in the axiom itself are the judgements of common sense, which are also mentioned as a 'criterion' in the corollary. Since Vico has already connected *il vero* with the 'universal and eternal' the axiom is asserting that where uniform judgements of common sense arise among different peoples independently of one another, they do so because they are a consequence of the same causes. This is clearly one of the main presuppositions of Vico's science: that uniform correlations are products of causal connections and are not to be dismissed as mere coincidences. This is confirmed by the fact that, as we have seen, Vico is prepared to reject the Epicurean hypothesis of chance on the grounds that when men act in the same ways 'the results of their so doing are always the same'.[2]

The corollary to the axiom makes four claims which could be read as indications of the method whereby we are to reach the 'universal and eternal'. Taken in this way they can be stated as follows:

(1) The axiom establishes common sense as the criterion by which may be defined what is certain in the natural law of the gentes.

(2) The latter is reached by understanding the 'underlying identity' which obtains among nations in respect of their natural law.

(3) From this identity we can derive a mental dictionary for assigning origins to all the various languages.

(4) By means of this dictionary we arrive at the 'ideal eternal history' which determines the history in time of all the nations.

The suggestion would thus be that we search first for invariable correlations in the natural law of different peoples. We then abstract from this a 'dictionary' of people's needs and utilities, i.e. of the things which determine their social activity for which there are appropriate linguistic expressions. Finally, from this in turn we abstract the complex set of laws (the 'ideal eternal history') which determines the sequence of changes all actual histories will incorporate. The method would therefore involve the use of induction and comparative analysis. By a series of steps a set of empirical laws would

---

[1] Element XIII, *S.N.* 145. I have modified Bergin and Fisch's translation here, translating Vico's *unità* as 'identity' rather than 'agreements' and his *intendere* as 'understanding' rather than 'recognising'.

[2] *S.N.* 1108.

be established which would explain what was common in the history of all nations. For convenience I shall call this the inductive thesis.

In favour of this account is the undeniable fact that comparative research, albeit often of an idiosyncratic nature, plays a large part in the *Scienza Nuova*. As an example of this we may consider Vico's claim that all nations, at a certain stage in their careers, must develop belief of a pantheistic kind. To support this thesis Vico offers an analysis of the myth of Jove, in which it is claimed that the myth, in its original meaning, embodied such a belief. Further, he tries to show, by a series of similar analyses, that all nations had, at some time in their history, a God who was the same as Jove in all but name.[1] It might thus seem that Vico's claim that every nation must have a pantheistic stage in its career is an inductive conclusion.[2]

It is also to be noted that in his account of the history of philosophy Vico praises philosophers such as Socrates and Plato, to whom he attributes use of the inductive and synthetic method, and criticises others such as Aristotle and Zeno, to whom he attributes a deductive method:

The former [Aristotle] taught by syllogism, a method which deduces particulars from their universals rather than uniting particulars to obtain universals...Neither yielded anything more notable to the advantage of the human race. Hence with great reason Bacon, great alike as philosopher and statesman, proposes, commends and illustrates the inductive method in his [*Novum*] *Organum*, and is still followed by the English with great profit in experimental philosophy.[3]

The favourable character of Vico's remarks about Bacon and the English philosophers for their use of the inductive method, and his deprecating references to Aristotle for his employment of the deductive method, would seem to support the suggestion that Vico's method is itself inductive.

[1] *S.N.* 380.

[2] Croce detected such a method in Vico and, although wanting to write it off as a mistake on Vico's part, characterised it as inductive, describing the 'ideal eternal history' as the product of an 'empirical science of man and society' which was 'inductive and psychological'. See *The Philosophy of Giambattista Vico*, p. 35. More recently Matteo Iannizzotto has supported the view that Vico's method was essentially inductive, leading only to knowledge of the probable. See *L'Empirismo Nella Gnoseologia di G.B. Vico* (Padua 1968), chapter VIII.

[3] *S.N.* 499. The reference here is to Boyle, of whose work Vico is generally thought to have had some knowledge. See F. Nicolini, *La Giovinezza di Giambattista Vico* (Bari 1932), pp. 113–14.

Nevertheless a number of considerations can be brought forward to show that the inductive thesis is incorrect and rests upon a misunderstanding of what Vico was trying to do. The following four are perhaps the most important. They serve also to provide a foundation for coming to a more acceptable view.

It should be noted first that the inductive thesis presents no solution whatsoever to the main problems with which the *Scienza Nuova* is, at least according to Vico, concerned. It has been argued above that the doctrines developed in the 'Elements' and in the section on 'Method' are claimed to establish the scientific principles necessary for a correct account of history, e.g. for the account summarised by Vico in his Chronological Table. Further, Vico's criticisms of current historical practice have shown that he thinks this is in need of reform if historical knowledge is to be reached.[1] It is to be noticed, however, that the inductive method, while it might produce laws and hence be scientific, could not produce principles which would help solve problems of this kind, for the materials from which its conclusions were derived would themselves be (accounts of) historical facts. If, as Vico has claimed, the problem is to establish these facts themselves, the inductive method would be of no assistance since, in abstracting from such facts, it would necessarily presuppose them. An inductive method, of the kind sketched above, would be essentially a second-order procedure, the epistemological status of the results of which, even when properly carried out, would be dependent ultimately upon that of the first-order facts from which it was derived. It could not therefore provide whatsoever scientific principles were held necessary for the establishment of these facts. An acceptable account of Vico's method would therefore have to show that it was a method for the introduction of scientific principles into *history* and Vico's remarks must be read in the light of this aim.

Vico has also claimed that he is going to achieve this aim by creating a science in which the philosophers are to 'give certainty to their reasonings by appeal to the authority of the philologians' and the latter 'to give their authority the sanction of truth by appeal to the reasonings of the philosophers'.[2] But if his methodological remarks were taken to amount to an advocacy of inductive procedures it would

---

[1] See pp. 8–14 above for the development of these points.
[2] *S. N.* 140.

become impossible to see how the aim could thus be achieved. The 'reasonings' of the philosopher would presumably be the comparative analysis referred to above. But these could not give 'the sanction of truth' to the work of the philologian since they would presuppose it. Nor does there seem to be a place for any other kind of philosophical reasoning on this account.

A further connected difficulty here is that this view does not allow for the metaphysical character of Vico's account of man's historico-social nature. The latter might, at best, be an inductive hence empirical conclusion, i.e. a consequence of the acceptance of Vico's recommendations. It certainly could not be a principle providing a scientific basis for such conclusions, for it might even turn out to be falsified by them. If we suppose it to be a product of philosophical reasoning it could not give the sanction of truth to philological research since it would also presuppose the findings of that research.

Finally it must be noted that this interpretation of Vico's remarks is unable to explain why he should claim that we can have knowledge of the human world but not of the natural world because we can discover the principles of the one but not of the other in our own human mind. If knowledge were inductively established this reservation would be unintelligible since, as Vico pointed out when commending Bacon, the English were applying the inductive method successfully in 'experimental philosophy'.

For these reasons the inductive thesis must be rejected as inadequate. The essential point here is that it fails to come to grips with Vico's problem at the right level, for the laws in which it claims the 'ideal eternal history' consists would presuppose, and therefore could not support, historical fact. What is required is an interpretation which shows how 'philosophical reasoning' can contribute to the establishment of first-order historical facts of the kind which appear in Vico's own Chronological Table.

THE DEDUCTIVE THESIS

An alternative account which would have the merit of meeting Vico's problem at the correct level can be produced if we view Vico's remarks in the following way. Science is concerned with the universal and eternal. The introduction of scientific principles into history can be achieved only by basing the interpretation of the latter upon principles which govern the humanity of nations, i.e. upon the laws which govern the development of the empirical content of human nature itself. Such laws cannot be inductively established, since they would then presuppose the very facts to be based upon them. Nor, since they are empirical laws, relating to what actually happens, can they be established *a priori*. They can be established only by being shown to be involved in the constitution of historical facts themselves. The 'ideal eternal history' is therefore an empirical theory deduced from certain assumptions about laws, to which we commit ourselves when we interpret historical evidence in a particular way. These assumptions are necessary within such a system of interpretation but they are not *a priori*, for should no acceptable interpretation of evidence be possible by means of them they, along with the interpretations in question, must be rejected. Nor, again, are they inductive. They are, nevertheless, testable, not directly but via the acceptability of the facts to whose constitution they contribute.

This interpretation involves a number of distinct claims: the 'ideal eternal history' is deductive in form; its premisses are all necessary within the system, i.e. they are not themselves directly challengeable or testable, though the system is challengeable; the whole theory is empirically confirmable through the facts whose interpretation it makes possible; and if it is thus confirmed its propositions assume the status of laws. It is one thing, of course, to suggest that such a conception would solve the problems with which Vico is concerned and another to show that it is indeed to be found in Vico. The interpretation therefore requires to be supported by further textual analysis. Nevertheless, before undertaking this, it might be useful briefly to point out how it meets Vico's needs as they have so far come to light.

Vico has brought these requirements together in the claim that philosophy and history must so adapt as each to supply the other with what it has so far lacked: history to supply philosophy with the 'certain', philosophy to supply history with the 'true'. In the above interpretation these claims are to be understood in the following way. The 'certain' with which history will supply philosophy is a content of particular historical evidence to the conversion of which into intelligible, verified, historical fact, philosophical reasonings must be relevant. Through their intimate connection with this content, these reasonings can themselves be verified. Philosophy will therefore cease to concern itself with those purely conceptual truths with which it has formerly been concerned and come to be involved in our understanding of empirical truth.

Philosophy does this by supplying history with the 'true' which she has hitherto lacked. This breaks down into a number of claims. Philosophy will provide, first, theories about the nature of the subject-matter of history and the main categories required to understand it. These are Vico's theories of historico-social man and the nature of historical causation. As such they have no empirical content. They acquire the latter when they are used in the formulation of a general deductive theory about the course a nation's history must take, a formulation possible only by making assumptions about the laws which govern that history. By utilising the deductive consequences of these assumptions in his interpretations of historical evidence, the historian is able to give his work first a *systematic* character. This enables him to demonstrate the underlying unity in the institutions, thoughts and actions of a certain age. It enables him, further, to draw a clear distinction between the historically possible and the historically impossible and, similarly, between the historically necessary and the historically contingent, thus laying down precisely what kinds of explanations he can entertain with regard to a particular historical problem and what kinds are precluded. His work will therefore be freed of the charges of being unhistorical and arbitrary in character. Finally, in doing all this philosophy is providing a theory of knowledge in which history is accorded a status higher than that of any other intellectual activity, since the categories involved in its understanding are such as to render it more intelligible than other branches of knowledge.[1]

This interpretation would therefore provide a solution to the problems confronting Vico, though whether it is his theory remains to be seen. One further point must, however, be made about it as it has so far been stated. It has been pointed out earlier that the philosophical reasoning of which Vico's theories of historico-social man and historical causation are products differs from that involved in pro-

---

[1] This is a reference to Vico's claim that the principles of the historical world are to be found in our own human mind. It is fully discussed below, pp. 157–69.

ducing a systematic set of assumptions about the laws which govern man's history. The former involves the claim that there are such laws and of what sort they will be, the latter states the laws themselves. Moreover the claims that there are such laws and that they will be of an historical and sociological kind have conceptual but not empirical consequences for history, whereas the statements of such laws will have empirical consequences as well. Vico distinguishes these two kinds of reasoning, rather unsatisfactorily, as the 'general propositions' which are a 'basis of our science throughout' and the 'particular' propositions which 'provide more specific bases for the various matters it treats of'.[1] The philosophical account of man's nature and of historical causation is included in the general elements, and the account of the 'ideal eternal history' in the particular elements. The distinction is, however, more properly that between philosophy and a theoretical science or, in this case, since the laws are of an historical and sociological kind, a theoretical sociology.

Finally, before turning to investigate separately the various claims involved in this 'deductive' thesis it is necessary briefly to re-examine Element XIII and its corollary to see if it can be fitted in with this interpretation rather than with the inductive thesis previously considered. The passage offered support for the latter only if it was assumed that Vico was not concerned with the epistemological status of the historical facts between which the causal connections were to be established. This assumption has been shown to be unwarrantable. A further, equally challengeable, assumption made in the inductive interpretation of this passage is that the steps it outlines are in fact *procedural*, representing a series of rules to be followed for the establishment of the causal connections in question.

An alternative suggestion which is consistent with the view that Vico's concern is for the establishment of the historical facts themselves is that Vico is not here offering a series of methodological steps but is stating a number of formal relationships, in which the idea of common sense is connected to that of an 'ideal eternal history'. These statements would provide the conceptual basis for certain methodological recommendations but would not themselves constitute such

---

[1] *S.N.* 164. The first twenty-two elements (and Element CVI) are classified as general, the rest as particular.

recommendations. Taken thus the suggestion would work out in the following way.

The axiom itself asserts that where certain judgements of common sense occur in the case of all peoples independently, i.e. unknown to each other, this must be because they have their basis in certain (historico-sociological) laws. In suggesting that such a phenomenon 'must have a common ground of truth' Vico does not mean that judgements of common sense shared by different nations independently must form separate causal systems, which can then be discovered inductively. He means that any part of such a set of ideas or judgements must be a consequence of more fundamental laws which govern the development of the empirical content of human nature, i.e. historical and sociological laws. The corollary fills in certain sub-relationships involved in this over-all conception:

(1) Common sense determines the content of natural law and the interpretation of the latter must be undertaken in the light of this relationship.

(2) The necessary part of the content of natural law will be an identical element in the natural law of all nations.

(3) The conception of an identical element in the natural law of all nations implies ('thence issues') a mental dictionary (of the ideas and judgements involved in common sense) by which all linguistic evidence may be interpreted.

(4) The idea of a mental dictionary implies the concept of an 'ideal eternal history' which enables us to establish the histories in time of all nations.

Taken in this way the axiom is consistent with the main claims involved in the deductive account. It emphasises the point that the content of natural law is fully determined by common sense and this, in turn, by man's nature as it expresses itself in the 'ideal eternal history'. The question how the latter is to be established is not here touched upon, though it is clear that it must be established if we are to support any actual historical accounts.

It remains only to explain why Vico at this point should lay so much emphasis upon common sense and natural law since they are intermediate rather than fundamental causes in his science. The answer to this lies in the fact that, although not fundamental ontologically, they are of crucial importance methodologically. For it is at their level that the whole theory of historico-sociological laws becomes amenable to application in particular historical interpretations, since it is *via* common sense and the conception of natural justice to which this leads that man's nature conditions his actual historical institutions. Assumptions about common sense and natural law stand therefore in the closest possible connection to the interpretations of historical evidence upon which the credibility of the new science is to depend.

9

The ideal eternal history: its theoretical character

A first difficulty to be faced in maintaining the theoretical character of the 'ideal eternal history' is that Vico never explicitly ascribes such a character to it while, as we have seen, he approves of those philosophers such as Bacon who have adopted an inductive approach. This difficulty can be met by establishing the following three points:

(1) Although Vico does not ascribe a theoretical element to the 'ideal eternal history' as such he explicitly recognises such an element in his *science*.

(2) When he recognises such an element in his science he intends to include the 'ideal eternal history' in it.

(3) In describing Bacon's method as inductive Vico does not intend to deny that there is also a theoretical side to it. He is thus not using the word 'inductive' in an anti-theoretical sense, in which sense alone it can properly be used to describe the alternative account outlined in the last chapter.

Since the first and third of these points can be most easily established it will be convenient to commence with them.

Vico's explicit recognition of a theoretical aspect to his science is made in Element xxii, in which he divides the 'general Elements' into two groups. The first group (containing the philosophical theories so far discussed) comprise Elements v–xv. These 'serve for considering this world of nations in its eternal idea by that property of every science, noted by Aristotle, that science has to do with what is universal and eternal'. The second group (containing theories not yet discussed) comprises Elements xvi–xxii. These 'give us the foundations of the certain. By their use we shall be able to see *in fact* this world which we have hitherto studied *in idea*, following the method of philosophising that Francis Bacon, Lord of Verulam, did most to render certain, but carrying it over from the things of nature...to the civil institutions of mankind.'[1]

The distinction is between propositions elaborating the idea of the world of nations and propositions which give us the foundations for seeing this world in fact.[2] It is important to notice that, in using these elements to see *in fact* what has first been studied *in idea*, Vico takes himself to be extending Bacon's (inductive) method to the study of civil institutions. This suggests that he does not conceive the 'inductive' method to be wholly lacking in theoretical content.

This suggestion is confirmed by a later passage in which Vico discusses the relations between the propositions of philosophy and philology. The latter 'enable us to see in fact the institutions we have hitherto meditated in idea as touching this world of nations, in accordance with Bacon's method of philosophising, which is "think [and] see" (*cogitare videre*)'.[3]

Here Vico explicitly recognises the presence of a theoretical activity in Bacon's 'inductive' method. His approval of the latter does not therefore of itself suffice to falsify the deductive account of the 'ideal eternal history'. On the other hand these quotations do not themselves suffice to establish the latter, for it is by no means clear whether the 'theory' alluded to in them is meant to apply to the work of the philosopher in the broad sense, that in which it includes historical and sociological theory, or in the narrow sense, in which it excludes this. If Vico's references to the theoretical (the 'idea of this world of nations') are intended to refer only to his general theories about man's historico-social nature, it would remain possible that he thought of the establishment of determinate historico-social laws as a purely inductive matter. Certainly, as already pointed out, this would

[1] *S.N.* 163. My italics.
[2] Vico talks of seeing this world ' *in fatti*', i.e. in the facts.
[3] *S.N.* 359. The phrase ' *cogitare videre*' is Vico's mistranslation of Bacon's *Cogitata et Visa*, written between 1607 and 1609, a work of which probably only the title was known by Vico. See Paolo Rossi, *Le Sterminate Antichità* (Pisa 1969), p. 46. Since Vico considers that he is applying to the human world methods formerly applied only to the natural world, it is useful to recall here the account of the latter, given in the *De Antiquissima*, in which he approved of an approach he attributed to Plato, Pythagoras and Galileo in which physical facts were studied in the light of mathematical theories (see above, p. 80). The suggestion that in the *Scienza Nuova* Vico is thinking in terms of some relationship between scientific theory and empirical enquiry thus also derives support from Vico's earlier thought.

make it difficult to see how philosophy could thus provide philology with *il vero*, since it might turn out to be empirically false that man had the nature suggested, but the difficulty would reflect a major confusion in Vico's thought rather than a failure to interpret the latter correctly.

To decide between these alternatives it is necessary to turn to Vico's discussion of method, given, amongst other things, in a separate section from the 'Elements', called 'Method'. His first account is given in the following paragraph:

In search of these natures of human institutions our Science proceeds by a severe analysis of human thoughts about the human necessities or utilities of social life, which are the two perennial springs of the natural law of the gentes. In its second principal aspect our Science is therefore a history of human ideas.[1]

Vico mentions analysis (*analisi*) here but fails to define the term. It is not clear therefore whether he is thinking of the sort of comparative analytic activity proper to the inductive account, or of the deductive analysis proper to the alternative. That he is thinking of the latter, however, comes out in his next remarks in which he stresses the importance of a 'metaphysical art of criticism' which his science is to provide:

To determine the times and places for such a history – that is when and where these human thoughts were born – and thus to give it certainty by means of its own (so to speak) metaphysical chronology and geography, our Science applies a likewise metaphysical art of criticism with regard to the founders of these same nations...And the criterion our criticism employs is that taught by divine providence and common to all nations, namely the common sense of the human race, determined by the necessary harmony of human institutions, in which all the beauty of the civil world consists.[2]

Combining these passages, the 'metaphysical art of criticism', which takes human common sense as its criterion, provides a 'metaphysical chronology and geography'. The latter is necessary to establish the *actual* times and places for the history of ideas without which the history of institutions cannot be understood. Metaphysics being that part of Vico's science which is concerned with the

[1] *S.N.* 347.
[2] *S.N.* 348.

(historico-social) nature of the world of human minds,[1] a metaphysical chronology and geography will provide an account of those conditions of human mental development which determine when and where certain ideas will be created. An actual history offers, of course, an account of the actual occasions upon which they were created. Since the suggestion is that knowledge of the metaphysical conditions is necessary before we can establish any such actual account it is clear that the former cannot be derived from the latter as the inductive interpretation would suggest. Since knowledge of the conditions which determine the birth and development of human ideas cannot be extracted from historical accounts themselves without presupposing the acceptability of these accounts, it must be sought in some other way, through an art proper to it.

The conception of a metaphysical art of criticism is thus clearly an indispensable part of Vico's account of method. It is that part of it which deals with the establishment of the conditions which determine the order of development of human ideas. The clearest account of this art is given in the introductory 'Idea of the Work', in a paragraph which I quote at length:

Moreover, it may here be pointed out that in the present work, with a new critical art that has hitherto been lacking, entering on the research of the truth concerning the authors of these same [gentile] nations...philosophy undertakes to examine philology (i.e. the doctrine of all the institutions that depend on human choice; for example, all histories of the languages, customs, and deeds of peoples in war and peace), of which, because of the deplorable obscurity of causes and the almost infinite variety of effects, philosophy has had almost a horror of treating; and reduces it to the form of a science by discovering in it the design of an ideal eternal history traversed in time by the history of all nations...For by virtue of new principles of mythology herein disclosed as consequences of the new principles of poetry found herein, it is shown that the fables were true and trustworthy histories of the customs of the most ancient peoples of Greece. In the first place, the fables of the gods were stories of the times in which men of the crudest gentile humanity thought that all institutions necessary to the human race were deities. The authors of this poetry were the first peoples...who founded the gentile nations with fables of the gods. And here, *by the principles of this new critical art, we meditate*[2] *upon*

---

[1] *S.N.* 2, 400.

[2] I have altered Bergin and Fisch's translation which here reads 'we consider at what'. Vico, however, uses the verb *meditare*. The more literal translation is important for it enables this passage to be connected with others in the *Scienza Nuova*

what determinate times and what particular occasions of human necessity or utility felt by the first men of the gentile world, they, with frightful religions which they themselves feigned and believed in, imagined first such and such gods and then such and such others. The natural theogony or generation of the gods, formed naturally in the minds of these first men, may give us a rational chronology of the poetic history of the gods. [In the second place] the heroic fables were true stories of the heroes and their heroic customs, which are found to have flourished in the barbarous periods of all nations; so that the two poems of Homer are found to be two great treasure houses of discoveries of the natural law of the gentes among the still barbarous Greeks.[1]

The first part of this quotation makes a number of claims already considered. Vico is to introduce a new critical art, hitherto lacking, by which philosophy is to reduce philology to a science. This has so far been impossible because of the 'deplorable obscurity of causes and almost infinite variety of effects' of human affairs. But the critical art will remedy this state of affairs, by discovering these causes in the form of an 'ideal eternal history traversed in time by the histories of all nations'. Philosophy will thus make philology scientific by providing it, in the shape of the 'ideal eternal history', with an account of the *causes* of historical change.

The second part of the quotation offers examples of the new metaphysical criticism at work. Vico first refers to new mythological principles *by virtue of which* it will be shown that the fables of the gods were products of a mode of thought in which men personified and deified their thoughts about human necessities and utilities, and that the heroic fables were true stories of the heroes and their customs. In the light of these principles the Homeric poems are to be seen as expressions of two very different modes of human thought. And by virtue of this we put ourselves in a position to use poems as historical evidence and to find in them historical accounts of the natural law of the gentes.

Thus far, the suggestion is that philology becomes scientific when historical evidence is interpreted in the light of *general* theories of the causes and significance of evidence of that type, theories which involve, of course, accepting that evidence as the product of a certain historical and sociological being. But the new critical art amounts to

(351–9) which make it clear that the meditation in question involves meditation of the idea of a thing and that this is a philosophical as opposed to philological activity.
[1] *S.N.* 7. My italics.

more than just this insistence upon interpreting historical evidence in the light of general philosophical theory. For Vico claims in addition that 'by the principles of this new critical art, we meditate upon what determinate times and what particular occasions of human necessity or utility felt by the first man...they imagined first such and such gods and then such and such others'. Moreover, the outcome of this meditation is described as a 'rational' and not a temporal chronology, i.e. the same sort of chronology that is referred to elsewhere as 'metaphysical'.[1]

The first thing to note here is that the critical art produces a *determinate sequence* of human feelings of necessity and utility (i.e. judgements of common sense), and an equally determinate sequence of imagined deities by which early man represents these to himself. It is clear that it is of a sequence of this sort that Vico is thinking when, in the first part of the quotation, he attributes to philosophy the discovery of the 'ideal eternal history'.

It is important also to note that these determinate sequences are presented as an outcome of meditation, for this indicates that Vico is still dealing with a philosophical as opposed to a philological or factual enquiry. But since philosophy deals with the 'universal and eternal', it is clear that Vico intends that phrase to include the causal relations by means of which he wishes to explain these early theistic beliefs. The sequence of deities is 'rational' because, despite the fact that it involves causal explanations, it is an outcome of philosophical meditation and not of empirical research.

The 'ideal eternal history', of which this determinate sequence is a part, is thus a theory about the determinate causes of determinate kinds of human phenomena. It is, moreover, a product of philosophical reflection or reasoning. It is not the product of an inductive enquiry for, as Vico's references to the Homeric works indicate, it makes possible the correct interpretation of historical evidence.

From this it would seem that the new critical art involves interpreting historical evidence in the light both of general philosophical theories about the nature of man and of hypotheses about the determinate conditions under which he will act in certain equally determinate ways. These conditions being of an historico-sociological kind, Vico's claims about them may properly be called 'socio-

---

[1] *S. N.* 348. Quoted above, p. 99.

logical'. And since they are also a product of reason or meditation and not of empirical research, they may be called 'theoretical'. Vico thus includes in his conception of philosophy an activity which may correctly be distinguished as 'theoretical sociology'.

A properly constructed science of this sort ought to enable one to predict what, *under certain instantiated conditions*, men will do. In the passage from the section on Method, Vico follows the remarks considered above by a claim of precisely this sort:

> The decisive sort of proof in our Science is therefore this: that, once these institutions have been established by divine providence, the course of the institutions of the nations had to be, must now be and will have to be such as our Science demonstrates, even if infinite worlds were born from time to time through eternity, which is certainly not the case.[1]

There are two points to be noted here. Vico plainly takes himself to be offering a theory whereby the institutional pattern of a nation's history can be predicted. He is giving an account of those determinate conditions under which certain other determinate conditions must follow. He also implies, however, the possibility that these conditions may not be instantiated. Hence the force of the provisos that this pattern will obtain '*once* these institutions have been established by divine providence' and that it would occur infinitely if an infinite number of worlds (of nations) were to be born. His denial that the latter will occur shows that Vico does not think that his Science can establish that a nation should be born, only what will happen to it if it is born, i.e. only what will happen if certain conditions are instantiated. Vico is therefore offering a hypothetical, predictive theory about the conditions under which institutions will develop in certain ways.

[1]   *S. N.* 348.

10

The ideal eternal history: its deductive character

The claim that the 'ideal eternal history' is a theoretical construction suffices to refute the suggestion that its propositions might be empirical generalisations, inductively established. It does not, however, establish the further thesis, which must now be considered, that the 'ideal eternal history' is wholly deductive in character.

The source of the difficulty about the formal character of the 'ideal eternal history' lies in the fact that Vico describes his method in two apparently incompatible ways. On the one hand he commends the 'inductive' method of Bacon, although, as we have seen, he uses this term in an idiosyncratic way. In contrast to this he also dwells upon the quasi-geometric character of the 'ideal eternal history':

Our Science therefore comes to describe at the same time an ideal eternal history traversed in time by the history of every nation in its rise, development, maturity, decline and fall...Now as geometry, when it constructs the world of quantity out of its elements, or contemplates that world, is creating it for itself, just so does our Science [create for itself the world of nations], but with a reality greater by just so much as the institutions having to do with human affairs are more real than points, lines, surfaces and figures are. And this very fact is an argument, O reader, that these proofs are of a kind divine and should give thee a divine pleasure, since in God knowledge and creation are one and the same thing.[1]

The suggestion that the 'ideal eternal history' is constructed in the same manner as geometry might seem to support the suggestion that it is deductive in character. But this conclusion would be warranted only if it could be shown that Vico thought geometry itself to be a deductive science. And in the above quotation Vico makes only two

[1] *S.N.* 349.

positive remarks about geometry, that it is constructive ('it constructs the world of quantity') and that it itself provides the principles of construction (it 'is creating it for itself'), neither of which entail that it is deductive. In fact they amount to little more than an assertion of the creative theory of knowledge formulated in the *De Antiquissima*.

The principal reason why the 'ideal eternal history' has been thought to be non-deductive in character is that this has been thought to follow from Vico's rejection of Cartesian rationalism and, in particular, from his substitution of the creative theory of knowledge for Cartesian 'deduction' based upon clear and distinct ideas. Some scholars have been prepared to admit that the lay-out of the *Scienza Nuova* itself, with its section of 'Elements', in which are included axioms, definitions and postulates, reflects the influence of Descartes, but treat this solely as a surface characteristic, which is not reflected in the fundamental structure of the work.[1] Support for the non-deductive view is also found in Vico's complaints against Aristotle's conception of syllogistic deduction and the sorites of Zeno, which appear in the *De Antiquissima* and reappear in the *Scienza Nuova*.[2] Other scholars, however, have held that Vico's appeal to English empiricism does not exclude more rationalistic elements in his thought.[3]

The question to what extent the 'ideal eternal history' is deductive in structure is best settled by turning from Vico's explicit but obscure remarks about it to its manner of construction itself. For this purpose it will be most convenient to consider that part of it in which Vico deals with the development of the institutions of primitive ('poetic') man for it is here that the principles underlying its construction are most clearly revealed. The reason for this is that in constructing this part of human history Vico was dealing with a period for which there existed little or no evidence in his own time. What he did therefore was to work out that part of the 'ideal eternal history'

---

[1] See, for example, Max H. Fisch's essay, 'Vico and Pragmatism', in *Giambattista Vico, An International Symposium*, edited by G. Tagliacozzo and H. White, pp. 408–14.   [2] *S.N.* 499.

[3] Among these Paulo Rossi includes the definitions and axioms of the 'Elements', Vico's use of the geometrical method, his stated requirement that the new science must assume no previous historical knowledge (*S.N.* 349), and the use of generalisations and theoretical models in the construction of the 'ideal eternal history'. See *Le Sterminate Antichità* pp. 46–9.

which would be relevant to the actual history of the period in considerably more detail than that worked out for later periods, and then offer it as an actual historical account of the period. This lapse on Vico's part has the consequence that here, as nowhere else in the *Scienza Nuova*, the manner of construction of the 'ideal eternal history' is fully revealed. The following account is therefore drawn from Book II of the *Scienza Nuova* which purports to be, and in its later but not earlier stages is, an account of actual history.

Vico begins with the claim that an account of the common sense of early man must begin with an account of his nature.[1] He then proposes such a principle, that before human nature develops through social, civilising influences, man knows of things only what he perceives of them.[2] Poetic man must therefore have been incapable of abstract or rational thought but possessed nevertheless of keen senses and a vigorous imagination. From here Vico goes on to build up a picture of the world as it must have seemed to such a man. Because he was ignorant he would be curious about the causes of things[3] and would attribute a divine nature to these causes.[4] In attempting to understand these causes he would consider them as beings or parts of beings similar in nature to himself, i.e. he would personify what he saw.[5] In such circumstances he would naturally go on to personify the sky itself, and such natural phenomena as thunder and lightning, coming to think of the former as the mightiest of the gods and the latter as his means of communication with them.[6] Thunder and lightning

---

[1] 'From these first men, stupid, insensate and horrible beasts, all the philosophers should have begun their investigations of the wisdom [i.e. the common sense] of the ancient gentiles', *S.N.* 374.

[2] 'And human nature so far as it is like that of the animals, carries with it this property, that the senses are its sole way of knowing things.
  Hence poetic wisdom must have begun with a metaphysics not rational and abstract, like that of learned men now, but felt and imagined as that of these first men must have been, who, without power of ratiocination, were all robust sense and vigorous imagination', *S.N.* 374–5.

[3] 'This metaphysics was their poetry, a faculty born with them (for they were furnished by nature with those senses and imaginations); born of their ignorance of causes, for ignorance, the mother of wonder, made everything wonderful to men who were ignorant of everything,' *S.N.* 375.

[4] 'Their poetry was at first divine, because as we saw in the passage from Lactantius, they imagined the causes of the things they wondered at to be gods', *ibid.*

[5] 'At the same time they gave the things they wondered at substantial being after their own ideas, just as children do', *ibid.*

[6] 'Thereupon a few giants...raised their eyes and became aware of the sky. And because in such a case the nature of the human mind leads it to attribute its own

were thus the first words of a 'real' language by which the gods spoke to man. The emotional force of this divine fable of Jove was so great that the creators of the fable themselves would come to believe it while they would extend the concept of Jove until it embraced the whole experienced world.¹ Other parts of nature would thus become elements in the language by which Jove communicated with men and the need to understand this language would necessitate the development of a science of divination, the purpose of which was to discover the precise meaning of Jove's commands.²

It is necessary next to take note of a systematic relationship which holds between that part of the 'ideal eternal history' summarised above and a series of axioms, given in the second set of elements, i.e. in those which are said to be 'particular' and to provide 'more specific bases' for the matters treated in the *Scienza Nuova*. The Elements which are relevant to this part of the 'ideal eternal history' run from XVIII to XXXVII. Vico describes them as revealing 'the beginnings of divine poetry or poetic theology'.³

The first point to note is that in the above part of the 'ideal eternal history' Vico makes a certain assumption about the function of religious institutions in primitive societies. The justification for this assumption is given in Element XXXI, where it is stated in the form of an axiom:

Whenever a people has grown savage in arms so that human laws no longer have any place among it, the only powerful means of reducing it is religion.

This axiom establishes that divine providence initiated the process by which the fierce and violent were brought from their outlaw state and by

nature to the effect, and because in that state their nature was that of men all robust bodily strength, who expressed their very violent passions by shouting and grumbling, they pictured the sky to themselves as a great animated body, which in that aspect they called Jove...who meant to tell them something by his bolts and by his clap of thunder', *S.N.* 377.

¹ 'And by the trait of the human mind noticed by Tacitus, whatever these men saw or imagined or even made or did themselves they believed to be Jove; and to all the universe that came within their scope, and to all parts, they gave the being of animate substance.' *S.N.* 379.

² 'The first men, who spoke by signs, naturally believed that lightning bolts and thunderclaps were signs made to them by Jove...They believed that Jove commanded by signs, that such signs were real words, and that nature was the language of Jove...The science of this language the gentiles universally believed to be divination, which by the Greeks was called theology, meaning the science of the language of the gods', *S.N.* 379.

³ *S.N.* 191.

which nations were instituted among them. It did so by awakening in them a confused idea of divinity.[1]

The axiom is thus offered as an explicit statement of the sociological assumption on which the account rests. It is to be noted that the axiom purports to state the sufficient and necessary conditions under which human behaviour can be modified in certain specified conditions ('whenever a people...the only powerful means...').

A second requirement to which Vico's account must conform, in view of his metaphysical theories, is that men's institutions should be explained as their own creations, reflecting their own natures. The account of institutions must therefore be based upon an account of these natures and, as we have seen, Vico offers such an account. The supposition upon which this rests is, however, again made clear in Element xxxvi, which states that 'imagination is more robust in proportion as reasoning power is weak'.[2]

Given that early man's belief in God (itself a sociological necessity) cannot be explained by an intellectual grasp of the reasons which might bring a more rational being to accept such a belief, the next part of Vico's task is to construct an alternative account of his acceptance of such a belief. The remainder of the above part of the 'ideal eternal history' is largely taken up with this. The most important steps involve the claims that 'God' is at first little more than a name for the unknown causes of things, that early men would attribute sentience to everything, that they would personify these unknown causes and attribute their own barbaric natures to the person thus created. They would finally come to think of the sky itself as a cruel, retributive being, and natural phenomena as the language of this being.

The justification for each of these steps is again given in the 'Elements'. The claim that God is the concept of the unknown (efficient) causes of things is supported by Element xxxiii which states that 'the physics of the ignorant is a vulgar metaphysics by which they refer the causes of things they do not know to the will of God without considering the means by which the divine will operates'.[3] The fact that this physics has a metaphysical character is itself explained by the natural propensity men have for attributing their own nature to anything of which they are ignorant: 'when men are ignorant of the natural causes producing things and cannot even

---

[1] *S.N.* 177–8.   [2] *S.N.* 185.   [3] *S.N.* 182.

explain them by analogy with similar things, they attribute their own nature to them. The vulgar, for example, say the magnet loves iron.'[1] The same axiom explains why they should take thunder and lightning to be a language by which this God communicates with them and why the nature they ascribe to him should be cruel and retributive.

It would be tedious to extend this analysis further since its completion would require taking account of the whole of the 'ideal eternal history' and noting the relationship in which the claims it embodies stand to nearly all the more specific Elements up to Element cxiv. It is beyond doubt, however, that in these Elements Vico is offering a set of propositions from which can be deduced the character, content and history of a certain set of beliefs, practices and institutions. Such an account is quite properly described by Vico as an 'ideal eternal history': 'ideal' in the sense that is a statement of what is necessary and not of what is actual; 'eternal' in the sense that, being validly deduced from a set of axioms, it deals with timeless truths. The latter are statements of hypothetical necessities for one could not deduce from these axioms alone that any such set of beliefs, practices and institutions, i.e. any such 'ideal eternal history', had ever had historical instantiation, since none of them carry any existential commitment.[2]

The clear evidence of the deductive character of the 'ideal eternal history' shows that the influence of rationalism upon Vico far from being restricted to the literary form in which the *Scienza Nuova* was cast, affected in a fundamental manner the formal characteristics of

---

[1] *S.N.* 180.

[2] I exclude here two further types of propositions, referred to as 'postulates' of which there are a few examples in the 'Elements'.

(1) There are some postulates such as Element ciii: 'The postulate must needs be granted that on the shore of Latium some Greek colony had been set up, which after conquest and destruction by the Romans, remained buried in the darkness of antiquity' (*S.N.* 306). This is a particular historical claim and is existential in character. It is included in the 'Elements' because there is no direct historical evidence for it and its defence involves assuming the kind of historical evidence which the 'ideal eternal history' makes possible.

(2) There are also a few postulates in which Vico makes some historical assertions of a more general character, such as in Element lvi: 'the first authors among the Orientals, Egyptians, Greeks and Latins and, in the recourse of barbarism, the first writers in the modern languages of Europe, were poets' (*S.N.* 224). This states the consequence of applying the 'ideal eternal history' to the interpretation of some general historical evidence. Like (1) it is existential in character and is not itself part of the 'ideal eternal history'.

the system of knowledge Vico was trying to formulate. It shows also that when Vico drew his parallel between the way in which geometry creates the world of quantity out of its own elements and that in which his science creates 'the world of nations' he did not intend to deny the deductive character of either science. As in his remarks about geometry in the *De Nostri Temporis Studiorum Ratione*,[1] he is not denying that deduction is a proper part of demonstration; he is suggesting that it is not in itself sufficient for demonstration and that it must be allied to some guarantee, such as that provided by the conventional aspect of geometry, that its rules are adequate to its subject matter. Neither his rejection of Cartesian 'deduction' nor of the Aristotelian syllogism imply a rejection of the place of deduction in a science. His rejection of Cartesian deduction rests primarily upon a denial of the adequacy of the criterion of 'clear and distinct ideas' rather than that of some further formal feature which a system of thought as such should possess.[2] His criticisms of Aristotelian deduction similarly are directed against its sterile and unproductive character and reflect his dissatisfaction with its failure to be synthetic (i.e. constructive) rather than with its deductive character.[3] What Vico wants to create in its place is not a non-deductive science but one which is both synthetic and deductive.

The best support for this view is to be found in the thoroughly synthetic character of the axioms from which the 'ideal eternal history' is deduced. This is so evident, indeed, that they have often been taken for empirical generalisations. This view, however, is mistaken for, although it correctly emphasises the synthetic character of the axioms, it confuses the question of the origin of the axioms with that of their logical status within Vico's science. In origin most of them are undoubtedly historical. Many are attributed (and often misattributed) by Vico to a wide number of classical authors and antiquarians such as Tacitus,[4] Lactantius Firmianus,[5] Varro,[6] Iam-

---

[1] See above, p. 77.

[2] Cartesian deduction was nothing but a sequence of connected intuitions, each intuition having for its content a 'clear and distinct idea'. No new criterion was, however, introduced in the notion of a sequence of these, i.e. a deduction. Once Vico had rejected the capacity of the criterion of distinctness to guarantee the truths in question, rejection of the Cartesian concept of deduction followed as a matter of course.

[3] *S.N.* 499.   [4] *S.N.* 121, 183.

[5] *S.N.* 188.   [6] *S.N.* 196.

blichus,[1] whose own evidence for them was clearly inductive. Others are simply the fruits of Vico's own observation. But once incorporated into Vico's science, in the form of the axioms from which the 'ideal eternal history' is deduced, they assume the character of propositions which are necessary within, i.e. unchallengeable within, the system. Consequently any prior inductive support there may have been for them becomes irrelevant, based as it would be upon epistemological approaches to history which Vico has rejected as inadequate. Even one's own observation, as the discussion of *Cogito* in the *De Antiquissima* has shown, cannot guarantee knowledge.

[1] *S.N.* 207.

11

The ideal eternal history: its sociological content

If the foregoing account is correct the connection between Vico's metaphysical theories and scientific history is achieved by means of the 'ideal eternal history'. The latter is a scientific theory, embodying the determinate empirical presuppositions required to interpret man's actual history in the light of the metaphysical theories. Since these theories involve the assertion that man is both sociologically and historically determined, the 'ideal eternal history' must have two dimensions: an account of the empirical content of the system of social relationships which must obtain in any given historical age; and a theory about the historical laws upon which the development of this content depends.

These empirical theories presuppose the metaphysical theories and it is a mark of Vico's analytical grasp of what he is doing that when he gives his summary of the content of the 'ideal eternal history' in Book IV of the *Scienza Nuova*, sub-titled *The Course the Nations Run*, he introduces it with a clear account of the non-empirical (i.e. metaphysical) categories presupposed. He mentions first the historical theory of three natures, according to which every nation must undergo three discernible stages of development. He then writes:

For the nations will be seen to develop in conformity with this division by a constant and uninterrupted order of causes and effects present in every nation, through three kinds of natures. From these natures arise three kinds of customs; and in virtue of these customs three kinds of natural law of the gentes are observed; and in consequence of these laws three kinds of civil states or commonwealths are instituted. And to the end that men who have come to human society may on the one hand communicate to each other the three kinds of all the aforesaid major institutions, three kinds of languages and as many of characters are formed; and to the end that they may on the other hand justify them, three kinds of jurisprudence assisted by three kinds of authority and three kinds of reason in as many of judgments. The three kinds of jurisprudence prevail in the three sects of times which the nations profess in the course of their lives. These [eleven] triadic special unities, with many others that derive from them...are all embraced in one general unity. This is the unity of the religion of a provident divinity, which is the unity of spirit that informs and gives life to this world of nations.[1]

Two kinds of order or pattern are distinguished here. In the first sentence Vico refers to an order which is revealed in the sequence of three kinds of human nature involved in the history of all nations. This is a genetic or historical order, described by Vico as causal. In referring to it he is making a direct application of his metaphysical claim that the human past is historically conditioned.

In the rest of the paragraph Vico refers to two distinct aspects of a different kind of order. There is first a series of sociological relationships which obtain between the various kinds of institutions in any society. In his account of this series of relationships Vico is making a more detailed statement of the metaphysical basis of his theory of sociological conditioning: the customs mentioned are man's institutional practices, the claim that a certain kind of natural law is observed in virtue of these practices, a reiteration of the metaphysical claim that it is of the nature of natural law that it should be determined by common sense, i.e. by the necessities and utilities men feel in their various institutional rôles. The theory set out in the 'Elements', is, however, extended in a number of ways. The character of the State is now said to be a consequence of that of natural law and whole new dimensions of human activity are brought in under the concept of a human institution, so that the latter comes to include men's language, writing, jurisprudence, authority, judgements and reason.

The second aspect of this second pattern mentions human nature again but in this instance claims that from it 'arise' the various kinds of human institutions. Vico is here referring to the modifications of men's minds, i.e. to the most general and most basic characteristics of the human mind at any given stage of its development. It is necessary at this point to recall the account given in Elements XIV

[1] *S.N.* 915.

and xv in which Vico claimed that these modifications and human institutions were related as necessary and sufficient conditions of certain features of each other.[1] Thus, according to the theory of these Elements human nature consists in certain fundamental modes of thought and feeling which are present in, and colour, each and every institution within a given historical society.

In the passage under consideration, however, a somewhat different claim is made. Human nature affects the character of all institutions but it does so by affecting in turn each of the kinds of institution in the hierarchical series. Thus from it 'arise' first certain kinds of customs, from these certain kinds of natural law and from these in turn certain kinds of civil states. Similarly, though it affects on the one hand the character of language and writing and on the other that of jurisprudence, authority and so on, these kinds of institution exist for the communication and justification of matters pertaining to the more practical institutions and to that extent presuppose them.

There is, however, no contradiction between the two passages. Vico's theory of modifications is certainly intended to explain the unity of any given system of institutions by explaining the unity of belief and attitude upon which it rests. At the same time, however, Vico wants to assert that it is of the nature of some institutions causally to presuppose others. The suggestion of a historical transmission of beliefs and attitudes in the above passage is simply a consequence of the combination of these two claims. In suggesting that the modifications of mind revealed in the natural law of a nation are products of the modifications revealed also in its customs, Vico does not intend to deny either that it is the same modifications or that if, *per impossibile*, there could be a code of natural law not causally dependent upon institutional practices, certain parts of its character would be determined by the very same modifications as they are when it is dependent upon such practices.

It would not be possible within the scope of the present work to undertake a detailed analysis of the more specific claims Vico has here put forward about the relationships in which the various kinds of human institutions stand to one another or how the whole of these stand in relation to the theory of the modifications of the human mind. It is important, however, to note that Vico clearly distinguishes these

---

[1] *S.N.* 147–8. For discussion of this point, see chapter 4 above.

non-empirical theories from the empirical theories embodied in his account of the 'ideal eternal history'. For this again reveals Vico's grasp of the notion that the rôle of metaphysical theory in his science is to govern in the first place the organisation of material in the 'ideal eternal history' and hence, through it, the organisation of material in actual historical accounts. To show how Vico's metaphysical claims function in this way, it is easiest to extract from Book IV of the *Scienza Nuova* those paragraphs in which Vico summarises that part of the empirical content of the 'ideal eternal history' relevant to the history of poetic man.

The account begins with a summary of the nature (i.e. the 'modifications of the mind') of poetic man. This was 'a poetic or creative nature which we may be allowed to call divine, as it ascribed to physical things the being of substances animated by gods, assigning the gods to them according to its idea of each...Furthermore it was a nature all fierce and cruel; but, through that same error of their imagination, men had a terrible fear of the gods whom they themselves had created.'[1] In consequence of this 'the first customs were all tinged with religion and piety',[2] 'the first [natural] law was divine for men believed themselves and all their institutions to depend on the gods, since they thought everything was a god or made or done by a god',[3] and 'the first [governments] were divine, or, as the Greeks would say, theocratic, in which man believed that everything was commanded by the gods. This was the age of oracles, which are the earliest institutions we read of in history.'[4]

Vico next offers an account of the language appropriate to such a society:

the first...was a divine mental language by mute religious acts or divine ceremonies, from which there survived in Roman civil law the *actus legitimi* which accompanied all their civil transactions. This language belongs to religions by the eternal property that it concerns them more to be reverenced than to be reasoned, and it was necessary in the earliest times when man did not yet possess articulate speech.[5]

Such a language has its own appropriate characters which were also

divine, properly called hieroglyphics, used, as we have shown above, by all the nations in their beginnings. And they were certain imaginative univer-

---

[1] *S.N.* 916.   [2] *S.N.* 919.
[3] *S.N.* 922.   [4] *S.N.* 925.
[5] *S.N.* 929.

sals, directed naturally by the human mind's innate property of delighting in the uniform. Since they could not achieve this by logical abstraction, they did it by imaginative representation. To these poetic universals they reduced all the particular species belonging to each genus, as to Jove everything concerning the auspices, to Juno everything touching marriage and so on.[1]

Finally a summary of the jurisprudence of the age is offered: 'the first [jurisprudence] was a divine wisdom called mystic theology, which means the science of divine speech or the understanding of the mysteries of divination. This science of auspicial divinity was the vulgar wisdom whose sages were the theological poets, who were the first sages of the gentile world.'[2] The first authority was 'the authority of property ownership...This authority had its source in divine governments from the time of the family state, in which divine authority must have been vested in the gods, for it was believed, fairly enough, that everything belonged to the gods.'[3] The first kind of reason or right was 'through the auspices, the oracles and other corporeal signs regarded as divine messages because they were supposed to come from the gods, whom the gentiles believed to be corporeal'.[4] And the first legal judgements were 'divine' for 'as there were no civil authorities ruling by law, the family fathers complained to the gods of the wrongs done to them...and called the gods to bear witness to the justice of their causes'.[5]

From this summary we can see how in the 'ideal eternal history' a determinate content is organised in accordance with a formal socio-logical theory which itself satisfies the requirements of certain meta-physical claims. The determinate content is given in the account of poetic man's world. His nature is imaginative, cruel and barely rational. His beliefs derive from associative and analogical rather than rational kinds of thought. By the operation of these he conjures up a pantheistic world of which he is a small part. This belief affects his customs, all 'tinged with religion and piety', leading him to a conception of justice in which the 'just' is what the gods command and to the creation of a system of oracles by which the content of these commands can be established and put into operation through an

---

[1] *S.N.* 933. [2] *S.N.* 938.
[3] *S.N.* 944. [4] *S.N.* 948.
[5] *S.N.* 955.

appropriately organised kind of government. The language of such a man would be primarily a language of religious acts, since the function of language in such a society would be to worship the gods. The characters in such a language would consist in hieroglyphics since men would create them by use of their imagination and not their reason. Jurisprudence would be a science of the auspices, created by men in response to their need to discover the commands of the gods in whom would be vested the first kind of legal authority.

This content is organised in accordance with two of the patterns distinguished above. First it is organised in accordance with the theory of determinate sociological relationships. Poetic man's theological system of government depends upon his concept of natural law, the latter is determined by his customs and these in turn by his fundamental world-picture.

Second, however, the whole network of institutions, taking the latter term in its widest possible sense, is affected by human nature. The same imaginative, non-rational faculties which condition primitive man's customs, religion, and theocratic beliefs, condition also his language, his conception of natural justice and the organisation of his legal system. Yet they do this by means of the series of sociological relationships. Vico's account of the latter is thus constructed in such a way that it satisfies the requirement that the constituents of the human world derive from the nature of its creators. Were the latter to change, as it does according to Vico's conception of historical man, the content but not the structure of the human world would also change.

One of the things that Vico is doing here is emphasising, and making it possible to apply, the suggestion that a certain kind of *unity* obtains among the institutions of any given historical society. It is clear, however, that this is not a conceptual or logical unity. The institutions of a society form a unity in the sense that they are structured by the human capacities and modes of thought proper to the people who have created them, but the unity of these capacities is not derived from any purely logical principle of unity. There *is* some sort of principle which connects these capacities – man cannot, for example, be both imaginative and rational at the same time. But although this principle reflects some fundamental truth about human nature, it is not a truth that cannot be denied without self-contradiction.

It is necesary also to note here that Vico does not believe that only one such unity can pervade any given society. In insisting that the character of, say, the government or jurisprudence of a society must reflect certain traits of human nature he does not want to deny that one of them, which occupies a less fundamental place in the hierarchical scheme of sociological relationships, might for a time continue to have characteristics which were determined by the human nature of a previous historical age. People's habits and beliefs do not change all at once and at all periods in human history there will be some classes in society who will see certain proposed changes as an improvement and something to be welcomed and others as a deterioration and something to be resisted.

There are many examples in the *Scienza Nuova* which confirm the fact that some agents in a given society may reflect a human nature which is not identical in development with that which conditions its other institutions. This is, indeed, precisely how Vico explains the fact that at the appropriate stage in history the feudal hierarchy will form aristocratic commonwealths to resist the demands of their dependents. That such examples do not constitute a failure on Vico's part to adhere to his general theoretical claims can be seen in his account, in Chapter XIII of Book IV, of how this can occur with regard to the sequence of governments outlined in the 'ideal eternal history':

> But to leave no point of doubt concerning this natural succession of political or civil institutions, we shall find that the succession admits of mixtures, not of form with form (for such mixtures would be monsters) but of a succeeding form with a preceding administration. Such mixtures are founded on the axiom that when men change they retain for some time the impression of their previous customs.
>
> Hence we say that the first gentile fathers, passing from bestial life to the human, retained, in the religious times in the state of nature under the divine administrations, much of the savagery of their recent origins...and that likewise in the formation of the first aristocratic commonwealths the private sovereign powers remained intact in the hands of the family fathers, just as they had held them in the previous state of nature.[1]

Vico did not therefore claim that in a given society all belief and activities must, of necessity, reflect the same modifications of the

---

[1] *S.N.* 1004–5.

human mind, though he did claim that they must, of necessity, reflect some such modifications. This is a point of considerable importance for its bearing upon the concept of the historically possible which, as we have seen, is a concept which Vico had accused his predecessors of failing to understand.[1] For Vico an activity is historically possible if it presupposes an institution which is historically possible, and an institution is historically possible if it is determined either by the human nature reflected in the other more fundamental kinds of institutions in that society or in those of that society in a prior state of historical development. It is not historically possible if it reflects modifications of a more developed kind than those proper to the society in which it arose.[2] It is clear that the distinction between historical possibility and impossibility depends upon, and involves the application of, some sort of necessity which determines the genetic growth of human nature, from which it can be decided what is to count as a higher or lower state of its development.

[1] See the account of the conceit of scholars in chapter 2 above.
[2] Cf. *S.N.* 344, where Vico claims that the account of the sequence of institutions given in the 'ideal eternal history' is the only one historically possible: 'Consider, finally, if in these occasions, places and time we can conceive how other divine benefits [i.e. other institutions] could arise by which, in view of the particular needs and ills of men, human society could be better conducted and preserved.'

12

The ideal eternal history: its historical content

The genetic pattern which Vico attributed to history and which he describes in the 'ideal eternal history' is most commonly put in the form of a tripartite scheme of development. Vico distinguishes between three ages which characterise the history of every nation, or between three human natures which, ultimately, determine this division, or between three stages through which any single kind of institution must develop genetically. The fully worked out scheme is a consequence of the sociological theories discussed in the preceding chapter conjoined with the philosophical claim that the human nature upon which the products of a given age depend itself develops and a theory about the determinate stages by which it does so. The relevant philosophical theory here has already been discussed as it represents the account of man's historical nature given in the general Elements. This chapter will therefore be concerned to establish certain points about the determinate pattern Vico ascribed to the history of every nation.

Typically Vico names each of the three divisions in words which describe one of its main features. The first nature is 'poetic', 'creative' or 'divine' because it is a nature in which the imagination, playing a dominant rôle, creates a religious world-view which affects the character of all institutions.[1] The second nature is 'heroic' because it is a nature which recognises and honours force, heroism and valour, and allocates social, economic, legal and political status on this basis.[2] The third nature is 'human' for those who possess it have the power to reason about things and to understand their true nature.[3] Corresponding to this sequence of three natures there is a

[1] *S.N.* 916.   [2] *S.N.* 917.   [3] *S.N.* 918.

sequence of three ages, also called poetic, heroic and human. Each of these represents a system of institutions which must develop as a consequence of the human nature which then obtains. Finally within this sequence of three ages any single institution or sub-system of institutions such as those of political or legal life will be found to develop through a sequence in which it successively takes on the characteristics of the three natures.

As an example of this scheme in operation we may consider Vico's account of the 'ideal' history of natural law. In the summary in Book IV the account of the three natures of man is followed by an account of three kinds of law: 'the first law was divine for men believed themselves and all their institutions to depend on the gods, since they thought everything was a god or was made or done by a god'.[1] This is followed by heroic law which is a

law of force, but controlled by religion which alone can keep force within bounds where there are no human laws or none strong enough to curb it. Hence providence ordained that the first peoples, ferocious by nature, should be persuaded by this their religion to acquiesce naturally in force, and that, being as yet incapable of reason they should measure right by fortune, with a view to which they took counsel by auspicial divination.[2]

The third is 'human law dictated by fully developed human reason'.[3]

In this sequence the character of law is determined by the nature of man. The latter evolves through two stages in which men are 'as yet incapable of reason' to a third in which there is 'fully developed human reason'. The character of men's conception of natural law varies in direct relationship with these changes.

This history of law is expounded more fully in the concluding set of particular Elements.[4] Here a distinction is drawn between the 'strict law' of the first and second ages, and the 'mild law' of the third. The difference is further described as that between law which is applied according to its 'certitude' and backed by authority and law which is applied because it is 'whatever impartial utility dictates in each case'.[5]

'Strict law' is the law of men who lack the power to reason about the

---

[1] *S.N.* 922. [2] *S.N.* 923.
[3] *S.N.* 924. [4] *S.N.* 319–29.
[5] *S.N.* 323.

nature of things, i.e. about themselves, society, law, the nature of different kinds of legal offence and so on. Because they lack the capacity to reason about these things they are unable to apply law in the light of any real understanding of the things with which law is concerned. They can therefore do no other than apply, in the most literal possible manner, the very words in which laws are framed. Such a law is 'harsh but it is certain'.[1] This literal application is the 'certitude' of the law. Accepted without any understanding of the true nature of law it can be applied only when there are authorities who can enforce it. It thus requires the context of imaginative, theological belief which first gives rise to the idea of authority. It is therefore a product of human nature but not of 'fully developed human reason'.

'Mild law' is the law of a human nature in which the capacity to reason has so developed that men are capable of understanding the nature of things: 'the natural equity of fully developed human reason is a practice of wisdom in affairs of utility, since wisdom in its broad sense is nothing but the science of making such use of things as their nature dictates'.[2] Equity is thus the principle which informs the highest kind of law, a principle, moreover, which can only be operated when man can understand the nature of things. This understanding is, however, something that can only be achieved in a society that has undergone the appropriate historical development.

The changing principles which determine the history of law are thus explained by the development of man's understanding itself. When man thinks of himself as part of a pantheistic world the law is one thing. When he thinks of himself as receiving the law from the gods via intermediaries whose authority is based upon respect for force, it is another. When his intellect is such that he can understand his own nature and the true nature of the law it is something else again.

It is to be noted that this account rests upon a thesis concerning the principles of development of human nature. The claim is that human nature develops from a state in which its primary activities are sensory and imaginative and in which its conceptual world consists

[1] *S.N.* 322. [2] *S.N.* 326.

largely of an imaginative objectification of its own characteristics, to a state in which it can understand its own needs and requirements and create institutions fit to satisfy these. The guiding principles of history are therefore those on which the development of human nature itself rests.

Vico presents his summary of the 'ideal eternal history' in such a way as might suggest that the principles upon which the development of human nature depends are themselves extra-historical in character. For if the history of human institutions is determined by the development of human nature it would seem that the latter cannot itself be conditioned historically. It must therefore be determined by some extra-historical principle which we should have to discover before we could truly understand history.

An interpretation such as this would seem, for example, to support those commentators who have identified Vico's theory of historical causation with Hegel's 'cunning of reason', in which the progress of historical institutions is based upon a necessity which is ultimately metaphysical, and hence extra-historical, in character.

It is important, however, to realise that, whatever the overt resemblances between Vico's account of man's ascent to reason and that to be found in Hegel,[1] the principles which in Vico's theory determine the development of human nature are historico-sociological in character. The development of human nature on which Vico rests his account of the genetic pattern is something that occurs in and through the historical and sociological context in which men act. It has none of the extra-historical character of Hegel's concept of Reason.

This point is most easily demonstrated by focusing upon one important difference between the rôles assigned to Reason in the two schemes. In Hegel there is no upper limit to the process by which Reason brings about its own development. In Vico, on the contrary, not only is there an upper limit but human reason deteriorates and is eventually replaced by the poetic modes of thought in the return to barbarism with which the 'ideal eternal history' ends. Were it the case that Vico shared with Hegel the view

---

[1] Pietro Piovani has shown how superficial are many of the commonly accepted points of resemblance between Vico and Hegel. See 'Vico without Hegel' in *Giambattista Vico: An International Symposium*, eds. Tagliacozzo and White.

that history was a consequence of the self-development of Reason he should either have gone on, as Hegel did, to accept the proposition that there was no upper limit to this process, or find a ground, *within the concept of Reason itself,* why its progress should be halted and reversed.

In fact, however, Vico offers an explanation of a very different kind for this reversal. The reason why, in his account, man's intelligence itself begins to deteriorate as soon as man has acquired the power to understand the nature of things, is that this understanding immediately erodes the basis of all those sociological conditions, particularly those which presuppose belief in a provident divinity, which have hitherto caused man to adopt the civilised habits alien to his fallen and vicious nature. In other words, in Vico's account, Reason can only develop in certain historico-sociological conditions. And as soon as it develops to the point where it can itself become a *condition* of history there is an immediate end to historical development and Reason itself declines.

Vico did not therefore attribute to Reason an innate capacity for self-development nor did he include it among the causes of historical development. As the example considered earlier shows, the fundamental cause of historical change is human nature as it develops in historico-sociological conditions. The human nature from which all else 'arises' is not something which can exist, or even be thought of as existing, separately from the network of human institutions. It is nothing more than those general attitudes of mind, general beliefs and values shared by an historical society and appearing in all its products, which are themselves conditioned by that society's past. It is not something over and above the customs and laws of men. It is expressed in them. Their history is its history.

The sequence of three natures which determines the ideal history of a nation is not therefore some non-historical principle from which the principles of historical change can be deduced. It is, rather, an overarching historical principle expressing a theory about the way in which human institutional history must itself develop. It is, in other words, simply an historical theory.

Further support for this view comes from Vico's claim, in the introductory paragraph to the summary of the 'ideal eternal history',[1]

---

[1] *S.N.* 915. See above, pp. 112–13.

that 'the nations will be seen to develop in conformity with this division [i.e. into the ages of gods, heroes and men] by a constant and uninterrupted sequence of causes and effects present in every nation, through three kinds of human natures'. The more or less outright identification of the causal development of a nation with the sequence of human natures precludes the possibility that the latter can stand outside the 'uninterrupted sequence of causes and effects'.

In emphasising the difference between Vico's conception of human nature as the ultimate determinant of human history and Hegel's conception of the self-development of Reason as the ultimate determinant, one must be careful not to suggest that there is no proper conception of self-development in Vico at all. It is clear that the changes that occur in human nature are thought of as a development for they are acquired by virtue of a causal, historical process. They also, however, constitute a process of self-development, since there is nothing beyond its own past to which we may turn to find the causes of this change in human nature. The changes of attitudes, beliefs, and values in which it consists are changes which men are constrained to make because of the attitudes, beliefs and values embodied in their institutional system as they receive it at any given period in history. It is genuine self-development because it is genuine historical development.

This is best illustrated by reference to the passages in the 'Elements' (LXIV–LXVIII) in which Vico sets down the genetic principles of the 'ideal eternal history':

The order of ideas must follow the order of institutions.

This was the order of human institutions: first the forests, after that the huts, then the villages, next the cities, and finally the academies.

Men first feel necessity, then look for utility, next attend to comfort, still later amuse themselves with pleasure, thence grow dissolute in luxury, and finally go mad and waste their substance.

The nature of peoples is first crude, then severe, then benign, then delicate, finally dissolute.

In the human race first appear the huge and grotesque, like the cyclopes; then the proud and magnanimous, like Achilles; then the valorous and just, like Aristides and Scipio Africanus; nearer to us, imposing figures with great semblances of virtue accompanied by great vices, who among the vulgar win a name for true glory, like Alexander and Caesar; still later the melancholy and reflective, like Tiberius; finally the dissolute and shameless madmen, like Caligula, Nero and Domitian.

This axiom shows that the first sort were necessary in order to make one man obey another in the family state and prepare him to be law-abiding in the city state that was to come; the second sort, who naturally did not yield to their peers, were necessary to establish the aristocratic commonwealths on the basis of the families; the third sort, to open the way for popular liberty; the fourth to bring in the monarchies; the fifth to establish them; the sixth to overthrow them.[1]

In these passages Vico states first a genetic sequence of systems of human institutions. This is followed by a genetic sequence of the main elements which determine common sense in these institutional circumstances (necessity, utility, comfort, etc.) and of the main characteristics which human nature will have in them (crude, severe, benign, etc.). Then comes a sequence of paradigmatic figures for each type (the cyclopes, Scipio Africanus, Alexander, etc.).

In connection with the sequence of paradigmatic figures, and the kinds for which they stand, two important points are made. First, each type is necessary for the proper functioning of its own appropriate mode of political organisation. The huge, for example, ensure obedience in the family-state, the proud establish the contractual element of the aristocratic commonwealth. Secondly, however, each kind of figure also provides some sort of human characteristic which is a necessary condition of the development of the next mode of political organisation. Thus, in developing obedience in the family-state man acquires the basis of a capacity to abide by law without which the city-state could not develop; in developing a certain 'valour and justice' in the aristocratic commonwealths he acquires capacities without which a system based on popular liberty could not be operated. From this it is clear that each phase in the genetic sequence is a necessary condition of the next phase because in it man acquires a certain human capacity or disposition without which the institutions of the next phase could not be created. Human nature thus develops within the historical, institutional contexts in which men exist. It is not something which can develop apart from these.

Vico's genetic pattern is thus an historical theory about the

[1] *S.N.* 238–44.

determinate sequence of conditions of institutional life in which alone man can develop those social capacities in which his human nature consists and upon which the character of his historical development depends. It can, for convenience, be thought of as a single historical law, but it is more properly a statement of the historical character events will exhibit in consequence of a number of different laws.

13

Philosophy and historical interpretation

In the foregoing account the 'ideal eternal history' has been presented as a deductive theory about the path a nation's history must take. The demonstration of the necessity for this path involves a philosophical theory about the nature of historical causation and the application of this theory in certain determinate assumptions about the historico-sociological laws which govern the development of human institutions. The necessity which is thus demonstrated is, it must be noted, purely hypothetical or conditional. In the 'ideal eternal history' the account of any one stage of the genetic pattern can be shown to entail that of the next, or the account of the character of any one institution at a given historical stage to entail that of another at the same stage, because the assumptions made about the relevant historico-sociological laws support such implications. There is, however, nothing that philosophy can do to take us out of the realm of the possible into that of the actual, by showing that this theory is true of *our* human nature rather than merely of some conceptually possible human nature. For Vico has rejected any suggestion that history is metaphysically determined and therefore can offer no metaphysical demonstration of the necessity for the historico-sociological assumptions from which his historical pattern is deduced.

The establishment of the truth of these historico-sociological claims is the work of philology which, as we saw, is to 'give certainty to the reasonings' of the philosopher[1] by enabling us 'to see in fact the institutions we have meditated in idea as touching this world of nations in accordance with Bacon's method of philosophising which is "think [and] see" (*cogitare videre*)'.[2]

[1] *S.N.* 140.   [2] *S.N.* 359.

The connecting link between philosophy and philology lies in the conception of a 'mental dictionary', mentioned in Element XIII, 'for assigning origins to all the diverse articulated languages'. This is an essential element in Vico's science and it is important to come to a clear understanding of it.

Vico explains the idea more fully in Element XXII where he writes:

There must in the nature of human institutions be a mental language common to all nations, which uniformly grasps the substance of things feasible in human social life and expresses it with as many diverse modifications as these same things may have diverse aspects. A proof of this is afforded by proverbs or maxims of vulgar wisdom, in which substantially the same meanings find as many diverse expressions as there are nations ancient and modern.

This common mental language is proper to our Science, by whose light linguistic scholars will be enabled to construct a mental vocabulary common to all the various articulate languages, living and dead.[1]

The key expression here is 'the substance of things feasible in human social life' which this mental language expresses. For it is precisely these things with which common sense is concerned. In other words, the content of the mental language common to all nations is the conceptions (judgements) of common sense, which are common to all nations. The claim is that, although different nations have a different verbal language for expressing these conceptions, the conceptions themselves are the same. This is confirmed by the fact that, in his reference to the proverbs which prove his point, Vico refers also to 'maxims of vulgar wisdom', which are part of the general common sense of poetic man.

Vico is thus making explicit something that follows from his general conception of human social nature. Just as man's institutions are historically and sociologically determined, i.e. are the consequence of historico-sociological laws, so also is man's practical thought. To adapt one of Vico's favourite examples, it would be no more possible for poetic man to have a law based upon the conception of impartial utility than it would be possible for him to inaugurate a democratic, political system. These practices and conceptions can exist only where certain appropriate historical and sociological conditions obtain. Then, however, their existence is necessary.

Vico is thus putting forward a claim about the objectivity of social

[1] *S.N.* 161–2.

possibilities. It must again be emphasised that the possibilities are not objective in any metaphysical or transcendent sense. Vico is not claiming that the possibilities which men can grasp are determined *a priori*, or by causes obtaining outside the world of human society and human thought. They are, on the contrary, determined by the historical and sociological conditions of a society, of which man's capacity to feel certain needs and think in certain ways is itself an indispensable part. It therefore makes no difference whether we think of the possibilities as determining man's thought or of men creating the possibilities themselves by thought. For to consider something an historical possibility is to think of it as conceivable by a certain kind of historical agent and both it and he are products of the same historico-sociological situation.

Two points must be made about the central claim itself before considering its rôle as the connecting link between philosophy and philology. First, one must distinguish between the conception of such an objective, historically and sociologically determined, mental language and any claim about some determinate historico-sociological conditions and their consequences. A theory of the former sort would be a metaphysical theory and, as such, would be presupposed by a theory of the latter kind which would be an historico-sociological theory. In the axiom under consideration Vico is making an assertion only about the conception of such a mental language, hence his claim is purely metaphysical. His recognition of this point is revealed by his claim that 'there *must* in the nature of human institutions'[1] be such a mental language. The distinction must, however, be observed because, although it is true that the kind of historico-sociological theory Vico formulates presupposes the metaphysical claim, theories of both kinds are necessary in order to enable linguistic scholars to carry out their work.

Secondly, to reinforce a point made earlier, the mental language is not to be established inductively, i.e. it is not to be discovered by empirical research into the correlations between the social conceptual vocabularies of different nations. Vico makes this quite clear by his remark, to which we shall return shortly, that 'this common mental language is proper to our Science, *by whose light* linguistic scholars will be enabled to construct a mental vocabulary common to

[1] *S.N.* 161. My italics.

all the various articulated languages, living and dead'.[1] If scholars require the mental language in order to construct a mental vocabulary they cannot derive it from the latter.

It is possible now to enquire how the theories in question will enable linguistic scholars to carry out their work. Vico discusses this in a number of different places and from a number of different points of view in the *Scienza Nuova*. It is necessary therefore to take these separately, beginning first with a passage in the 'Elements' in which he gives 'a part of the principles of the ideal eternal history' since this reveals that determinate historico-sociological theories are required before the linguistic scholar can accomplish his task in the way envisaged. Vico begins with a very general, but nevertheless most useful, statement of a certain historical principle:

> The human mind is naturally inclined by the senses to see itself externally in the body, and only with great difficulty does it come to understand itself by means of reflection.
>
> This axiom gives us the universal principle of etymology in all languages: words are carried over from bodies and from the properties of bodies to signify the institutions of the mind and spirit.[2]

This axiom itself is, of course, simply a very general statement of the same genetic principle expressed in the 'three natures' thesis. Vico has derived from this the etymological principle that words first arise in an era when men, ignorant of the causes of things and unable to reason about them, clothe them with objectified features of their own mind.[3] Later, when men can reason about human institutions and creations these same words are used to express their new conceptions of things.

[1] *S.N.* 162. My italics.   [2] *S.N.* 236–7.

[3] *S.N.* 405: 'It is noteworthy that in all languages the greater part of the expressions relating to inanimate things are formed by metaphor from the human body and its parts and from the human senses and passions. Thus, head for top or beginning; the brow or shoulders of a hill; the eyes of needles and of potatoes; mouth for any opening; the lip of a cup or pitcher; the teeth of a rake, a saw, a comb; the beard of wheat...The farmers of Latium used to say the fields were thirsty, bore fruit, were swollen with grain; and our rustics speak of plants making love, vines going mad, resinous trees weeping. Innumerable other examples could be collected from all languages. All of which is a consequence of our axiom that man in his ignorance makes himself the rule of the universe, for in the examples cited he has made of himself an entire world. So that, as rational metaphysics teaches that man becomes all things by understanding them, this imaginative metaphysics shows that man becomes all things by *not* understanding them'. Cf. the relevant Element xxxii, *S.N.* 180–1.

The principle is also, however, described as 'the universal principle of etymology in all languages'. It is thus one of the principles which are proper to Vico's conception of a science. In other words, Vico has derived from the 'ideal eternal history' a principle by virtue of which etymology itself will become a scientific discipline.

In the above statement of the genetic thesis, the principle is expressed in terms of a certain kind of development of the human mind. Since, as we have argued earlier, it is part of Vico's view that the human mind is historically and socially conditioned, precisely the same principle can be expressed in terms of a genetic sequence of institutional developments. It is interesting to note therefore that Vico continues his exposition by restating the principle in terms of such a sequence:

The order of ideas must follow the order of institutions.

This was the order of human institutions: first the forests, after that the huts, then the villages, next the cities, and finally the academies.

This axiom is a great principle of etymology, for this sequence of human institutions sets the pattern for the histories of words in all the various native languages. Thus we observe in the Latin language that almost the whole corpus of its words had sylvan or rustic origins. For example, *lex*. First it must have meant a collection of acorns. Thence we believe is derived *ilex*, as it were *illex*, the oak (as certainly *aquilex* means collector of waters); for the oak produces the acorns by which the swine were drawn together. *Lex* was next a collection of vegetables, from which the latter were called *legumina*. Later on, at a time when vulgar letters had not yet been invented for writing down the laws, *lex* by a necessity of civil nature must have meant a collection of citizens, or the public parliament; so that the presence of the people was the *lex*, or 'law', that solemnised the wills that were made *calatis comitiis*, in the presence of the assembled *comitia*. Finally, collecting letters, and making, as it were, a sheaf of them for each word, was called *legere*, reading.[1]

In these paragraphs Vico begins with the philosophical claim that the order of development of (social) ideas is determined by the order of development of institutions. Next he formulates an historico-sociological theory, i.e. a determinate genetic sequence of different kinds of institutional system. The character of this sequence as an historico-sociological theory is made clear in the claim that it 'sets the pattern for the histories of words in the various languages'. Finally he presents us with one of his many examples of faulty etymological

[1] *S.N.* 238–40.

interpretation. The fault, however is unimportant. What counts is the principle upon which the interpretation is carried out. In this the historico-sociological sequence is taken for granted. It provides the assumptions about the institutional context of men's lives which make possible both an interpretation of the words they used, and an interpretation of the changes in meaning which the words would undergo as the possibilities of life, and thus the meanings of the words, are determined in accordance with this sequence.

In the above section Vico presents his principle in relation to its bearing upon the problem of the historical development of the meaning of words. As such its bearing upon the possibility of scientific etymology is obvious. As regards its philosophical importance Vico is insisting that any account of the change in meaning of a given word or system of words must, since many words are internally related in meaning, be accompanied by a demonstration of the real, i.e. objective, possibility of the sequence of conceptions in which this account consists. In a sense Vico's complaints against his fellow-historians for their unhistorical interpretations of documentary evidence represents a detailed demonstration of their failure to observe precisely this requirement. Thus, their attempts to show that the Egyptian hieroglyphics were a language for the concealment of erudite philosophical truths is rejected because a scientific approach to the whole question of ancient Egyptian history can only go to show that there was no objective possibility of the development of the conceptions these hieroglyphics were claimed to conceal. Once the nature of poetic man is investigated the hieroglyphics can be seen in their true light, i.e. as a picture language which conveys meaning through natural and non-conventional relationships with its objects.[1] Similarly the attempt to show that in early Roman times a political system of popular liberty obtained, with the consequences this entailed for the intepretation of later Roman political, legal and economic history, is rejected because such a system, and the conceptions on which it rests, is a real possibility only at a comparatively late stage in a nation's career.[2]

The principle is also, however, applied by Vico in a rather wider way. Not only is it necessary to show the objective or real historical

[1] *S.N.* 435.
[2] *S.N.* 104–13. Cf. chapter 2 above for an exposition of these mistakes.

possibility of the sequence of meanings involved in the interpretation of the history of words, it is necessary also to show the possibility of the function which is attributed to the various kinds of language under any given interpretation. Thus, where in a later age poetry is a means of amusement or pleasure, in the world of early man it is the natural expression of his first attempts to understand and control his environment. Early fables and myths are not therefore consciously distorted accounts of an imaginary world but the natural expression of a metaphysical view. The figures of speech which abound in these early myths, simile, metaphor, synecdoche, metonomy and so on, were not evolved, consciously or otherwise, in an attempt to increase the imaginative enjoyment these tales could produce but simply represent the only way in which early man could think about things, given the state to which his institutional history had developed his capacity for thought. For in this state those connections of thought content which, in a later, more developed age, would depend upon abstract reasoning, were effected by these figures of speech themselves.[1]

Vico's conscious grasp of the connection between his historico-sociological theories and the assumptions underlying the interpretation of any historical evidence comes out in the last set of general Elements, numbers XVI–XXII, which, he says, 'give us the foundations of the certain'.[2] In these he states explicitly the implications which his philosophical and historico-sociological theories have for the interpretation of history.

First, vulgar traditions become an important source of historical evidence for 'they must have had public grounds of truth by virtue of which they came into being and were preserved by entire peoples over long periods of time'.[3] Vico does not state what traditions he has in mind here but it is clear from his own use of tales of the Trojan war and of Romulus and Remus that he is thinking of traditions held by a nation about its own past history. He does not, of course, intend to suggest that such traditions, in the way in which they are later received, represent the literal truth. Indeed it is precisely because they fail to do this that his science is necessary, hence 'it will be another great labour of this Science to recover these grounds of truth – truth which, with the passage of years and the changes of

---

[1] *S.N.* 400–11.   [2] *S.N.* 163.   [3] *S.N.* 149.

its languages and customs, has come down to us enveloped in falsehood'.[1]

A number of claims are involved here. First any public belief is a human creation. It wins assent because it satisfies human needs and because it answers to the mentality of those who feel these needs.[2] Thus, for example, the tales which later generations received of the gods of poetic man were once expressions of belief fitted to the needs and mentality of poetic men. This being the case their value as historical evidence is clear: they can be used to verify hypotheses about the nature, speech and mentality of poetic man.[3]

But this cannot be done directly since in the course of being handed down through the ages each tale has been re-interpreted and modified, to some extent *re*-created, by successive generations in the light of their own understanding. At each successive stage the changed significance of the tale depends upon the human nature of the age.

The task of the *Scienza Nuova* is therefore to provide principles whereby this sequence of historical reinterpretations can be retraced and the tale stripped of its successive accretions until it is revealed in the form in which it was originally created. Then, and only then, can it be used as evidence for the times in which it was created.

It is obvious, however, that the task cannot be accomplished if the tale is used solely as evidence for the original times in which it was created since the task involved at each stage of the enquiry, i.e. the task of seeing how any later age has attached a different significance to the tale, is precisely the same as that involved in establishing how its first creators thought of it. If the tales of poetic man have been received by us only as modified by heroic man, and if we have to understand how these modifications have affected the tale before we can recapture poetic man's original creation, we shall have to understand also the nature and needs of heroic man. The historian who wants to use popular traditions as evidence and to do so in a thoroughly scientific way cannot avoid committing himself to some

---

[1] *S.N.* 150.

[2] Here it is useful to recall Element XIV: 'The nature of institutions is nothing but their coming into being at certain times and in certain guises', *S.N.* 147.

[3] This follows from Element XV: 'The inseparable properties of institutions must be due to the modification or guise with which they are born. By these properties we may therefore verify that the nature or birth was thus and not otherwise', *S.N.* 148.

account of the development of human nature throughout the whole of a nation's history. Methodologically, the historian is committed to the unity of history.[1]

In effect this Element presents a plea for the critical historical usage of national traditions. The 'public ground of truth' it mentions is simply the historically and socially conditioned human nature of which these traditions are a product. The *Scienza Nuova*, as Vico recognises, makes it possible to apply this insight systematically and objectively, that is to say, scientifically to history.

Element XVII applies the same considerations to the question of linguistic evidence: 'the vulgar tongues should be the most weighty witnesses concerning those ancient customs of the peoples that were in use at the time the languages were formed'.[2] Language, as one institution among others, has been created to fulfil human necessities and utilities. It can therefore also be used to confirm accounts of those other customs and institutions with which it is related for this purpose.

The suggestion that language is a 'witness' is worthy of note. A witness is not an authority but some person or thing which can be used to confirm or refute an account. In Vico's case the account in question is that made possible by the 'ideal eternal history'.

For the historian language is especially important since it is one of those human activities of which, through writing, a permanent record has been left. It is therefore of special value in the recovery of those other customs and institutions in which the historian is interested. Vico here suggests that it does this not merely by describing them, in which case its value would be limited to those comparatively few occasions on which people have set down in writing descriptions of the social or political scene. It helps also by revealing them incidentally, for in language are expressed those social ideas and conceptions which are a necessary part of the different kinds of human activity and institution.

Element XVIII is similarly concerned with the use of the study of language in history: 'A language of an ancient nation which has

---

[1] This important point is not mentioned in the group of general Elements themselves but in a separate general Element no. CVI, which Vico states near the end of the whole set of Elements: 'Doctrines must take their beginnings from that of the matters of which they treat', *S.N.* 314.

[2] *S.N.* 151.

maintained itself as the dominant tongue throughout its development should be a great witness to the customs of the early days of the
world.'[1] Vico goes on to add that this axiom entitles us to use both the
Latin and German languages to prove the natural law of the gentes.

This Element adds to the previous one in only one way. Vico is
drawing attention to the extra importance of those languages which
have remained in use throughout the development of a nation, i.e.
where the natural development of the nation, and hence of the
language, has not been affected by such external factors as conquest
from abroad. In these circumstances, and where the nation concerned was an ancient nation, we are in a position to use linguistic
evidence to confirm accounts of early world history.

The final Elements in this section are not, properly speaking,
general Elements at all, for they mention two particular pieces of
historical evidence, the Law of the Twelve Tables and the Homeric
poems and indicate how they are to be used in the light of the
theories put forward in the *Scienza Nuova*. Thus the Law of the
Twelve Tables is 'a great witness of the ancient natural law of
the gentes of Latium'[2] and not, as Vico's opponents had argued,
an importation from Greece. The Homeric poems are 'civil histories
of ancient Greek customs', and thus 'two great treasure houses of
the natural law of the gentes of Greece'.[3]

Vico's full account of the interpretation of the Homeric poems is set
out in Book III of the *Scienza Nuova*. It is not possible within the scope
of this essay to undertake any detailed discussion of it. But it is worth
while briefly to draw attention to some of the ways in which it is
related to Vico's philosophical and historico-sociological theories.

The relationship to Vico's philosophical theories comes out most
clearly in two aspects of his interpretation of Homer. First, there
is his rejection of the current view that the writings of Homer were
the product of a sophisticated philosophical mind, whose purpose
it was 'to tame the ferocity of the vulgar'.[4] Vico presents a series
of arguments against this account of Homer's purpose, pointing out
that the language with which ferocious deeds are described in Homer
implies admiration and not disgust for them, and that the villainies of
the gods seem to be enjoyed by the writer.[5] Homer's sophistication is

---

[1] *S.N.* 152.   [2] *S.N.* 154.   [3] *S.N.* 156.
[4] *S.N.* 782, 780.   [5] *S.N.* 782.

likewise called in doubt for he applauds as clever decisions of sheer stupidity,[1] thinks of drunkenness as a permissible antidote for an uneasy mind, and so on.[2]

Vico ends this series of detailed points with a paragraph of some significance:

Such crude, coarse, wild, savage, volatile, unreasonable or unreasonably obstinate, frivolous or foolish customs...can only belong to men who are like children in the weakness of their minds, like women in the vigour of their imaginations, and like violent youths in the turbulence of their passions; whence we must deny to Homer any kind of esoteric wisdom.[3]

It will be seen that the conclusion here presupposes a claim about the unity of culture of any given society. Vico realises that, taken in isolation, some parts of the Homeric tales can be construed to embody philosophical truths as his opponents have claimed. Such a possibility can never be ruled out, on purely logical grounds. Vico's claim is, however, that it is historically impossible. For a mind which can delight in cruelty, immorality and drunkenness cannot, at the same time, be capable of lofty philosophical speculation. The philosophical presumption underlying this argument is that the two modes of human nature are so diverse, and can develop only in such diverse historical and sociological conditions, that they could not be parts of a single human nature.

The second way in which Vico's philosophical theories underly his interpretation of Homer is to be seen in his virtual dissolution of the figure of Homer himself into a poetical type. There are two stages in this dissolution, of which the first is both more fundamental, and carried out more completely, than the second.

For Vico any human creation is largely, even if sometimes indirectly, an historico-sociological creation. A poem, a play, a political rôle, may be the direct creation of a particular historical individual, but the latter cannot help but create in the light of needs, utilities, attitudes, feelings, thoughts and so on, which he possesses by virtue of his upbringing in certain historico-sociological circumstances shared by many others. The poet writes to satisfy needs felt by himself and his audience and these vary in different historical and sociological contexts. The historical interest in a poem thus lies in discovering those historico-sociological circumstances which alone

[1] S.N. 783.   [2] S.N. 784–5.   [3] S.N. 787.

can explain the real significance of the poem. If we wish therefore to understand the Homeric epics as they were understood by their creator we need to understand something, not about the individual psychology of an (albeit anonymous) historical person, but about the historical and sociological circumstances which can produce the modes of human experience shared by the poet and his audience. In short what we need to know is what kind of society could produce such poems, written or related in such language, expressing such sentiments, feelings and attitudes, and for what purposes or to satisfy what needs, utilities or pleasures.

The first part of Vico's approach to Homer, therefore, involves an attempt to establish the historico-sociological circumstances to which we must turn for a full understanding of the poems. The assumptions of this enquiry, taken in conjunction with the theory that any given society is unified by communal modes of thought and attitude which are the products of the history of its own institutional developments, directly support Vico's conclusion that the *Iliad* and the *Odyssey* were products of different historical societies. Again the basic argument is the same. Anybody who examines carefully the kind of knowledge, kind of attitude, kind of human nature expressed in the *Iliad* and that expressed in the *Odyssey* will see that they cannot both be products of the same historical and sociological conditions.

The poems of Homer are thus explained by Vico as a later compilation of the products of earlier ages. This conclusion leads directly to Vico's second claim, that Homer himself may never have existed as an actual historical person, and that he may have been the personification of a *social* type, the Greek rhapsodes, whose function it was to relate these tales. Hence Vico investigates resemblances between Homer and the rhapsodes, their mutual blindness, poverty, indefinite age and so on, coming to the conclusion that Homer was probably a personification of these traditional tellers of tales. In this way also, he is able to resolve some of the difficulties involved in the concept of a single spatio-temporal Homer for he can argue that 'the Homer who was the author of the *Iliad* [i.e. one set of rhapsodes] preceded by many centuries the Homer who was the author of the *Odyssey* [another set] '[1] and that the two Homers came from different geographical areas.

[1] *S.N.* 880.

The way in which Vico's historico-sociological theories enter into his interpretation of Homer may be dealt with much more briefly. Indeed, it is necessary only to refer to Element xx to establish this point. This Element, as mentioned above, though included in the general Elements is not purely philosophical since it mentions a particular source of historical evidence and a determinate historico-sociological hypothesis.

The Element itself states: 'If the poems of Homer are civil histories of ancient Greek customs, they will be two great treasure houses of the natural law of the gentes of Greece'.[1] It is to be noted that this axiom is put forward in the form of an hypothetical. The suggestion is that if the poems of Homer are taken in a certain way, they will constitute a certain kind of historical evidence. It must further be noted that the hypothetical involved in this claim involves reference to historico-sociological theory. For Vico is here hypothesising that the gods and heroes of the Homeric poems were the products of a human nature which imaginatively created poetical persons to stand for its own social institutions and narrated the history of these institutions in the form of myths and fables involving these persons. This hypothesis, however, is an instance of an historico-sociological theory for it alludes to a feature which, according to Vico, must arise in the development of all nations. Accordingly the theory itself can be found in the elements proper to the 'ideal eternal history'.[2]

In the above axiom therefore Vico is presupposing a historico-sociological theory in order to advance a historical thesis under which certain historical remains become a certain kind of historical evidence. This reveals the relationship in which historico-sociological theory stands to historical investigation in Vico's science.

Taken together Vico's metaphysical and historico-sociological theories are related to historical investigation in the following way. The philosophical theories provide the non-empirical assumptions about his subject matter which any historian must make, i.e. assumptions about the various kinds of facts which should enter into it, the way in which these should be connected and the kinds of explanations appropriate to them. In his metaphysical theories, Vico has claimed that human activities are historico-sociological products and that they

[1] *S.N.* 156.   [2] See *S.N.* 193–202.

are determined by empirical, historico-sociological causes. This implies that a proper historical account must make presuppositions about the empirical laws which govern historical facts. Vico's historico-sociological theories are statements of such presuppositions. This represents part of the meaning of Vico's claim that in his science philologists will 'give their authority the sanction of truth by appeal to the reasoning of the philosophers'.[1] It remains now to be shown how the reciprocal aspect of this relationship is to be achieved, i.e. how philosophers are to 'give certainty to their reasonings by appeal to the authority of the philologians'.[2]

[1] *S.N.* 140. [2] *Ibid.*

14

Philosophy and historical confirmation

Vico's most complete account of the support which empirical investigation gives to metaphysical and scientific theory is to be found in the last chapter of Book I, on 'Method'. It comprises the last of three 'proofs' which he offers for his Science. Since these proofs are not completely independent of one another, it will be necessary to consider all three.

The first proofs mentioned are the 'divine'[1] or 'sublime natural theological' proofs.[2] The first claim in this kind of proof depends upon the assertion that Vico has demonstrated the fact of providence, or God's influence, in history. For the reader of the *Scienza Nuova*

will find that he has thereby proved to the Epicureans that their chance cannot wander foolishly about and everywhere find a way out, and to the Stoics that their eternal chain of causes, to which they will have it the world is chained, itself hangs upon the omnipotent, wise and beneficent will of the best and great God.[3]

To demonstrate this claim Vico adduces three features of history as construed in his Science and shows that these correspond to, and hence can be thought of as consequences of, three aspects of God's nature. The three features are the 'natural customs'[4] or 'naturalness'[5] which are central to Vico's account; the order[6] which is integral to it; and the end, transcending men's particular ends,[7] to which human history is shown to be directed, i.e. the preservation of the

---

[1] *S.N.* 343.   [2] *S.N.* 346.
[3] *S.N.* 345.   [4] *S.N.* 343.
[5] *S.N.* 343–4.   [6] *S.N.* 343.
[7] *Ibid.*

human race on earth.[1] To these features there correspond respectively God's omnipotence, by virtue of which he can achieve his ends through man's natural customs, his wisdom, by virtue of which he disposes things in an orderly manner, and his goodness, by virtue of which he chooses for men an ultimate good beyond any which, in their fallen state, they could propose for themselves.[2]

In essence, the claim is that Vico's Science is to be accepted because it is consistent with, and makes intelligible, certain theological doctrines. It is clear that this cannot be thought of as an independent proof. The correspondences Vico mentions might well recommend his Science to someone who antecedently and independently believed in God's participation in history, for they might serve to show how a being with a nature such as God's could involve himself in human history. But the capacity of Vico's Science to do this would not constitute an independent proof of it, since such a demonstration would not recommend it to anybody who lacked other grounds for believing in God's participation in history.

Yet despite its lack of cogency this proof is important, for Vico develops it in such a way as to suggest that the three characteristics which his Science attributes to history serve to demonstrate it, irrespective of any possible connection between these characteristics and correspondent features of God. This line of argument first becomes apparent when Vico goes on to say something about our knowledge of the three characteristics of history: the naturalness will be demonstrated 'when we reflect with what ease the institutions are brought into being, by occasions often far apart and sometimes contrary to the proposals of man, yet fitting together of themselves'; the order will be revealed when we 'compare the institutions with one another and observe the order by which those are now born in their proper times and places which ought now to be born and others deferred for their birth in theirs' (i.e. when we observe that the sequence of actual historical events instantiates the order of events laid down in the 'ideal eternal history'); while the divine end is revealed when we 'consider, finally, if in these occasions, places and times, we can conceive how other divine benefits could arise by which, in view of the particular needs and ills of men, human society would

---

[1] *S.N.* 344.
[2] *Ibid.*

143

be better conducted and preserved'.[1] To this explanation Vico adds:

Thus the proper and continual proof here adduced will consist in comparing and reflecting whether our human mind, in the series of possibilities it is permitted to understand, and so far as it is permitted to do so, can conceive more or fewer or different causes than those from which issue the effects of this civil world.[2]

The suggestion is that Vico's Science is proved because, by virtue of its use of the concepts of naturalness, order and end, it makes possible the most complete yet economical causal explanations of human history accessible to man. This claim could obviously stand irrespective of any further claims about the connection between the instantiation of these concepts in history and certain aspects of God's nature.

Thus under the label 'divine proof' two different claims are being made. The first is that human history has been rendered consistent with God's involvement in the world. The second is that human history is only properly understood when its explanation involves use of certain concepts. The first claim presupposes too much to offer any strong support to the *Scienza Nuova*. And for the second to be decisive it still remains to be shown that the explanations Vico offers are indeed the most comprehensive yet economical possible within the limits of human understanding. Thus the second claim presupposes some criterion for establishing the nature of these limits, and a successful demonstration that Vico's explanations are the best available within them.

The next kind of proof is 'logical'[3] or 'philosophic'.[4] Vico's view of it is summed up in the following paragraphs:

The decisive sort of proof in our Science is therefore this: that, once these institutions have been established by divine providence, the course of the institutions of the nations had to be, must now be, and will have to be, such as our Science demonstrates, even if infinite worlds were born from time to time through eternity, which is certainly not the case.

Our Science therefore comes to demonstrate at the same time an ideal eternal history traversed in time by the history of every nation in its rise, development, maturity, decline and fall. Indeed we make bold to affirm that

---

[1] *S.N.* 344. [2] *S.N.* 345.
[3] *S.N.* 346. [4] *S.N.* 351.

he who meditates this Science makes it for himself by that proof 'it had, has and will have to be'. For the first indubitable principle posited above is that this world of nations has certainly been made by man and its guise must therefore be found within the modifications of our own human mind.[1]

Vico's first claim here is that, *given* the occurrence of certain initial conditions, he will show that human history must go through the sequence of institutional changes demonstrated in the 'ideal eternal history'. He will not therefore show that human history is necessary in any absolute sense, for the occurrence of its later stages is dependent upon that of an initial stage whose own occurrence is not demonstrable. But he will establish that, given such an initial stage, it must go through the sequence of other stages demonstrated in the 'ideal eternal history'. He will therefore show both that every phase in history is necessitated by an antecedent phase and that it itself necessitates a subsequent phase. In other words, he will show that his Science offers complete causal explanations of actual historical events.

Vico's second, and rather more obscure, claim is that this will be made possible because we can find 'within the modifications of our own human mind' the kind of causes relevant to this task. Thus here he seems to be referring to the criterion of the nature of human understanding presupposed by the second sort of divine proof. In fact, it is evident that the two claims involved in Vico's philosophical proof amount to a reassertion of the second, non-theological, kind of divine proof. For the complete causal explanations involved in the philosophical proof are precisely what the concepts of naturalness, order and end were claimed to make possible; while the appeal to the 'modifications of our own human mind' is a direct reference to the criterion of human understanding presupposed in the divine proof. Consequently Vico's philosophical proof, since it is largely a restatement of the claims involved in the second kind of divine proof, presupposes a successful demonstration that his explanations are the best possible within the limits of human understanding.

This demonstration is what is dealt with in Vico's third kind of proof, his 'philological proofs'.[2] There are a number of these which are most easily stated in his own words:

---

[1] *S.N.* 348–9.   [2] *S.N.* 351.

(I) Our mythologies agree with the institutions upon which we have meditated,[1] not by force and distortion, but directly, easily, and naturally. They will be seen to be civil histories of the first peoples, who were everywhere naturally poets.

(II) The heroic phrases as here explained in the full truth of the sentiments and the full propriety of the expressions, also agree.

(III) The etymologies of the native languages also agree, which tells us the histories of the things signified by the words, beginning with their original and proper meanings and pursuing the natural progress of their metaphors according to the order of ideas, on which the history of languages must proceed.

(IV) The mental vocabulary of human social institutions...is exhibited to be such as we conceived it.

(V) Truth is sifted from falsehood in everything that has been preserved for us through long centuries by those vulgar traditions which, since they had been preserved for so long a time and by entire peoples, must have had a public ground of truth.

(VI) The great fragments of antiquity, hitherto useless to science because they lay begrimed, broken and scattered, shed great light when cleaned, pieced together and restored.

(VII) To all these institutions, as to their necessary causes, are traced the effects narrated by certain history.

These philological proofs enable us to see in fact the institutions we have meditated in idea as touching this world of nations, in accordance with Bacon's method of philosophising, which is 'think [and] see' (*cogitare videre*). Thus it is that with the help of the preceding philosophical proofs, the philological ones both confirm their own authority by reason and at the same time confirm reason by their authority.[2]

It will be seen that in part these paragraphs simply repeat the claims about the relationship between philosophy, historico-sociological theory and history discussed in the foregoing chapter. (V) and (VI) reassert the historical value of the vulgar traditions and 'the great fragments of antiquity' (i.e. Homer and the Law of the Twelve Tables) when treated in the manner made possible by Vico's Science. (I) to (IV) refer to Vico's determinate historico-sociological interpretations, i.e. both to the theories he has formulated and to the particular historical interpretations which 'agree' with them.

---

[1] Vico's '*le cose le quali si meditano*' is translated by Bergin and Fisch as 'the institutions under consideration'. This loses the force of Vico's use of *meditare* which is always a philosophical activity. I have accordingly altered their translation to take account of this.

[2] *S.N.* 352–9.

(VII) refers to the conception of historical causation employed in these interpretations.

In addition to repeating these claims, however, a new element is added. By approaching historical evidence in the above way we are able 'to see in fact the institutions we have meditated in idea', i.e. we convert historical evidence into historical fact by the use of historico-sociological theory. Conversely, however, these theories, the institutions meditated in idea, are 'confirmed' by the self-same historical facts. Vico here refers explicitly to a process of mutual confirmation: 'the philological proofs both confirm their own authority by reason and at the same time confirm reason by their authority'.

At the risk of being repetitive it is worth emphasising the consequences this claim has for the two main interpretations hitherto offered of Vico's account of historical laws. First it rules out any quasi-Hegelian interpretation which construes Vico's laws to be statements of some sort of metaphysical necessities. For Hegel the laws of history can be deduced *a priori* and, hence, though they illuminate historical facts they cannot be verified by them. For Vico, on the other hand, the laws can be verified only by the facts whose construction they make possible. There is thus no possibility of their being known *a priori*. The quasi-Hegelian account is ruled out, in effect, by Vico's claim that in his Science reason is confirmed by the authority of philology.[1]

The opposite mistake is to overemphasise the purely empirical aspects of Vico's Science at the expense of its theoretical content, leading to an account of its laws as empirical generalisations. If, however, history cannot be pursued scientifically without making presuppositions about the conditions which determine fact, including presuppositions about historico-sociological laws, such laws cannot be derived from the facts since they are involved in their

[1] In offering a Hegelian interpretation of Vico, Croce was not, of course, unaware of the difficulty of reconciling the metaphysical character he ascribed to the laws involved in the 'ideal eternal history' with Vico's demand for empirical confirmation. He dealt with it by suggesting that, in the end, Vico simply failed to see that if the determinate events of history were metaphysically necessary, empirical confirmation was 'superfluous' (*The Philosophy of Giambattista Vico*, p. 41). Croce was forced into having to maintain this thesis by his failure to understand either the reciprocal character of the relationship between philosophy and philology, or the different functions which metaphysical and empirical theory have in the *Scienza Nuova*.

establishment. The suggestion that they are to be established inductively simply involves a *petitio principii*. The inductive thesis is therefore ruled out by Vico's insistence that in his Science philology is confirmed by reason.

Vico thus attributes rôles of equal importance to philosophy and philology by insisting upon their epistemological interdependence. Knowledge of human history is possible only under two conditions. The historian's interpretations of historical evidence must involve the consistent and rigorous application of testable theories about the determinate conditions which affect history, i.e. of empirical theories. The latter must themselves, however, be such as systematically to presuppose acceptable philosophical theories about the nature of their subject matter.

Attention has recently been drawn to certain resemblances between Vico's methodological recommendations for history and those now employed in the natural sciences.[1] The foregoing analysis might seem to suggest that there is a close parallel with the hypothetico-deductive method. The 'ideal eternal history' would thus be a deductive, empirical hypothesis which, when confirmed by the facts, attains the status of a statement of historical law. There is a striking passage in the *Scienza Nuova* in which Vico comes close to a literal endorsement of this suggestion. This occurs in connection with his discussion of his claim about the significance of the Publilian Law in Roman history:

If we read further into the history of Rome in the light of this hypothesis [concerning the Publilian Law] we shall find by a thousand tests that it gives support and consistency to all the things therein narrated that have hitherto lacked a common foundation and a proper and particular connection among themselves...whereof this hypothesis should be received as true. However, if we consider well, this is not so much a hypothesis as a truth meditated in idea which later will be shown with the aid of authority (*con l'autorità*) to be the fact...This hypothesis gives us also the history of all the other cities of the world in times we have so far despaired of knowing. This then is an

---

[1] Paolo Rossi emphasises Vico's use of theory as 'an instrument for the guidance and control of experience'. See *Le Sterminate Antichità*, pp. 48–9. Max Fisch has also drawn attention to the importance of hypothesis and experiment in Vico's theory of knowledge. See 'Vico and Pragmatism', in *Giambattista Vico, An International Symposium*, edited by G. Tagliacozzo and H. White.

instance of an ideal eternal history traversed in time by the histories of all nations.[1]

Vico here begins by referring to his account of the meaning of the Publilian Law (i.e. that it marked a change in the Roman constitution from an aristocratic to a popular commonwealth) explicitly as an hypothesis (*ipotesi*). As such it makes possible a consistent interpretation of the evidence for a difficult and obscure part of Roman history by providing 'support and consistency...a common foundation and a proper and particular connection among themselves' for 'all the things therein narrated'. This constitutes a series of tests for it, by passing which 'it should be accepted as true', i.e. which thus give it a *prima facie* claim to truth.

Thus far Vico is considering what is clearly a particular historical thesis. In effect he is claiming that such a thesis first enters history as an hypothesis but takes on the status of a *prima facie* truth when shown to make possible a consistent, interconnected interpretation of evidence relating to a wider area of historical fact. Its successful involvement in the latter serves, to some extent, to confirm it.

But in the middle of the paragraph Vico begins to modify these claims: 'if we consider well' the hypothesis becomes 'a truth meditated in idea' later to be established as fact with the help of authority. As such it gives us part of the history of all cities (at a comparable stage of their development) and is thus an example of part of an 'ideal eternal history'.

It is clear that Vico is not suggesting that the hypothesis becomes a 'truth meditated in idea' by virtue of the *prima facie* confirmation it first receives through its successful involvement in a particular account of Roman history. The latter gives it a degree of support as a particular historical claim but does not, of itself, suffice to turn it into a 'truth meditated in idea'. To accomplish this we are required to 'consider well', take it as an hypothesis not merely about Rome but about all the other cities in the world, i.e. as part of an 'ideal eternal history' and confirm it by appeal to the authority of the philologians. The suggestion is that by reflection we formulate the theoretical (i.e.

---

[1] *S.N.* 114. Quoted also by Paolo Rossi, *Le Sterminate Antichità*, p. 48. I have altered Bergin and Fisch's translation of Vico's expression *con l'autorità* from 'authoritatively' to 'with the aid of authority' because he intends here to refer specifically to the technical 'authority of the philologians' by which the truth of things meditated in idea is confirmed.

philosophical and causal) presuppositions upon which a particular historical claim rests, and seek to give them the status of philosophical truths and causal laws (and thus of things which can be legitimate parts of a science) by the kind of confirmation appropriate to each.

What Vico is doing in this passage is showing how a proposition which begins life as a *particular* historical hypothesis is transformed in three successive phases. It becomes a *prima facie* historical truth by being shown to be involved in the successful interpretation of a larger but nevertheless equally particular part of history. It becomes theoretical when by reflection we isolate and inspect critically the philosophical and scientific theories it presupposes. Since its ultimate acceptability rests upon these theories they must themselves be established by methods appropriate to them, i.e. in the case of the philosophical theories by satisfying the appropriate philosophical criteria and in the case of the scientific theories by widespread empirical confirmation. The latter will not, of course, be different in kind from that whereby the original hypothesis was given a *prima facie* status as a particular historical truth. It will, however, involve the application of the same method to a much wider range of historical evidence, a range sufficient, indeed, to verify or falsify statements of law. Until this is achieved the proposition cannot be considered to have been confirmed as part of an 'ideal eternal history' and thus has not cast off its purely hypothetical character.[1]

---

[1] Failure to attend to the above passage explains why many commentators have given an incorrect account of the nature of the two kinds of propositions, i.e. philosophical and scientific, upon which the 'ideal eternal history' rests. For, because Vico very frequently refers to some historical source, such as a passage from a classical writer, or a verbal tradition, when taking over some proposition, particularly some scientific proposition, and because these propositions were often originally inductive generalisations, it has been assumed that they must also have the status of inductive generalisations in his own Science. The above account makes it clear, however, that Vico was aware that a proposition can have a series of different functions as it is involved in the procedure of working towards scientific knowledge, so that if it might be first entertained because it seemed like a true inductive generalisation, its final acceptance in a science can still depend upon its success in fulfilling a very different function. Thus to take the most obvious of countless examples in the *Scienza Nuova*, the tripartite division into the divine, heroic and human ages, is taken over by Vico from an Egyptian tradition (*S. N.* 173). But for the Egyptians it was a particular thesis about the history of the world prior to their own time, whereas, we have seen, for Vico it finally becomes a scientific law. Thus it is important to distinguish the source of the propositions in Vico's Science from their logical status.

In many respects, therefore, this passage confirms the foregoing interpretation of the methodological aspect of the *Scienza Nuova*. Scientific theories enter into history in the form of testable, deductive hypotheses, to be granted or denied the status of laws according as their truth is shown to be necessary to that of any scientific history whatsoever. Vico is trying to show how, in making particular historical claims we make various philosophical and empirical assumptions about their subject matter and is insisting that the adequacy and truth of these assumptions simply cannot be taken for granted in a science. In particular, such empirical assumptions as receive confirmation by their involvement in acceptable historical accounts lose their hypothetical but not their conditional character.

It is nevertheless clear that the above account does not explain the whole of what Vico is suggesting. For it fails to give any exact meaning to Vico's claim that the hypothesis first under consideration is, even before its confirmation as an element in an 'ideal eternal history', i.e. as a scientific law, 'not so much a hypothesis as a truth meditated in idea'. Since this is a point of considerable significance it is important to note that it is not simply one of those isolated, random remarks which abound in the *Scienza Nuova* and which make its interpretation so difficult. The same qualification reappears in another passage in the 'Elements' in which Vico is discussing the account of the origin of cities given in the 'ideal eternal history':

If such an origin of cities (which later we find to be the fact) were offered as a hypothesis, it would command acceptance by its naturalness and simplicity and for the infinite number of civil effects which depend upon it as their proper cause. In no other way can we understand how civil power emerged from family power and the public patrimony from the private patrimonies.[1]

The claim is that even prior to empirical confirmation, i.e. were the explanation offered merely as an hypothesis, there would be a presumption in its favour because of its naturalness, simplicity (i.e. economy) and relevance to an infinite number of phenomena. It is to be noticed, however, that these criteria, upon which the presumption depends, are the very same criteria as those involved in Vico's divine proof and, indeed, that there, as here, they enable us to claim that an explanation which conforms to them offers the only possible way in which whatever it explains can be understood.

[1] *S.N.* 264.

It is clear therefore that the propositions embodied in the 'ideal eternal history' are not epistemologically neutral prior to their empirical confirmation and that, as a result, Vico cannot be interpreted as offering a straightforward version of the hypothetico-deductive method as it is currently conceived. For it is not a requirement in the usual account of the hypothetico-deductive method that the propositions from which the conclusions of the hypothesis are drawn should have any antecedent epistemological status. It is sufficient that they should have a certain logical form and by virtue of this be capable of operating as premisses in valid deductive arguments. Their epistemological status depends entirely upon the extent to which their deductive consequences correspond to certain knowable features of the real world, i.e. of a world, be it the natural or historical world, the epistemological status of which is not in doubt. If this situation is compared with that which confronts Vico in his attempt to produce a science of history, it is clear that although it is necessary that the basic empirical theories of his Science be such as can be used to support valid deductive arguments, there can be no straightforward appeal to an external historical reality for confirmation, since the epistemological status of the historical world is precisely what requires to be established.[1]

In the light of these considerations it is necessary to accept that Vico's remarks about his proofs do not suffice to establish the epistemological status of his Science. In his philological proofs he has claimed that the confirmation of his empirical theories is provided by their capacity to support acceptable interpretations of historical evidence, but has failed to provide the independent criterion of acceptability which this position requires. He has, it is true, suggested that his theories have an antecedent epistemological status but this has turned out to depend upon criteria involved in his divine and philosophical proofs and, as was pointed out above, these presuppose the acceptability of the historical accounts his Science makes possible. It does not, however, follow from this that Vico's position involves a vicious circle. Rather what he is suggesting is that it is a necessary but not a sufficient condition of their truth that empirical theories and historical accounts should stand in the relationship outlined. Empirical theory makes it possible for the historian to take

[1] See chapter 8 above.

the evidence in a certain way and to construct certain kinds of historical accounts from it, the intelligibility of which is of the same kind as that of the theories themselves. Were the theories to fail to do this they could not be true, but their capacity to do so does not of itself establish their truth. For a sufficient condition of their truth it must be shown that they, and they alone, provide the only possible understanding of the events in question. Thus Vico's three kinds of proof presuppose a further, yet more ultimate, criterion upon which his claims about the epistemological status of Science finally depend. It is necessary therefore to turn to his most fundamental remarks about his theory of knowledge to discover what this is.

15

Theory of knowledge

At the end of the 'Elements', in perhaps the most famous passage in the *Scienza Nuova*, Vico states his fundamental epistemological principle in such way as to show that he fully accepts the need for the independent criterion presupposed by his various proofs and is prepared to provide this:

Now in order to make trial whether the propositions hitherto enumerated as elements of this Science can give form to the materials prepared in the Chronological Table at the beginning, we beg the reader to consider what has hitherto been written in the whole of gentile knowledge, human and divine. Let him see if it is inconsistent with the above propositions. Whether with all or some or one. For inconsistency with one would amount to inconsistency with all, since each accords with all. Certainly on making such a comparison he will perceive that all that has so far been written is a tissue of confused memories, of the fancies of a confused and disordered imagination; that none of it is begotten of intelligence which has been rendered useless by the two conceits enumerated in the Axioms. For on the one hand the conceit of the nations, each believing itself to have been the first in the world, leaves us no hope of getting the principles of our Science from the philologians. And on the other the conceit of the scholars who will have it that what they know must have been eminently understood from the beginning of the world, makes us despair of getting them from the philosophers. So, for the purposes of this Science we must reckon as if there were no books in the world.

But in the night of thick darkness enveloping the earliest antiquity so remote from ourselves, there shines the eternal and never failing light of a truth beyond all question: that this world of civil society has certainly been made by men and that its principles are therefore to be rediscovered within the modifications of our own human mind. Whoever reflects upon this cannot but marvel that the philosophers should have bent all their energies to the world of nature, which, since God made it, He alone knows; and that they should have neglected the study of the world of nations which, since men made it, men could come to know.[1]

It is important to notice how, in the first paragraph, Vico commences by raising the question of the formal adequacy of his Science but finishes by discussing its truth. The initial question raised is whether or not his Elements can 'give form' to the historical scheme previously outlined in the Chronological Table as they are supposed to do.[2] But Vico is prepared to allow that different sets of Elements could 'give form' to historical schemes other than his, such as those against which, in his notes on his Chronological Table, he has so far proposed only historical arguments. Such a concession is implied in his preliminary suggestion that other sets of elements ('the principles of any subject in the whole of gentile knowledge, human and divine') be tested for compatability with his own. Thus Vico is not suggesting that his set of Elements is the only one which is formally adequate or conceptually possible. His subsequent reference to the two conceits as a source of the inadequacy of rival sets of principles is meant only to explain how they come to be arbitrary and unhistorical but not to imply that they are conceptually impossible.[3]

Were Vico claiming that sets of Elements which were incompatible with his own allegedly self-consistent set should be rejected solely by virtue of that fact, his claim would have to be rejected. For he would be taking the self-consistency of a set of Elements to be a sufficient condition of their acceptability whereas it is, at most, a necessary condition.

But Vico shows that he is fully aware of this point in the second paragraph by introducing the further claim that what distinguishes his Elements is that they are connected to a 'truth beyond all question'. The rejection of other sets of principles is thus justified not by their incompatibility with a given set of mutually consistent principles but by their incompatibility with a set which is both mutually consistent and true. This implies that the requirements of

---

[1] S.N. 330–1. I have altered Bergin and Fisch's translation to capture Vico's suggestion that the principles of historical knowledge are to be 'rediscovered' rather merely than 'found' within the human mind. This corresponds more closely with Vico's use of the verb *ritruovare*, the importance of which will appear later in this chapter.

[2] See chapter 1 above for a statement of Vico's claim.

[3] See chapter 2 above for an account of the arbitrary and unhistorical nature of rival systems of thought.

'knowledge' are not exhausted by the formal self-consistency of a set of claims, for self-consistency is a necessary but not a sufficient condition of their truth.

The truth which is now introduced to complete the conditions of knowledge is stated twice. It is first put forward as the claim that because history is a human product its principles are to be 'rediscovered within the modifications of our own human mind'. This formulation is so vague, however, that it might well be nothing more than a restatement of the purely metaphysical principle that history, being a human product, must be explained by certain aspects of human nature, rather than a claim about our knowledge of these. In his second statement of the principle, however, Vico makes it clear that he is making an epistemological claim, for here the concept of knowledge is explicitly mentioned: men can know the world of human history because they have themselves made that world, whereas only God can know the natural world, because he has made that world. It is clear that here, for the first time in the *Scienza Nuova*, Vico is referring to a creative theory of knowledge which is, at least verbally, very similar to that developed in the *De Antiquissima*.[1]

There are two preliminary points to be noted about this principle. First it presupposes the metaphysical theories put forward in the 'Elements'. For the principle that 'the world of civil society has certainly been made by men' can be nothing other than a reassertion of Vico's claim that human institutions are made by men sharing a historically and socially conditioned nature. It is thus a principle of historical causation.

Second, however, there is the assertion that because men have themselves made the historical world 'its principles are therefore to be rediscovered within the modifications of our own human mind'. This is a claim about our knowledge of the principles necessary for the historian to do his work properly. It is suggested that, by appeal to the 'modifications of our own human mind' the historian has access to certain principles upon which historical truth itself rests. This is emphasised even more strongly in a later passage:

Our Science therefore comes to describe at the same time an ideal eternal history traversed in time by the history of every nation in its rise, development, maturity, decline and fall. Indeed we make bold to affirm that he who

[1] See chapter 7 above.

meditates this Science narrates to himself this ideal eternal history so far as he himself makes it for himself by that proof 'it had, has and will have to be'. For the first indubitable principle posited above is that this world of nations has certainly been made by men, and its guise must therefore be found within the modifications of our own human mind. And history cannot be more certain than when he who creates the things also narrates them. Now as geometry, when it constructs the world of quantity out of its elements, or contemplates that world, is creating it for itself, just so does our Science create for itself the world of nations, but with a reality greater by just so much as the institutions having to do with human affairs are more real than points, lines, surfaces and figures are.[1]

The comparison between historiographical and geometrical construction again indicates that Vico is restating the creative theory of knowledge of the *De Antiquissima*. But new principles have been introduced into the account leading to the assertion that historical knowledge is 'more real' than mathematical knowledge. Historiographical creation involves the construction of the 'ideal eternal history' upon principles of necessity ('by that proof "it had, has and will have to be"') derived from 'within the modifications of our own human mind'. Historical knowledge is therefore rendered more real than geometrical knowledge for by involving use of the true principles upon which institutions are based it transcends the purely conventional nature of geometrical truth.[2]

The fundamental problem of Vico's theory of knowledge, and that

[1] *S.N.* 349.

[2] In view of Vico's frequent yet often mystifying claim that Plato is one of his major philosophical ancestors, it is worth noting that there is an interesting parallel between Vico's and Plato's accounts of the way in which the limitations of mathematical reasoning are transcended in philosophy. It was noted earlier (see p. 80, n. 2 above) that in one passage in which he commended Plato Vico seemed to have in mind the paragraph in *The Republic*, Book VII, 531, in which Plato expressed his preference for a mathematically based science of harmonics against an acoustically based science. In the account of the various kinds of knowledge, in which this passage appears, Plato expresses his admiration for the deductive character of mathematics while yet having reservations about the fact that the mathematician can do no better than assume the truth of the propositions from which his conclusions follow. This limitation is transcended only by dialectic, through which the philosopher can come to have knowledge of an 'unhypothetical' first principle, on which the epistemological superiority of philosophy depends. Similarly in the *Scienza Nuova* for the first time Vico finds the purely conventional aspect of mathematics a limitation. In the above passage the suggestion is that this limitation be transcended by an appeal to some knowledge derived from 'within the modifications of our own human mind'. It is at precisely this point, it should be noted, that the theory of knowledge of the *Scienza Nuova* departs from the purely conventional theory of the *De Antiquissima*.

about which there has been least agreement among commentators, concerns the nature of these principles or, what is the same thing, of the mind of which they are modifications. On any account it is clear that Vico is appealing to some point of identity between man as historical agent and man as historian as a ground for the possibility of historical knowledge. Yet there are difficulties in all the interpretations which have so far been suggested.

Croce, as we have seen, construed Vico to mean that the mind which is active in creating the concrete events of history is literally identical with the mind which later reconstructs and knows these events as history. The mind referred to here being identified with objective reason, the principles necessary for this reconstruction, the 'modifications of our own human mind', were therefore to be established by a philosophy of mind which undertook 'to determine the forms, categories or ideal moments of mind in their necessary succession'.[1] This necessary succession of phases of human mental development, when applied to the interpretation of historical evidence, would produce 'living history'.[2] Philosophy would thus supply us with an *a priori* key to the interpretation of history.

An undeniable merit of Croce's view is that it provides a clear sense for Vico's claim that knowledge of the modifications of our mind will enable us to introduce principles of *necessity* into history, i.e. enable us to see history as that which 'had, has and will have to be'. Yet, as we have seen, by claiming that these principles are to be derived by some sort of metaphysical deduction, and hence must be statements of metaphysical necessities, Croce's view fails to make sense of Vico's opposition to Spinozistic and Stoic determinism,[3] or of his insistence upon the *reciprocal* nature of the epistemological relationship between philosophy and philology.[4] A further difficulty which Croce overlooked here was that his account failed also to explain why Vico should think that he could justify the claim that the historical world was knowable to man whereas the natural world was not. If the appeal to the 'modifications of the human mind' is an appeal to a knowledge which Reason can provide *a priori* of certain metaphysical necessities, there would appear to be no obstacle to its providing us with knowledge of both the historical and the natural worlds. Indeed,

---

[1] *The Philosophy of Giambattista Vico*, p. 39.   [2] *Ibid.* p. 34.
[3] See above, pp. 22–3.   [4] See above, pp. 84–6.

Hegel who did hold such a theory, did not restrict the field of application of Reason in this way but thought that the categories it deduced were as applicable to a philosophy of nature as to a philosophy of history. For these reasons it would seem improbable that Vico was using the phrase 'the modifications of our own human mind' to refer to an *a priori* understanding of certain metaphysical necessities.

A second possibility is that Vico is referring to some knowledge we can gain about ourselves by introspection, which is then presupposed in the interpretation of history. There are, however, at least two strong objections to this view. First, we must note that, at best, what introspection could reveal would be something about the content of our natures as they exist in a given set of historical and social circumstances. But one of the errors Vico has been concerned to combat is the assumption that the content of human nature is fixed and constant throughout all historical periods and is thus not affected by different historical and social conditions. His conception of human nature as something of which a part, at least, is historically and socially conditioned would thus rule out this suggestion.

Second it is also to be recalled that for Vico knowledge must be of the causes of things. In the *De Antiquissima*, as we saw,[1] he denied that consciousness of one's mental states was the same as knowledge of them, on the ground that mere apprehension of one's thoughts did not give one knowledge of their cause, i.e. of the mind which made them. Mere consciousness of one's thoughts, feelings, motives, and so on, which is all that introspection could give us, would not therefore be knowledge. For the latter we would require also an account of those (historical and social) conditions which cause men to have such thoughts, feelings and motives.

A third, more promising, interpretation, recently suggested by Sir Isaiah Berlin, is that Vico is alluding to a hitherto unrecognised 'sense of knowing basic to all humane studies. The sense in which I know what it is to be poor, to fight for a cause, to belong to a nation, to join or abandon a church or a party, to feel nostalgia, terror, the presence of a god, to understand a gesture, a work of art, a joke, a man's character or that one is transformed or lying to oneself.'[2] These things are known

[1] See chapter 7 above.
[2] 'Vico's Concept of Knowledge' in *Giambattista Vico, An International Symposium*, p. 375.

in the first place, no doubt, by personal experience; in the second place because the experience of others is sufficiently woven into our own to be seized quasi-directly, as part of constant intimate communication; and in the third place by the working (sometimes by a conscious effort) of the imagination... This is the sort of knowing which participants of an activity claim to possess as against mere observers; the knowledge of the actors as against that of the audience, of the 'inside' story as against that obtained from some 'outside' vantage point; knowledge by 'direct acquaintance' with my 'inner' states or by sympathetic insight into those of others.[1]

Finally, this sense of knowing is 'neither deductive, nor inductive (nor hypothetico-deductive), neither founded on a direct perception of the external world nor a fantasy which lays no claim to truth or coherence'.[2]

The suggestion is that, *qua* human beings ourselves, we have knowledge of a special but unanalysable set of characteristics to be found only in human actions and creations. Derived largely from our experience of ourselves as agents in our own world, this knowledge is used, in the form of imaginative insight, to establish the full significance of the actions and creations of history.

A strong point in favour of this view is its capacity to explain what Vico means when he describes his empirical hypotheses as something more than hypotheses, as 'truths meditated in idea', and ascribes to them a power to 'command acceptance' because of their naturalness, simplicity and fruitfulness, a power independent of whatever empirical confirmation can be afforded them.[3] Interpreted in the light of Berlin's account, this would mean that we recognise in certain hypotheses a possible mode of human conduct independently of any empirical evidence of their factual truth. We do this because, so to speak, in becoming human agents, we ourselves acquire a knowledge of the ways in which it is possible for, and characteristic of, human beings to act. Acceptable historical hypotheses would have, as it were, an intrinsic plausibility which they would gain by embodying this knowledge.

Yet, despite the obvious merits of this suggestion, there are difficulties in it as well. First, like the previous account considered, it seems to conflate *coscienza* with *scienza*. The latter requires an account of the causes of things, and, as Vico pointed out in his

---

[1] *Ibid.* pp. 375–6.   [2] *Ibid.* p. 376.   [3] See chapter 14 above.

objections to Cartesianism in the *De Antiquissima*, mere apprehension of inner, psychological states does not give knowledge of those states since it does not reveal their causes. Thus we would not be entitled to *scienza* of terror or nostalgia merely by virtue of ourselves feeling terror or nostalgia. For *scienza* here we would require knowledge of the conditions under which terror and nostalgia arise.

Second, there is the connected difficulty that in this interpretation the expression 'our own human mind' is taken to refer to one's own individual mind or another's individual mind. Knowledge of the modifications of mind is accordingly derived from experience of one's own inner states or by direct insight into those of others. But this is to put the whole matter on too individual a level, for the kind of knowledge one would thus acquire could not be a possible basis for the kind of historical accounts Vico offers. In the latter the whole weight of explanation is thrown upon the historical and social conditions in which men find themselves, which determine a large part of the content of their character, thoughts, attitudes and desires. Individual factors as such are rarely mentioned by Vico for the reason that he believed that institutional systems cannot endure without a common, public support.

It is evident, if we attend to the passage quoted at the start of this chapter, that what Vico's appeal to the 'modifications of our own human mind' is intended to do is establish the historical and social plausibility of the account his Science makes possible, for it is largely this that is lacking in the accounts of his rivals. The latter, as we have seen, are accused of producing accounts which are either unhistorical or arbitrary and Vico has tried to overcome these defects by insisting upon the importance, on the one hand, of the concepts of historical relativism and historical determinism and, on the other, of man's social nature, in any acceptable account of human history. If this is so, then his appeal to the 'modifications of our own human nature' to guarantee the truth of his explanations must be an appeal to some prior knowledge the historian has of what is historically and socially possible.

It would be tempting to conclude that what Vico is suggesting we need knowledge of here, antecedent to that of our determinate, empirical theories, is of certain purely formal things, such as that institutions affect human nature, determine social decisions and are themselves determined by the historical conditions in which they arise or are modified, in other words, of the things put forward by Vico in his metaphysical as distinct from his historico-sociological theories. But it is clear that, although these theories are presupposed by Vico's determinate empirical theories, they are only necessary and not sufficient conditions of the plausibility of the latter.[1]

To see what more Vico can be referring to here it is necessary to turn to two of his other references to the modifications in question. The first of these has already been discussed, in connection with Vico's claim that the history of (poetic) man 'should have begun with metaphysics which seeks its proofs...within the modifications of the mind of him who meditates it'.[2] The outstanding point about this passage is that Vico goes on to base his account of poetic man's history upon the principle that in its primitive stages the senses are human nature's sole mode of knowledge and that therefore poetic man's view of the universe must have been based upon sense-experience, feeling and imagination. It would not be 'rational and abstract like that of learned men now'.[3] The claim is thus that the historian by appeal to the modifications of his mind can gain knowledge of modes of thought more primitive than those which are involved in the practices of his own society. Moreover, and even more importantly, what he thus gains is knowledge of the content of human nature and hence of the causes and content of human history.

The suggestion that knowledge of the modifications of mind is knowledge of the content of human nature is carried forward in a second passage, to which we must now turn. This occurs immediately after the long quotation with which this chapter commenced. Having claimed that the principles of human history must be found within the modifications of our own human mind, Vico proceeds: 'Now since this world of nations has been made by men, let us see in what institutions all men agree and always have agreed. For these institutions will give us the universal and eternal principles (such as

---

[1] In an earlier discussion of this point I argued that in this reference to the modifications Vico meant to assert the claim that we gained knowledge of the purely formal conditions of history by reflection upon our experience of ourselves as agents in our own historically and socially conditioned world. But although I still think this is part of what Vico means I now think it does not go far enough and that this position must be modified as follows below. See 'Vico's Science' in *History and Theory* vol. IX, no. 1 (1971), 73–4.

[2] *S.N.* 374. See chapter 4 above for a discussion of this passage.   [3] *S.N.* 375.

every science must have) on which all nations were founded and still preserve themselves.'[1] The principles which he then adduces are in fact the three principles of absolute common sense without which, he asserts, no civilised social life could develop in any nation.

It is noticeable that the beliefs involved in these principles, i.e. of religion, marriage and burial of the dead, are very different from the kind of modification mentioned earlier. The former were modes of functioning of the human mind, of the sort which, while always accessible to all men, could be of greater or less importance in societies at different levels of historical development. The content of absolute common sense, however, is a set of beliefs, shared by all societies at all times in their history. It is particularly important to note that they are institutional beliefs, i.e. beliefs which men naturally develop when, given their particular kind of nature, they are in certain kinds of institutional situations.

Finally, in this connection, it is necessary to recall the relationship which obtains between the three principles and men's vicious nature. The claim that these principles represent the minimal conditions of social cohesion and development presupposes the account of man as a self-centred, short-sighted creature, incapable of developing socially were his development to depend solely upon decisions of his own personal making. Yet, as we have seen,[2] there would be no self-contradiction in the concept of a society which did not include these institutions. Nor, similarly, would there be a self-contradiction in the idea of man's individual nature being such that, without existing in the suggested kind of institutional context, he should, by dint of his own personal efforts, seek and contrive to create the conditions of a progressive and just social life. It follows therefore that neither the three principles nor man's vicious nature are conceptually necessary. They represent, rather (together with the thesis about the genetic development of human nature), the most fundamental factual presuppositions of Vico's Science.

If this is so, it is not enough to represent Vico's reference to the modifications of our own human nature as an appeal to knowledge of the purely formal conditions of history. It is certainly true that this is

---

[1] *S.N.* 332.
[2] See chapter 3 above for an analysis of the relationship between the three principles and individual man's vicious nature.

part of what he is claiming. But he wants also to claim that we can learn something fundamental about the content as well as the form of human nature. Thus, in addition to learning that human nature can develop only historically or genetically, we learn also that it does so only through a sequence of stages correspondent to the doctrine of three natures upon which the 'ideal eternal history' rests, i.e. that the capacity to reason is something which can develop only by virtue of going through the sensible and imaginative stages of experience. It is something in fact, which can exist only as a modification of other modes of mental functioning. Again as well as learning that human beings can develop certain capacities and feelings only in a social context, we learn also that they will develop more human capacities only when the institution of religion causes them to feel shame, that of marriage to feel love and that of burial of the dead to feel a concern for the right conduct upon which the future welfare of their souls will depend. Thus the modifications of our own human mind is a source of two kinds of knowledge: of the formal conditions of history, as outlined in Vico's metaphysical theories; and of certain fundamental truths about the content of human nature, which operate as the most basic factual presuppositions of the 'ideal eternal history'.

It is necessary to notice two features of this account, which are ordinarily thought to be incompatible but which go a long way towards explaining the unique character of Vico's later theory of knowledge. The sociological conditions involved in the theory of absolute common sense and the historical sequence involved in the doctrine of three natures are contingent, or natural, necessities of human history. Yet, while maintaining this, Vico wants also to find in them an intelligibility which distinguishes the kind of understanding involved in historical knowledge from that involved in the purely physical sciences, and which elevates the former above the latter.

The claim that there is some causal knowledge which is contingent and yet differs in intelligibility from the equally contingent, causal knowledge of the natural sciences is the most fundamental and yet most difficult in the *Scienza Nuova*. The difficulty here is to see how Vico can maintain his claim that causal knowledge of the human world is more intelligible than that of the natural while accepting that both are contingent.

To understand what Vico means here it is useful to refer first to his often reiterated suggestion that our understanding of children is an aid to our understanding of poetic man. Vico often, in fact, refers to the age of poetic man as 'the childhood of the human race', supporting his account of the propensities natural to poetic man by reference to what we know is natural to children. For example, Axiom *L* and its corollary read:

In childhood memory is most vigorous and imagination is therefore excessively vivid, for imagination is nothing but extended or compounded memory.

This axiom is the principle of the expressiveness of the poetic images that the world formed in its first childhood.[1]

The principle put forward here concerns the cause of poetic imagery, and the appeal to the parallel case of children is intended to support the principle by rendering it intelligible to us. Yet it is to be noted that since children do not, merely by thinking imaginatively, know *why* they think imaginatively, we could not reach knowledge of the causal principle merely by remembering how we used to think as children. Children, in fact, have mere *coscienza* of their world, whereas Vico's claim is that by appeal to the modifications of the human mind we can come to have *scienza*, i.e. causal knowledge.

Vico's appeal to our knowledge of childhood is *not*, therefore, to be understood as an appeal to mere memory of how a child sees his world. It is, I suggest, rather to be understood as an appeal to adult reflection upon childhood. The point to note here is that a rational adult has both the possibility of remembering the world of childhood and of reflecting upon what it was about one's mode of consciousness that made one's world like that. His understanding will not therefore be identical with that of the child precisely because, where the latter will be an unreflective, immediate awareness of the world as conditioned by certain mental capacities and as involving certain modes of belief, the adult's will be reflective and will involve knowledge of the causes of that awareness and those modes of belief. Thus it is by virtue of his capacity, in respect of his own childhood, to *reflect* upon his own earlier beliefs and so to have knowledge of its causes, that the adult can have *scienza* where the child can only have *coscienza*.

In a parallel way Vico draws attention to the fact that judgements of common sense are 'without reflection'[2] whereas those of the his-

---

[1] *S.N.* 211–12.   [2] *S.N.* 142.

torian are not. Indeed, when he explains why it is that the real knowledge that the *Scienza Nuova* contains has been overlooked in favour of the pseudo-knowledge of the natural sciences, it is to the difficulty involved in reflection that he alludes:

this aberration [i.e. the neglect of historical knowledge] was a consequence of that infirmity of the human mind by which, immersed and buried in the body, it naturally inclines to take notice of bodily things and finds the effort to attend to itself too laborious, just as the human eye sees all objects outside itself but needs a mirror to attend to itself.[1]

It might be tempting to take this to mean merely that men are naturally inclined to attend to the physical world rather than to the mental world. But this would be incorrect. On Vico's view, natural science is itself a human construction but, since it is pursued without regard to the manner in which its beliefs are formed, i.e. to the causes of its beliefs, it is simply a species of *coscienza*. The complaint is not against man for having beliefs about the external world but for having failed to reflect upon how he came to have these beliefs and, hence, for ascribing to them a false epistemological status. If we think of the matter in terms of Vico's analogy involving the eye and the things we see by means of the eye, the natural scientist is in the position of concerning himself solely with the things seen and ascribes to them a spurious epistemological self-dependence. The historian, on the other hand, understands the thing seen (by the historical agent) as a species of naturally (historically and socially) conditioned belief, the principles of which he can gain by reflecting upon the causes of his own mental development and social activity.

The concept of *reflection* is therefore the crux of Vico's later theory of knowledge. Vico is claiming that by self-conscious reflection upon our own ways of seeing our world and our own attitudes to it, we can come to understand what are the natural propensities which cause these. We can, for example, think through the stages of our own mental development and see how, for example, the rational thought to which we eventually aspire, is a genetic modification of other modes of thought based upon certain natural propensities. Again, we can think about the reasons why we adopt our various attitudes towards

[1] *S.N.* 331. Cf. also *S.N.* 236: 'The human mind is naturally inclined by the senses to see itself externally in the body and only with great difficulty does it come to understand itself by means of reflection.'

our conduct and see how much of the latter depends upon certain feelings of obligation and of duty and how, if society lacked certain institutions, these would simply not exist.

It is necessary to stress here, that the knowledge we thus acquire is not conceptually necessary. Vico is not saying that we could not conceive of beings to whom rational thought, or a sense of shame, or feelings of duty towards their family, were innate and not historically acquired capacities. These are, obviously, conceptual possibilities. What he is claiming, however, is that such possibilities could not constitute a recognisable mode of human conduct and that a history which embodied such assumptions would not be our history.

The identity between historian and historical agent, upon which the possibility of history itself depends, is therefore more than purely formal. It involves in addition an identity of fundamental genetic and social structure which is, in the last analysis, contingent or factual. For Vico, the peculiar intelligibility of history rests upon insights into our own nature which are accessible to us by virtue of our capacity to reflect upon ourselves in our various social and historical activities, so that we can be aware not merely of the different ways in which we see and react to our world but also of the different conditions which cause us to see and react thus.

In view of the importance of this topic for an understanding of Vico's philosophy it is worth concluding with some brief indications of the extent to which the foregoing account makes sense of the more important claims Vico himself makes. First, we may consider the suggestion that his empirical theories are, prior to historical confirmation, not mere hypotheses but 'truths meditated in idea'. In the light of the foregoing interpretation this is to be understood to mean that Vico's empirical claims are of the right kind formally and that such factual suppositions as they make about human nature are correct. It is, of course, still conceivable that the formal categories and factual assumptions we make may not enable us to produce an acceptable account of history. But the conclusion to be drawn here is not that the categories and factual assumptions are wrong but that what we are dealing with is not the history of *man* in any intelligible sense of that word. This would not, however, be a purely nominal claim for the point would be that we should be precluded from a certain kind of understanding of the events in question if we had to deny ourselves what we can learn by reflection upon our own most fundamental natures.

Secondly, the above interpretation explains also why Vico, while asserting the methodological similarity between investigation of the human and natural worlds, should want to reserve the term 'scienza' solely for the former. The relevant methodological similarity lies in the fact that both require empirical confirmation, which is available only in a discipline having the formal structure of a science. The epistemological superiority of the human sciences stems from the fact that in them alone our prior knowledge of certain basic experiential truths about human nature involved in them enables us to recognise not merely that a given explanation is true but also to understand it in a special way. For example, it would be possible, if the formal structure of our explanations were all that we could take for granted, to construct 'historical' accounts in which we could recognise no intelligible human activity. This, indeed, is what happens, on Vico's view, in the case of the kind of explanations offered in the natural sciences. A consequence of this possibility would be that we could never conclusively verify any given historical account, nor the empirical theories it presupposes, since we could never finally rule out the possibility that other theories might not support other interpretations of the events in question. On Vico's account, however, this possibility can be eliminated by virtue of the fact that reflection can give us antecedent knowledge of the truths about human nature which are to be embodied in our theories and hence in our historical accounts. This alone would not, of course, suffice to verify any given account, but taken in conjunction with the confirmatory procedures which the formal structure of a science makes possible, it allows us to go beyond any degree of mere certainty we can achieve in the natural sciences and come as close as is possible to fully guaranteed knowledge.[1]

---

[1] Vico frequently compares the kind of knowledge made possible by his *Science* with God's knowledge, e.g. the reader of the *Scienza Nuova* should experience 'a divine pleasure, since in God knowledge and creation are one and the same thing' (*S.N.* 349). At the same time, however, he expresses certain reservations which indicate that they are not meant to be identical. Thus the *Scienza Nuova* is described as containing the most satisfactory set of doctrines available to the human mind 'in the series of possibilities it is permitted to understand and so far as it is permitted to do so' (*S.N.* 345). The point to note here is that God knows the natural world because he has made it, whereas man has only the *possibility* of knowledge of the historical

A third feature of the foregoing account is that it makes sense of Vico's assertion that the historical world is knowable insofar as there is some identity between man as historical agent and as historian. The well-known difficulty raised by this claim is that of finding a sense of identity to give it even an appearance of cogency. If, for example, we take the reference to man here as a reference to individual man as such we are left with an obvious *non sequitur*. For the individuals who appear in history are, for the most part, not the same individuals as those who seek later to understand it. On this view there would therefore be no reason why historians should find the principles of their subject within their own individual selves or within their experience as individual selves.

A *non sequitur* arises also if we take Vico to be referring to man conceived of under any of the determinate historical or social conditions which determine the content of *relative* common sense. For the conditions which make possible the writing of a refined and intelligible history of, say, heroic man are very different from those which determine the historical and social content of the nature of heroic man himself. Thus, again, there would be no reason·why an historian should find the determinate conditions which explain the nature of heroic man by recourse to those which explain his own.

The difficulty is resolved, however, if the modifications to which Vico refers are taken to include both the formal conditions of human development, together with the basic facts about human nature contained, on the one hand, in the related theories of fallen man and absolute common sense and, on the other, in Vico's genetic thesis. For these formal and factual conditions hold throughout history, in the world in which the historian himself lives as much as in that in which the historical agent lives. History is thus a uniquely human form of knowledge made possible by the exercise of self-reflection which is in itself a uniquely human capacity.

world because he has made it. The reason for this difference lies in the fact that God's making is metaphysical (i.e. he is the ultimate cause of actual, natural phenomena) whereas the historian's making consists in producing *accounts* of the activities and creations of past man. The production of such accounts can never be completely parallel to metaphysical creation because they always involve an appeal to something beyond the historians own activity, i.e. the evidence, which is both a condition of, and a limitation upon, historiographical creation. Thus the historian's remaking can never be the same as divine making, for the latter involves creation *ex nihilo*, whereas the former takes place within certain limitations.

169

16

The character of Vico's theory of knowledge

In the foregoing chapters I have argued that Vico's *Scienza Nuova* contains a highly sophisticated theory of knowledge, involving the claim that historical knowledge is superior in intelligibility to physical knowledge. Vico supports this claim by arguing that the following conditions are independently necessary and jointly sufficient for historical knowledge whereas something correspondent to the first of the three would be both necessary and sufficient for purely physical knowledge:

(1) It must be fully scientific and thus must include knowledge of the kinds we would now think of as appropriate (*a*) to philosophy, (*b*) to a theoretical science, i.e. a science here involving social and historical theory and (*c*) to an applied science, i.e. a science in which evidence is interpreted in the light of the foregoing kinds of theory.

(2) The historical and social theories in (*b*) here are statements of certain basic factual properties of human nature. These are contingent and hence natural rather than metaphysical in any *a priori* sense. They are also, however, intelligible to human beings in a way in which the equally natural properties of the physical world are not.

(3) The intelligibility of these fundamental factual properties is accessible to men by virtue of their capacity for self-reflection, i.e. by virtue of the fact that they can not only see their world in various ways and act in it accordingly but they can also reflect upon the social and historical conditions and causes of this and thus understand why they see and act as they do.

In this concluding chapter I shall briefly discuss certain aspects of these claims, taking them in their connection with the problem of history with which, in a sense, Vico's thought itself begins and ends.

I

We might begin by considering what is involved in the claim that history, if it is to be a branch of knowledge at all, must be pursued scientifically. In the light of what Vico has said about the relationship between philosophy and philology, its most obvious implication here is that the historian should become on the one hand both more systematic and theoretical and on the other more genuinely empirical in his approach to his subject. One imagines that the suggestion that these two aims must be pursued together is not likely to find favour with many historians themselves. They would approve of the demand to adhere to the facts but see this as in principle irreconcilable with any demand for the more systematic use of theory. Thus, for example, it has been a constant source of objection to Toynbee that he has done violence to the facts in the interests of his theories and in so doing has elevated systematic at the expense of empirical considerations in his treatment of history. Similarly, as we have seen, Croce found such a tendency in the *Scienza Nuova* itself, for Vico 'if he found himself faced by uncertain facts, instead of patiently waiting till the discovery of further evidence should dispel the doubt...cut the knot by accepting the fact in conformity with laws'.[1] No doubt there is an element of truth in Croce's charge, insofar as it relates to Vico's work as an historian. What Croce failed to see, however, was that even had Vico been blameless in this respect, he would not thereby have been able to establish the facts in total independence of assumptions about laws. For, if the foregoing account is correct, one of Vico's central points is that (general) facts and laws are mutually supporting or, when the position is too indeterminate to talk of facts and laws, putative facts and putative laws are mutually supporting. It follows that we cannot consider the facts out of relation to some or other theory. When we seem to be unfair to the facts in the interest of the theory, this is certainly an indication of the inadequacy of the theory in hand but not an indictment of the demand for theory as such. Indeed, on this view, the charge that a certain theory forces us to misconstrue the facts carries with it an implicit reference to the preferability of some alternative theory to which the historian commits himself in indicating that aspect of the facts to which justice has not been done.

---

[1] *The Philosophy of Giambattista Vico*, p. 41.

It is never a question of theoretically committed accounts of the facts giving way to accounts lacking such commitment but, rather, of accounts committed to inadequate theories giving way to accounts involving more adequate theories. Historians would therefore be correct to insist that we should try to reach a just view of the facts but would fall into error if they thought this could be reached without some theoretical commitment.

It must be emphasised here that Vico's claim is one which applies only to what we might call first-order history, i.e. to an enquiry which seeks to establish and throw light upon what happened without presupposing some epistemologically prior accounts. Such first-order history might be contrasted with the work of thinkers such as Toynbee and Spengler (to which Vico's is often erroneously assimilated) which presupposes first-order histories and uses them to provide inductive support for certain historical laws.[1] The claim that first-order history involves theoretical commitment does not, of course, carry with it the claim that second-order history involves such commitment at the second-order level. Since the findings of such a second-order enquiry pre-suppose first-order histories, they can be used neither to re-evaluate them nor, in the case of any conflict, to rectify or change them. For, even if it were thought that such a second-order approach could produce historical laws, these laws would not, by this manner of establishment, thereby be shown to be implicit in the first-order accounts of the facts and would not therefore be involved in any questions relating to the validation of the latter. Should, therefore, a conflict arise over the facts as presented in a second-order history and in some first-order histories the former can and must be abandoned without involving any necessary commitment to some other second-order account. But when a conflict arises over the facts as presented by different first-order histories, the very giving of an account of the unsatisfactory features involved carries with it an implicit commitment to some other putative account and the putative laws upon which that must rest.

Vico's claim is therefore about the place of theory in first-order history. He did not, in the *Scienza Nuova*, make any explicit remarks

---

[1] Such second-order accounts are methodologically akin to the inductive interpretation of Vico discussed and rejected above. See chapter 8.

about historians who attempt to establish the laws of history inductively from such first-order histories. But not only is acceptance of his claim compatible with rejection of second-order history and historical laws thus established, it also throws considerable doubt upon the scientific status of the latter; for it raises, in crucial form, the question of the relationship between the laws which presuppose first-order histories and those involved in the establishment of the latter. If Vico is correct it would seem that second-order historical laws could be genuine laws, stating the determining conditions of the phenomena in question, only if they were derived from first-order histories involving either those same laws or laws from which they could be deduced.

At first sight this might not seem obvious. Why could it not be the case that, by a comparative analysis of factors appearing in many different first-order histories, invariable connections between phenomena could be established even though the causal connection of these phenomena is not established within each history itself? Why, it might be asked, could we not establish the law that whenever a certain feudal institution, a, arises, it is always accompanied by a certain set of economic needs, b, felt by people in a certain social and legal position, c, by means of a comparative analysis of different historical accounts? The legitimate establishment of such a law would, of course, require a statement of the conditions entitling us to claim that a certain institution as it appeared in a work of French or Italian history was the same institution as appeared in a work on British history. But given that this could be done, and that the same could be done for the other factors involved in the correlation, could we not then claim to have established an historical or an historico-sociological law?

Given that this could be done we might well be able to accept the claim; but, Vico would ask, how could this be done without presupposing the very law in question? For if the acceptance of first-order historical accounts involves accepting general theories about the nature and determining conditions of the phenomena appearing in these accounts, the fact that the same phenomena appear in the different histories can be established only by showing that the latter involve the same theories. Thus where the second-order historian hopes to establish the law, if and only if a and b, then c, his right to describe any particular phenomenon, as mentioned in a first-order historical account, as an instance of *a*, *b*, or *c*, depends upon his right to assume that the law in question holds of that phenomenon. His procedure at this level begs the point at issue. If on the other hand, he asks himself how the nature of the phenomenon in question can be established *within* any first-order account he will, according to Vico, have to conclude that this can only be done when he can show of what law it is an instance.

It is necessary, therefore, to distinguish the two levels at which systematic, theoretical commitment might be involved. Vico's claim is consistent with the possibility that a conflict could arise between the demands of systematic theory and factual accuracy where these are involved at different levels of enquiry, as in the case of a conflict between first-order and second-order history. It could thus allow the legitimacy of some of the criticisms levelled against, say, Toynbee and Spengler. It could not, however, allow what historians sometimes think follows from this: that there is in the very nature of the case a conflict between these demands. For at the level at which Vico is addressing the problem, the demand for factual accuracy can be met by empirical confirmation only when the latter involves the application of general theories about the nature of the subject-matter and the laws in conformity with which the latter behaves.

The claim is that scientific historical accounts of the facts can be established only when certain appropriate historico-sociological laws can be established; and this is accomplished only when certain historico-sociological theories can be shown to embody principles allowing for the most systematic, consistent and comprehensive interpretation of the evidence. It is necessary now to ask what can be said in support of this position, for it would seem obvious that in current historical accounts many facts are claimed to be known while few or no laws have been established. Moreover, it is often held that even if historians use laws it is no part of their job to establish them. Vico's claim thus conflicts both with current historical practice and theory.

Vico's position can be thought of as involving two connected assertions: that an historical account cannot be established empirically without establishing certain laws and that the latter must be historico-sociological in character. The justification of the first of these points may be made quite briefly, since the question has been much discussed in recent contributions to the philosophy of history. The point here is that history can only be put on a scientific footing if its methodology be such that it is always in principle possible to decide between conflicting historical accounts.

It is often thought that this condition can be satisfied in the following way. It is generally admitted that the relation between the evidence for and the truth of a general historical claim is never such that the claim in question is the only one which could conceivably be supported by the evidence. Alternative possibilities can, however, be ruled out in either of two ways: by appealing to the historian's general knowledge of human nature and social behaviour, or to his knowledge of other connected and relevant historical matters. It should be noted that the second of these alternatives involves the acceptance of other historical claims. Consequently it cannot, of itself, provide a sufficient condition for the acceptance of an historical claim. It is, however – and Vico laid great emphasis upon this – clearly necessary. The historian cannot consider any one claim without considering other relevant claims. And in doing this he cannot avoid commitment to the thesis that human beings exposed to the same historical and social conditions will be conditioned in precisely the same ways.[1] The historian's right to support an account of why, let us say, a particular medieval manor flourished and then declined by appeal to the presence of the same factors in the growth and decline of other manors presupposes that these are law-comformable phenomena with which he is dealing and that, implicitly, he is committing himself to some thesis about what the relevant laws are.

Historians are apt to protest that this view overlooks the importance of the differences between similar historical phenomena, as though the fact that there can be differences as well as similarities between them is incompatible with their law-conformable character. In fact, as we have seen, Vico does not want to deny that there are some aspects of human behaviour that are not dependent upon historical conditioning, though he would not be prepared to allow that those can have any fundamental effects upon human history.[2] More importantly, however, he would argue that the fact that an historian's

---

[1] The reader's attention is directed again to *S.N.* 141–4.
[2] See chapter 3 above.

use of comparative evidence to support explanations of behaviour commits him to causal laws, entails also that differences between different historical and social agents imply relevant differences in their historical and social circumstances. Methodologically the historian is as committed in the conclusions he wishes to draw from, and the significance he wishes to find in, differences of behaviour as he is in regard to similarities of behaviour. To deny this would be to introduce an arbitrary and, hence, unscientific element into the explanation of differences. This would have the ultimate consequence of making it impossible to find a defensible way of deciding what part of the explanation of a given phenomenon should depend upon its being conditioned by the same laws as other similar phenomena and what part should depend upon differences, the explanatory limits of which, being arbitrary, could not be curtailed. In the end therefore even explanations of similarities could not be scientifically established. Thus history could not maintain its pretensions to any scientific character, nor indeed could any other discipline, if all the time it had to allow for the unlimitable and uncircumscribable operation of a completely arbitrary element.

The historian's need to consider both similarities and differences of behaviour between different historical agents as relevant to his historical explanations thus commits him to theories about the conditions upon which these similarities and differences depend. But this, as we have seen, is only a necessary condition of history for while it will enable an historian to give a certain systematic and consistent character to his claims it will not suffice to justify decisions between different systems of claims which the evidence might conceivably support. History must, it is true, be pursued scientifically, but it must also be pursued more than scientifically, i.e. by maintaining its scientific form in conjunction with a certain kind of human or reflective insight.

II

History, Vico has claimed, must be a scientific enquiry. It must therefore have the systematic and objective character that is made possible only by means of the rigorous application of systematic theory. The theory involved must also, however, be formally of the right kind, that is to say, the categories involved must adequately represent the nature of its subject matter. These are the categories offered by Vico in his metaphysical theories, involving the basic claim that man is an historico-sociological being. This, as we have seen, means not only that the most fundamental aspects of human activity are social, involving relationships that are necessarily social, but that they also depend upon conditions that are necessarily historical. The social and historical dimensions of human activity may be, and indeed are, logically distinct but they are metaphysically related. Complete explanations of human conduct must therefore involve both.

The claim that history and sociology are distinguishable but complementary aspects of a single epistemological enterprise has implications for both the social sciences and history. Contemporary historians have largely accepted this point, in their practice if not in their theory. The principal way, indeed, in which contemporary history is to be distinguished from earlier varieties is the increased depth of explanation and understanding which it achieves by relating the aims and activities of individuals to their cultural backgrounds and the latter to the various kinds of conditioning which individuals receive when they operate within the different social, economic, political, religious and educational structures and so on, in which society consists. Even if it is true that historically this has been a consequence of the way in which our social and historical understanding has been transformed by the direct and (more often) indirect influence of Vico's successors, thinkers such as Hegel, Marx, Adam Smith and so on, it remains nevertheless an essentially Vichian insight. Contemporary historical practice, at least, thus conforms to Vico's metaphysical insights, though it is not as yet pursued with the attention to empirical theory advocated by Vico, and thus would not, on his view, merit the status of a science.

With the contemporary social sciences, however, the position is entirely different, for here enquiry into the social dimensions of life, present or past, is carried out with an almost entire disregard for its historical dimensions. Yet if Vico is correct such an approach must lose sight of something which is essential to the nature of the facts themselves.

This is perhaps most easily seen in the case of social scientists who have tried to establish social laws in a purely inductive way, i.e. by statistical correlations within a subject matter taken as known independently of any knowledge of the historical context in which it arose. If, as Vico claims, these historical conditions are necessary to the constitution of facts, the facts from which empirical correlations can be derived can only be shown to be the same in kind, and hence to provide a satisfactory basis for empirical generalisations, if they can be shown to have arisen under the same historical conditions. Yet that they have done so can only be shown by an historical enquiry into the facts themselves. This point was, in essence, made above in criticism of Toynbee's procedure and might seem to require no further elaboration here. It is possible, however, that some sociologists might not accept it as a legitimate criticism of their own use of inductive procedures on the ground that, where the facts dealt with by Toynbee are historical facts, and hence raise questions about one's right to treat as identical in kind facts about people living in different historical conditions, the facts dealt with by the social scientist are contemporary and thus do not raise the same questions. It might thus seem that social scientists who concern themselves with inductive generalisations about contemporary social (and non-historical) facts are immune from the criticism.

Vico's reply to this is obvious: the fact that the phenomena with which some social scientists are concerned are contemporary phenomena does not render them non-historical. Vico would therefore simply reiterate his point that to establish one's right to treat different social phenomena as instances of the same kind of thing it is necessary to show that they come about in the same historical conditions and that to do this we require to know their causes and hence the laws which govern the genesis of things of that kind. Some social scientists have tried to evade this conclusion by classifying facts according to criteria of their own devising; but such attempts, since they still have to make epistemological assumptions about the facts to be classified, fail to meet Vico's claim at the proper level of investigation and would thus beg the question at issue here. It clearly makes no difference whatsoever whether the facts which one is investigating are facts contemporary to oneself or not. Since Vico's claim is that *all* social facts are historical (or, more properly, that all human phenomena are conditioned socially and historically), it applies to facts in the investigator's present as well as in his past. The need to understand the historical dimension of human activity is thus not set aside merely by confining one's enquiries to contemporary activities.

III

The formal adequacy of the categories involved in the *Scienza Nuova*, although sufficient to distinguish the understanding the latter provides from that of any natural science is not, however, sufficient to establish the truth of the claims involved in one human science against those in another. Since the facts made available by *any* scientific history are bound to be theory-laden, there are no independent facts against which the merits of rival sciences can be tested. Vico therefore requires a further condition to distinguish other formally correct but nevertheless unacceptable human sciences from the *Scienza Nuova* and to show why the latter should be accepted but not the former.

This further condition as we have seen, is provided by Vico's appeal to the 'modifications of our own human nature', which constitutes a series of claims about certain factual human necessities. This appeal raises two questions. Is Vico correct in thinking that some independent knowledge of this sort will, together with the formal correctness of his science, suffice to establish its acceptability against its rivals? And, how can we come by such knowledge? I shall discuss these problems separately, in this and the following section.

The difficulty Vico has to face here is best revealed by considering how he could demonstrate the superiority of his account of history against others in which the explanations provided, though formally correct, seemed to us so bizarre that not only could we not accept them as true but we could not even understand them. There are a number of ways in which sciences which were formally of Vico's kind, and which accepted his account of the basic categories proper to human history might provide this. It is worth briefly listing some of these.

(1) Vico tells us that primitive man took thunder and lightning to be communications from Jove and thought that the physical world was a living being. The assumption here is that, however different the construction put upon his external environment, the latter is basically of the same sort as that in which the historian finds himself. That is to say, the assumption is that the historical agent lives in a spatio-temporal world of physical objects and material, vegetable and

animal phenomena of the kind in which the historian lives. It is, of course, a purely contingent fact that we live in such a world. Nevertheless, it is a fact that is of some consequence for history. For suppose, for example, that some historian chose to deny this assumption with regard to the physical environment of primitive man, but was prepared to endow the latter with the basic psychological and social capacities which Vico ascribes to him. He would arrive at an entirely different account of that part of the 'ideal eternal history' appropriate to early man and an entirely different interpretation of whatsoever evidence was relevant to this part of our history (such evidence could hardly be physical, given the nature of the hypothesis, but it might consist in traditional tales, handed on through the ages). The concept of a god could not have arisen by endowing natural objects with objectified and magnified human capacities, for there would have been no objects so to endow. The science of divination or the taking of the auspices could not have arisen in the way suggested by Vico because there would be no natural phenomena of the sort he assumes to provide the material for the practice of these sciences. The emotion of shame could not have arisen as he suggests, i.e. by performing acts of love under the cover of caves, for the concepts of cover and cave would have no applicability to such a world. It can be seen, therefore, that an historian who chose to deny this fundamental but contingent fact, i.e. that historians share the same kind of physical environment as historical agents, could not give the kind of account given by Vico.

Yet the account such an historian gave would not necessarily be formally of a different kind from that offered by Vico. That is to say, he might still be able to accept Vico's claim that man is an historical and social being, that man's mental capacities change and develop historically, that a large part, at least, of our human nature consists in the acceptance of beliefs and attitudes which presuppose social concepts and so on. He could accept this, of course, because the purely formal categories appropriate to Vico's conception of human history tell us about the generic character of the mental side of human activity. They tell us, that is to say, something about the nature of human belief but nothing about its specific content.

It has to be conceded, I think, that if an historian proceeded as above, his account of history might be such that it was formally correct and yet involved claims which were so bizarre that we not only could not accept them as true but we could not accept them as true because we could not really understand them. This would be because, as we have seen, many of the concepts involved in our understanding of Vico's account would have no applicability in the environment postulated by his rival and also because, without knowledge of the objective properties of the environment he does postulate, we would have no means of working out what sorts of concepts would be applicable to it by human beings living in it. As Wittgenstein pointed out, and as Vico would fully have agreed, the fact that we have the conceptual schemes we do have depends upon certain natural facts. Were the latter otherwise our concepts would also be otherwise. The possibility of cross-cultural understanding of the sort involved in history thus depends upon the common accessibility of certain natural facts.

(2) The same considerations can be applied *mutatis mutandis* to the fact that the historian must also share the same physical and sensory apparatus as the historical agent. It would be tedious to pursue this point at any length but it seems clear that were some historian to assume that historical man's sensory organs were other than ours, perhaps rather more like those of certain primitive animals than they now are, we should again find his historical account unintelligible. For we would be unable to understand what, in these circumstances, historical agents could be talking *about*. That is to say, we should not be able to understand what was being said because we would not have any idea about the reference of their remarks, even though formally these remarks might be of the same sort as our own.

In practice, of course, historians assume that historical agents share our physical world and our sensory and physical constitution. Nor is there any reason why they should not do so, for we can establish purely physical facts of this sort without dependence upon our interpretations of past conceptual schemes.

(3) The position is different, however, when we come to a third area of discourse, that which relates to the social world. For here we can find out what other social agents are talking about only by establishing the way they think about themselves, for social entities and relationships cannot be referred to without descriptions involving social concepts.

This difficulty might, of course, be overcome if we could assume that historical agents thought about their social world in the way we think about ours. But, as Vico's remarks about the natural law theorists reveal, this assumption would be incompatible with recognition of the fact that conceptual schemes themselves change and develop in history. It would seem therefore we must either approach the matter unhistorically or else admit that we have no way of coming to understand what historical agents were talking about in any of their social remarks.

The last conclusion is not, however, necessary. For it seems that we could go a considerable way towards establishing the content of past conceptual schemes if we had some prior knowledge of two things: that about which historical agents thought and the causes whereby they thought of these things in the way they did. Now it is knowledge of precisely these two kinds of things that Vico claims in his account of the three first principles, i.e. the three necessary conditions of social life, and in his account of the genetic sequence of mental development which is natural to man. For in his account of the three first principles, Vico is claiming that it would be impossible for there to be any social dimension to life, human nature being what it is, without the institutions of religion, marriage and burial of the dead. At the same time, however, institutions presuppose the concepts of institutions. It follows, therefore, that if these claims are accepted, we know, antecedently to any specific interpretation of past social conceptual schemes, that they will contain the concepts of religion, marriage and burial of the dead.

This knowledge alone, however, would not be enough to enable us to interpret past historical schemes correctly. For though we might now be able to lay claim to knowledge of some of the things historical agents thought about, we could still go wrong by ascribing to them unhistorical ways of thinking about these things. We could, for example, make the mistake of believing that they thought about marriage in the way we think about it. But this possibility could also, to a large extent, be obviated if we had some prior knowledge of the sequence of development of ways of thinking natural to man. For, given knowledge of, say, the associative and imaginative habits of mind in which the thought of primitive man largely consists, we could work out the kinds of ways in which he would think about the three necessary institutions and from these proceed to work towards other elements in his conceptual scheme.

It follows that Vico did not, as is so often asserted, believe in the absolute autonomy of different social conceptual schemes. He certainly accepted that they were different in many ways but at the same time his belief that they are all human creations and hence conditioned by certain fundamental features of human nature, led him to claim that there were certain notions common to them all. Moreover, the possibility of their becoming accessible to inhabitants of other cultures, as, for example, to historians, depended precisely upon the fact that not only were they creations of a common human nature but that this both gave them all some common content and provided the key to understanding what was not common to them.

It is an important feature of this account that, though it is a contingent matter that a certain development of thought is natural to man in certain circumstances, and that the three first principles are necessary (for they are necessary only given other factual properties of man), these are not matters which can be established by historical research. They are not historical truths for acceptance of them governs the establishment of historical truths. One could not therefore adduce historical evidence to support them for they are presupposed by the interpretation of any historical evidence. They must therefore be known antecedently to the latter. In this sense, and in this sense alone, are they *a priori*.

IV

It is necessary now to enquire into the adequacy of Vico's account of the source of this knowledge and whether this suffices to support his claim that we can find in certain fundamental contingent features of human affairs an intelligible character that we cannot find in the physical world. The suggestion is that we can acquire this knowledge by self-reflection, i.e. by reflecting upon our activities as social and historical agents. We thus come in the first place to see that we have certain natural traits and beliefs. We see for example that we all go through a sequence of phases of mental development in which we are, in turn, first imaginative, then punctilious and finally rational, in the sense of being able to distinguish an abstract principle from its application. We see also that certain social institutions provide a causal context for our social activities. So much is, indeed, available to us as a matter of mere observation. If we could not go beyond this we would, indeed, be able to produce some kind of causal account of our mental development, on the lines of the accounts given in the physical sciences. Nevertheless, these accounts would never amount to much more than the classifying of sequences of observed regularities and empirical correlations, and such intelligibility as they might have would never go beyond this.

We go beyond observation, however, by our capacity to reflect upon ourselves in these situations. When we do this we see not merely, for example, that we went through the natural sequence of mental development but that the later stages in it could not have been reached, by us at least, as limited human beings, except by going through the earlier stages. We see, for example, that we could not have acquired the capacity to think in the consistent and critical manner proper to rational adults except by having first been able to think imaginatively and associatively. For the capacity to think rationally is something we can acquire only by having our imaginative and associative principles of thought modified and corrected partly by the teaching and education we receive in society and partly by the failure of expectations based upon them. And this is because, from one point of view at least, human, rational thought is nothing but modified associative thought; it is, in other words, associative thought proceeding upon correct rather than purely natural principles.[1] It may therefore only be a contingent fact that man has these associative forms of mentality and that he receives the kind of teaching that he does or that he lives in a world in which they do not provide a sound basis for fulfilled expectation, but it is not merely a contingent fact that, given all these conditions, the earlier modes of thought will change into the later, nor that the later could not have arisen but for the earlier. Yet neither, on the other hand, is it a matter of conceptual necessity. Vico is not suggesting that we could not conceive a world in which some sort of beings existed who could acquire the capacity to think rationally without going through the prior phases of the developmental sequence. He would, however,

---

[1] This is an application of Vico's claim that the nature of human things is nothing but their coming into being at certain times and in certain guises.

deny that we could recognise in such beings any truly human nature, for the necessity to acquire reason in this way is part of what we recognise as our human nature.

The same considerations apply to the three principles. Reflection upon our activities as social beings leads us to see that did we not exist in the context of certain institutions and under the pressure of certain beliefs, our activities would be intensely egoistical for we can see that even when we are in such a context the impulse to egoistical action is always there and is only resisted by recourse to other motives and intentions which these institutions make possible. Without this context we would not be able to pursue any of the activities upon which human social development depends. Again there is no question of any conceptual necessity here. Vico is not denying that we could conceive of beings who could act benevolently in a non-institutional context – presumably he thought God could. But such beings would not be *human* beings. This is not, of course, merely a matter of the definition of the word 'human'. It is, rather, a claim to knowledge of our most fundamental contingent human properties, a knowledge accessible to us by means of our capacity to experience ourselves in our various social and historical rôles and activities and thus to see how some parts of them are conditioned and made possible by others. This capacity is not itself something which human beings possess throughout their history, but something they can come to possess when the nation of which they are a part has developed sufficiently to make this mode of consciousness possible.

In the end, therefore, Vico's conception of a *human* science, and his claim that this is epistemologically superior to any natural science, rests upon a thesis about the capacity human beings have for reaching self-understanding. The necessity to use this knowledge in constructing history makes demands upon the historian over and above those he already shares with the natural scientist. It also, however, allows him to offer explanations which are ultimately more intelligible than any which are available in the natural sciences.

17

Law, providence and the barbarism of reflection

The conclusion of the last chapter was that the *Scienza Nuova* should be thought of as providing the philosophical basis for a science of man's historical development. This has been disputed by a number of writers, some of whom I shall discuss in the next chapter, on the grounds that it does not acknowledge sufficiently the extent of the humanist influence upon Vico's thought. Since the point has been made, however, it is worth emphasising that, although the *Scienza Nuova* is meant to provide the philosophical basis for a science of history, it is a highly unusual sort of science. For, unlike many natural sciences, it is, in the last analysis, based upon insights about human nature. Since these are presupposed by historical interpretation, they cannot be falsified by empirical historical discoveries, for such discoveries themselves require interpretation and presuppose principles of interpretation and verification. The centrality which Vico accords to these insights provides one sense, therefore, in which his Science can be seen to be affected by his debt to his humanist predecessors.

There is, however, another way in which Vico's work shows the influence of his humanist predecessors upon him. This is in the constitutive role which he ascribes to rhetoric and to topics in the historical development of the social world. These are not matters to which I have paid detailed attention so far, subsuming them generally under what I have said about the role of common sense. Some commentators, however, who lay particular stress upon them, believe that they introduce considerations which are incompatible with the kind of interpretation which I have advanced. It would be useful, therefore, to investigate in more detail how these aspects of social life fit into the *Scienza Nuova* and whether or not their presence there is incompatible with the foregoing account. In what follows I shall discuss this question first in connection with Vico's theory of the development of law, which is one of the principal areas in which his view of the operation of these factors is evident. The results can, however, be generalised to his account of the historical development of other aspects of institutional life. Since the discussion has consequences for the account of providence offered in chapter 5, I shall then investigate its implications for that view. Since these raise further questions about his belief in the necessity for the barbarism of reflection and the metaphysical status of the recourse of the nations, I shall conclude the chapter by analysing and discussing his views about them.

THE DEVELOPMENT OF LAW

Vico's interest in law and his conviction of its importance in human social and historical life has already been stressed in earlier chapters. To take the analysis of his account further than I have so far, however, it is necessary to bring together three separate claims, some of which have been mentioned in different contexts. The first, which has already been touched upon,[1] is that there is a single sequence of laws pertaining to private rights which arises independently in the history of each nation or, more precisely, which would arise independently, if each nation were to develop in isolation or in relative isolation from all others.

According to this thesis, every nation will have a 'poetic' stage of law in which, for example, all ownership belongs immediately to God and mediately to the fathers.[2] The sequence of changes then proceeds as follows. First, in response to opposition from the *famuli*, the fathers join together to form the aristocratic state under the rule of a king. They are forced, however, to grant bonitary ownership of the fields to the workers who, in return, must accept the burden of the census and offer free service to the fathers in times of war. This law, the 'first agrarian law',[3] was granted in Rome, according to Vico, at the time of Servius Tullius. Next, when the nobles fail to respect the conditions of this law, the plebs bring about the creation

---

[1] See pp. 114–15 and 121–3 above.   [2] *S.N.* 256.   [3] *S.N.* 107, 265, 597, 600.

of the plebeian tribunes for the protection of bonitary ownership and have them accepted under oath by the nobility. Next again, however, when the plebeians become discontented both with the quality and the security of bonitary ownership, under which they are not permitted to bring civil actions when the laws are breached, they demand quiritary ownership of the fields, hitherto reserved to the nobility. This is the 'second agrarian law' of the ancient peoples.[1] In the case of Rome, Vico claims, this is what was involved in the demand for the Law of the Twelve Tables. But this still does not allow the plebs to enjoy security in their ownership because they lack the right to solemnised marriage and, hence, have no legitimate successors to whom to leave their fields. To rectify this they therefore proceed to demand the right of *connubium* or solemnised marriage and, since this requires access to the religion of the nobles, the right to the latter as well. Thus, by a series of steps involving an improvement in their status in private law, the plebs gain such an equality in civil status as, in the end, to require a change from the aristocratic form of the state to that of the free popular state. This change, according to Vico, occurred in Rome with the enactment of the Publilian law.

This sequence constitutes a part of the 'ideal' history of the 'natural law of the gentes'. Initially, the suggestion might seem to be that the various changes involved in it are *caused* by a common desire on the part of the legally underprivileged for an equal share in those necessities or utilities which society, at some given stage, can provide.[2] This is not, however, Vico's view. To see why it is not, we must turn to the second essential feature of his theory.

Although Vico believes that a struggle occurs over the possession of the right to different forms of necessities and utilities, he denies that the desire for the necessities and utilities is the *cause* of the just. To do so he introduces a distinction between occasion and cause. The desire for the necessities and utilities of life is characterised as the *occasion* of the just, whereas the *cause* is said to be the idea of equity itself. This idea, he continues, is 'eternal', although the seeds

---

[1] *S.N.* 109.

[2] *S.N.* 241. Vico here mentions the features involved in the total sequence, including the later comforts, pleasures and luxuries. The extension introduces nothing new in principle and for simplicity I shall ignore it here.

of it lie in man as part of his nature from the start of his historical development.[1]

To understand the significance of this point it is necessary to recollect Vico's belief that man becomes progressively more rational in the course of his historical development. A complete grasp of the principle of equity is available only in the third, 'fully rational' age but in neither the poetic nor heroic ages which precede it. This eliminates the possibility that a fully cognised or fully developed idea of equity could be the cause of the just, as it is exemplified in earlier periods. The suggestion is rather that when, upon the *occasion* of a desire for a greater share of the necessities or utilities of social life, legal disputes arise, a third factor becomes operative, the idea of what is *equitable in the circumstances* – i.e. a certain *apportioning* of the necessities and utilities – and it is this which determines what is decided. Thus, in the example given above, when the *famuli* seek those necessities which only the first agrarian law, that of bonitary ownership, can allow them, they accept that it is equitable in the circumstances that they should be subject to the census and should provide service for the nobles in times of war. Again, when the plebeians have gained quiritary ownership of the fields but cannot enjoy its fruits to the full without the right to lawful marriage and to the legitimation of their offspring, the arrangements arrived at involve a further appeal to what is thought to be equitable in the circumstances, although, of course, the circumstances will now have changed from those earlier. The claim that equity is the cause of the just can thus be understood as implying that any new legal arrangements are grounded on an ideal – the notion of what is just in the circumstances – which itself changes progressively as the circumstances in which it is invoked change.

It must be emphasised that this involves no appeal to some absolute or ahistorical standard of justice. On the contrary, the people of any

---

[1] *S.N.* 341. The claim is made much clearer in the *Scienza Nuova Prima* of 1725, hereafter *S.N.P.* References to this work are based upon the system of numbered paragraphs provided by F. Nicolini in his edition in volume 3 of the *Scrittori d'Italia* series, published by Laterza, Bari 1931. Translations of it are taken from *Vico: Selected Writings,* edited and translated by Leon Pompa, Cambridge University Press, Cambridge 1982. In paragraph 41 Vico writes: 'The word *caussa* is not used here, for the cause of the just is not variable utility [itself] but eternal reason which, in immutable geometric and mathematical proportions, distributes the various utilities upon the occasion of different human needs', pp. 100–1.

historical period will have inherited, in their positive law, the embodiment of an historicised ideal of the equitable. If that no longer seems adequate to the situation, any new changes must start from that point and be seen to be more equitable in the new circumstances. It follows from this that there is an inner rational thread in the sequence of such changes and that they cannot be cataclysmic. Attempts at cataclysmic change, even if initially achieved, will simply be modified to meet the standards which, in the light of this historical development of the concept of the equitable, are held to be appropriate. Men do not change their customs all at once, Vico asserts,[1] and since law exists by nature, i.e. in the nature of men,[2] neither does it change all at once but only by degrees and over a long time.

It is necessary now to turn to the third aspect of Vico's theory: the importance which he attaches to rhetoric in general and to topics in particular in reaching decisions in law and, ultimately, in the development of law. From what has been said so far, it would seem that Vico holds that all nations will have a history in which their legal structures exhibit a common pattern of development in response to a common set of ideas about what is just or equitable in the circumstances at any given stage. It might, indeed, look as though this ideal exists as some sort of historicised Platonic Idea, becoming ever more accessible as men grow more rational and more capable of grasping it. This is not, however, what Vico means, as becomes apparent when account is taken of his conception of the role of rhetoric and topics.

Although Vico stresses the importance of topics in his later works, in which the notion of an historical development of human culture and consciousness is central, it would be helpful to approach the issue by considering some of his earlier comments upon it. I shall therefore briefly discuss these first, before examining his later conception of topics and its relation to the development of law.

In general, topics is, for Vico, the art of knowing, and being able to summon, all the considerations relevant to the formulation of a true judgement. In *De Nostri Temporis Studiorum Ratione*, he alludes to it when arguing that topics has been ignored in the interests of criticism, with unfortunate pedagogic results for the young, who should be taught how to create arguments before being taught how

---

[1] *S.N.* 249. [2] *S.N.* 134–5, 309, 311.

to criticise them. Topics, which is appropriate to the creation of an argument, is the art of knowing all of the considerations which are, or might be, relevant in the circumstances. Although it is indispensable to the orator, it is also of great importance in courts of law, where it enables the lawyer speedily and effectively to adduce considerations in support of a client's case. It includes not only a knowledge of the law but relevant parallels and analogies drawn from common experience and likely to be persuasive when applied in argument in virtue of that fact. At this stage Vico distinguishes topics from criticism, which is concerned with the criteria necessary for the assessment of the validity of arguments, as found, for example, in the *Port-Royal Logic*. But although he complains about the over-emphasis upon criticism at the expense of topics, he refuses to deny the need for criticism. For, as he points out, a reliance upon topics without criticism can lead to an acceptance of the false.[1]

In *De Antiquissima Italorum Sapientia*, however, there is a change in his point of view. He turns to the subject here in the context of a discussion of Aristotle's account of the categories and of topics. These, he maintains, are useless if it is thought that they can provide a body of truths which can be used to support the conclusions of arguments. On the other hand, they are indispensable as a clue to the main general areas of human experience and learning to which one should turn in order to view some matter in an appropriate and relevant way.[2] He still maintains that there is a distinction between invention and validation and, indeed, criticises the Academicians for having concentrated upon invention at the expense of criticism and the Stoics for having done the opposite: 'both were wrong, for neither invention without judgement nor judgement without invention can be certain'.[3] When it comes to the question of certainty, however, he no longer

---

[1] *On the Study Methods of Our Time*, translated by Elio Gianturco, The Library of Liberal Arts, Bobbs-Merrill, Indianapolis 1965, part 3.

[2] *De Antiquissima Italorum Sapientia*, chapter 7, part V, 'On the Faculty Peculiar to Knowledge': 'Aristotle's categories and topics are therefore quite useless should anyone wish to discover anything new in them. For should anyone try to do so, he will, like some latter-day Lully or Kircher, resemble a man who knows the letters of the alphabet but cannot put them together so as to be able to read the great book of nature. But if the categories and topics are taken to be the indices and alphabets, as it were, of questions to be asked about the matter in hand, so that we have it in a clear perspective, nothing can be more fruitful for discovery', *Vico: Selected Writings*, p. 73.

[3] *Ibid*. p. 72.

suggests that this is solely a matter of logic. What is required instead is a *critical use* of the categories and topics, so that one can be assured that a judgement arrived at conforms to the best of public wisdom and is thus free of any private idiosyncrasy. The intention here is not to deny the need for valid reasoning but to insist upon the necessity to view the matter in question in the most complete and detailed way and for the judgement reached to be informed by public and professional wisdom.[1] Decisions in law are therefore to be reached by a full inspection of everything relevant to a case and by the critical application of the best of public – and, in this instance, legal – wisdom to it. It is important to note, however, that, on this modified view, there is nothing beyond these public procedures to which to appeal to guarantee the certainty of a judgement. If the procedures have been properly conducted, the judgement which ensues is certain and correct.

Vico's interest in the question of the relation between the procedures appropriate to the creation of a judgement and those appropriate to its criticism is carried over into the later works, culminating in the *Scienza Nuova*, but his views of their relationships are considerably altered as a result of the introduction of his systematic theory of the historical development of human consciousness. He still maintains that the purpose of topics is to make the mind inventive and that of criticism to make it exact.[2] But he has abandoned the claim that both are always present, for the nature of each is affected by the stage of development of the mind of the nation. Thus for poetic man there arises what he calls a 'sensory topics',[3] the function of which is to create meaning in the form of specific things or deeds – in law, for example, mancipation *vera manu*, i.e. with the actual hand or real force.[4] As we have seen,[5] however, since poetic man has no abstract concepts, he has no idea of a class or of an abstract universal. The meaning which is created by the 'sensory topics' is always an individual

---

[1] 'For the arts are the laws of literate states, since they are the observations of nature, which all the scholars accept, transformed into rules for the disciplines. Thus anyone who makes something by means of an art is certain that he has the agreement of all scholars. [But] should he not employ an art he will easily be deceived, since he will be relying on his own nature alone', *ibid.* p. 73.

[2] *S.N.* 498.

[3] *S.N.* 495, 699.

[4] *S.N.* 1027.

[5] See pp. 115–17 above.

meaning and the laws which emerge from it have no universality. What poetic man understands is only what *he* must do, not what *all*, or even *some*, must do. Nevertheless, because of their common origin in the 'sensory topics', the law by which any individual of a particular kind is bound will be the same as that by which a different individual of the same kind is bound. At this point, in the absence of any genuinely rational capacities, there is no art of criticism.[1]

In the period of Roman law, however, a change takes place. This is the age in which, Vico claims, ancient law was a serious poem and ancient jurisprudence a serious kind of poetry.[2] By this point the fathers have united in common cause against their rebellious *famuli* and have surrendered some of their private powers to create a public power under the control of the aristocratic sovereign. There must therefore be a sense of identity of interest among the fathers, and laws must be recognised by the individual as holding for a class of people and not just for himself. The universality of law, in other words, is beginning to emerge from the particularity of its previous mode. In these circumstances the *persona* or mask is invented to stand duty for the class: 'under the person or mask of the father of the family was concealed all his children and servants and under the real name or emblem of a house was concealed all its agnates and gentiles'.[3] This is the imaginative or poetic universal, in accordance with which whole fables were invented and, by extension, 'empty masks without subjects' are created for *iura imaginaria*, i.e. rights invented by the imagination. Thus the whole of ancient law becomes a serious poem, justified by an equally poetic jurisprudence.

At this stage it is necessary that law, although a product of the imagination, of which topics is the regulative art, be written. For since men have little or no capacity for interpretation informed by reason, the law must be as certain and as free from interpretation as possible. Hence arises the formulae in which the laws were expressed and which admit of no change, no addition or subtraction, whatsoever.[4]

Finally, however, in the third age of development, pure intellect is brought into play, making use of legal concepts which are both abstract and universal. The intellect is here concerned with the will which is expressed in the law, a will which is that of the citizens

---

[1] *S.N.* 495–8.   [2] *S.N.* 1036–7.   [3] *S.N.* 1033.   [4] *S.N.* 1036.

brought into agreement upon the idea of a *common* rational utility.[1] It is at this point, then, that the arts of topics and criticism come together in a mutual and fruitful collaboration. For it is only now that a decision can involve the agreement of *all* the people about what is equitable for all in the circumstances and this requires a critical examination of all the arguments and considerations which affect all the parties involved, understood both as instances of their respective classes and as citizens entitled to whatever, in that capacity, the fully developed concept of equity requires.[2]

Topics is thus essential to Vico's account of how law develops. Initially it is a means of bringing about particular, but uniform, judgements in irrational beings who are incapable of grasping any truths of law. Eventually, however, it becomes the method of argument and persuasion whereby, because critical assessments of the interests of all the classes concerned is involved, decisions or judgements of universality can be reached.

It remains finally to note Vico's reason for holding that it is by the use of topics, as thus conceived, that judgements of universality can be reached. In part this is to be found in his general distrust of *purely* abstract reasoning and of a rigid adherence to abstract rules. Despite this, however, he never denies the usefulness of rules and laws. For heroic man, indeed, as we have just seen, they are strict and binding. But although this is so because heroic man is incapable of following laws which are not strict and binding and although it is therefore a wholly appropriate state of affairs, it is far from being an ideal one. Hence Vico explicitly distinguishes it, as 'strict' law, from the 'mild' law which the fully developed concept of equity makes available.[3] But as laws become more universal and as man is more capable of understanding the will expressed in them – a will, that is, which embodies an ideal – so they should be treated more as guidelines, since, given the diversity of factors which may apply in specific disputes, their very universality precludes their rigid or over-riding application in any particular case. Judgements and interpretation are therefore indispensably involved. It is this which makes the presence of the affected parties in actual legal disputes so essential. Disputes often involve a variety of different considerations, but nobody, Vico

---

[1] *S.N.* 1038.   [2] *S.N.* 323–9.   [3] *S.N.* 327–8.

insists, is more interested in ensuring that the full effects of any particular decision will be equitable than the affected parties themselves.[1] Hence, if law is to be a living and developing body of rules and procedures, which is appropriate to people's real but changing needs, it must be mediated by an input of knowledge, both of fact and of desire, which expresses itself, in the first instance at least, only in actual legal cases and in the formulation and testing of actual legal judgements.

It may be wondered, however, whether this view is compatible with the claim that there is one specific sequence of legal development which is revealed in the history of every nation. For if topics and rhetoric are made so central to the process, it would seem that, given their different rhetorical capacities and powers of persuasion, different jurists would have different effects upon the growth of law in their nations, thus producing radically different sequences of legal development in different nations. On the face of it, the element of sheer chance, which is introduced into the process by a recognition of the importance of topics, seems incompatible with the claim that, in certain specifiable circumstances, at least, there can be only one such sequence.

To resolve this difficulty or, rather, to show that it need not arise on Vico's view, two points must be made. The first is that it is common sense which determines human choice about the necessities and utilities which are the two sources of the natural law of the gentes.[2] Common sense, however, as Vico insists, is a shared property, i.e. a property shared by a class, people or nation, dependent upon the degree of historical development involved.[3] Thus there is no question of the skills of individuals introducing an ineluctable element of chance or contingency into the sequence. If decisions which are taken under the influence of inspired rhetorical or juridical performances are not supported by common sense, they will simply fail to recommend themselves to the nation and be changed in favour of others which do.

This consideration, however, although helpful, does not wholly solve the problem. For, while it may explain why the development of the natural law of any one nation will not be affected by

---

[1] *S.N.* 951.   [2] *S.N.* 141.   [3] *S.N.* 142.

contingencies arising from individual rhetorical skills, it does not explain why the development of the concept of equity in *all* nations must follow the same pattern.

To answer this, we must return to the distinction between the *occasion* of the just, which is the desire for the necessities and utilities of life, and the *cause*, which is the ideal of 'what is just in the circumstances'. The idea here is of two components, one activating, the other resolving. What it is important now to note is that these are not merely contingently related. This is the point of the qualification that the cause is what is just 'in the circumstances'. For the circumstances to which Vico is referring are circumstances which arise from a dissatisfaction with the positive law of the times, a law which may enshrine, for example, the tyrannical and quasi-divine power of the fathers over the *famuli*, or the prerogatives of the heroes over the plebs. It is crucial to note, however, that positive law is not merely positive. It may have arisen in response to an earlier desire for access to the necessities and utilities of life, but its enactment is grounded upon an earlier ideal. Thus it involves the translation of an earlier notion of what is just in the circumstances into the institutional framework of society. In so doing, however, it alters the circumstances themselves, by legitimating a different balance of the distribution of necessities and utilities which, in turn, provides the context for the creation of a new ideal. This will then provide the grounds for new law upon the occasion of dissatisfaction with the consequences of the ideal embodied in present law. These ideals arise and develop in the course of actual judicial procedures because the latter alone provide a formal mode of access to the balance or imbalance of interests and responsibilities as people perceive them. The theory thus involves a dialectical relationship between natural and positive law. The natural law of one stage is incorporated in the positive law of the next. As a result, however, it alters the situation in such a way as to require a further development of the idea of equity, which becomes the cause, in the sense of the ground, of the next form of law. There is therefore an inherent instability in the whole process, which can be halted only when human rationality is so developed as to allow men to understand the real nature of equity.

The reason, therefore, why Vico believes that the development of law will be the same in all nations is that he believes that it is internal to human nature, *in its social dimension*, to have a capacity to develop the rational concept of equity – to be able to see, that is to say, from a certain institutional framework, perceived as inequitable, what more equitable situation must be created to resolve the problems engendered.[1] On this view, the notion of equity is, as it were, an idea innate to social man. It develops itself through a sequence towards its rational resolution under the stimulus of human self-interest but within the context of its own progressive embodiment in positive law. There need thus be no conflict between the claim that the means by which these stages are reached is the exercise of rhetorical and judicial skills, which reveal the totality of interests involved, and the claim that the sequence is necessary rather than contingent, for acceptance of new judicial procedures and laws depends upon an appreciation of the greater degree of rational equity expressed in them.

If this is so, it is possible to acknowledge the influence which Vico's interest in, and knowledge of, rhetoric and law had upon him, without needing to deny what so many parts of the *Scienza Nuova* clearly imply: that there is a necessity in human social and historical development. The arena in which the clash of considerations involved in the production of legal change takes place may well be that of everyday legal life, but the necessity in the sequence of changes which actually occurs depends upon a sense of the increasingly rational concept of equity which is being realised through them.

PROVIDENCE

From this perspective, it is possible to consider again the account of providence given in chapter 5, in which three senses of the concept were distinguished, i.e. the historical, the immanent and the transcendent. I do not wish to alter this classification of the ways in which Vico uses the notion, nor to withdraw the claim that, of the three

---

[1] This is stated more explicitly in *S.N.P.* 49, where Vico is more directly concerned with law: 'The natural law of the gentes is an eternal law. But just as within us lie buried a few eternal seeds of truth, which are cultivated gradually from childhood until, with age and through [various] studies, they develop into the fully clarified notions which belong to the sciences, so, as a result of [human] sin, within mankind were buried the eternal seeds of justice which, as the human mind develops gradually according to its true nature from the childhood of the world, develop into demonstrated maxims of justice', *Vico: Selected Writings*, p. 106.

senses, that of an immanent providence is philosophically the most fundamental in the work. My aim is rather to develop the latter notion further in the light of the results of the discussion of law above.

The problem posed by the concept of providence in the *Scienza Nuova* lies largely in reconciling the claims that men have made the world of nations and yet that that world has issued from a mind which is 'often unlike, at times quite contrary to, and ever superior to the particular ends that men had set themselves, which narrow ends, made means to serve wider ends, it has always used to preserve the human race upon this earth'.[1] Vico frequently refers to this mind as 'divine' or as 'superhuman'. In the *Scienza Nuova Prima*, where he first introduces the notion, he does so by means of the Platonic metaphor of two agents. The first is an architect, who is responsible for a plan, in the light of which an end, the preservation of man – despite his predilection for aims which would otherwise bring about his own destruction – is secured. The second is his servant, the artificer, who is responsible for the actualisation of this plan. The artificer, in turn, is identified with human will, when it is determined by the wisdom of mankind through the judgements of necessities and utilities, which are the sources of the natural law of the gentes.[2]

In chapter 5, this was interpreted as the problem of the heterogeneity of ends. What Vico is pointing out, and offering to explain, is a lack of fit between the activities inspired by the self-centred, unenlightened objectives which most human beings set themselves and the providential or beneficial results which, unintendedly, follow from them. Because of this lack of fit, these beneficial but unintended consequences are ascribed to some superhuman activity giving effect to the dictates of a superhuman mind. The solution proposed was that the references to the potentially destructive character of the objectives which most people set themselves relate to the particular ends which they propose to themselves as specific individuals, where little or no thought is given to the long-term, or even the relatively short-term, consequences which they might have for the social conditions in which people live and which are necessary for their survival. The references to a superhuman mind, on the other hand, relate not to the activity of some *deus ex machina* – although there are certain

---

[1] *S.N.* 1108. [2] *S.N.P.* 45–7.

exceptions to this – but to the role of communal wisdom or common sense in avoiding the destruction of civilised life which would otherwise occur.

This analysis, I still believe, is largely correct. The modification which can be introduced into it is simply that which is involved in recognising the inherently progressively rational nature of the process by which institutional changes occur. This is exemplified in the foregoing account of the development of the natural law of the gentes, in which the capacity progressively to embody more adequate ideals in positive law, under the double influence of individual human desire and common sense, provides a model whereby one can understand why the process should be beneficial and, ultimately, providential.

There are two reasons why this process should be thought of as providential. The first lies in the fact that God has given man an inherently rational *social* nature which, in conjunction with his inherently unenlightened *individual* nature, provides a means whereby he can rise from a state of bestiality to one of the highest intellectual refinement. It is important to notice that on this view the social and the individual features of human nature are equally necessary. Man needs to have a predominantly self-interested individual nature if there is going to be any departure from some existing institutional situation. For if the only element involved were his inherently rational social nature, there would be nothing to activate a change which would call his social wisdom into play in such a way as to require its further development. An appeal to his social nature alone would not, of itself, suffice here since, at the stage to which it had developed, it would have satisfied itself in the ideals already incorporated in the existing situation. What is required in addition, therefore, is a source of disruption, such as that provided by human self-interest, which is sufficient to threaten the destruction of society unless there are further developments in the ideals which determine the preservational, institutional structure of society.

The second reason why the theory is seen as an expression of providentiality is the *necessity* which it involves, which Vico consistently links with the idea of the influence of providence. The crucial point here is that the individual desires, which are the occasion of change, and the ideals which arise from common sense, which are the basis of the causes of change, are not merely contingently linked.

For although, as Vico constantly asserts, individual man always wishes to act under the impulse of particular self-interested desires which, were they the only operative factors in the situation, would bring about the dissolution of society, the conception of self-interest which is involved here is constantly developing in a way which is reflected in the wider social and legal structure. Thus, for example, as we have seen, the fathers' conception of what is in their self-interest is identified with what is in the interest of their families but not of their *famuli*, and protection of this conception of their self-interest is embodied in the positive law of the heroic period. Hence, when the fathers abuse their powers over the *famuli*, they do so in the interests of their families, which they identify with their own. In so acting, however, they reveal also that the ideal expressed in the positive law of their age is inadequate to the permanent well-being of the society of which they are a part. For, if they wish to preserve themselves and their families, the law must be seen to be in need of change in the light of some ideal which can commend itself to a more universal form of common sense, a form which can take cognisance, and command the assent, of more than the limited classes with which their sense of their own interests is identified. This means that their desire for self-preservation can be satisfied only if there is an expansion in the content of their concept of the self and of their self-interest. It is this which forces them to accept higher ideals of justice, and to incorporate them in new forms of positive law. Thus it is the necessity to incorporate an expanded concept of self-interest into the substance of law itself, which forces them to search for, and to acquiesce in, more universal concepts of justice than those which already exist. The fact that all the developments which take place in law are, therefore, necessary, if the contents of an existent sense of self-interest is to be protected from destruction, implies that because, in the end, man is necessarily social, the connection between what is in his self-interest as, originally, he narrowly conceives it, and what is in his self-interest as, progressively and more universally, he comes to conceive it, is necessary rather than contingent. This is the second reason why Vico consistently describes these developments as providential.

It is necessary to turn now to two difficulties which might seem to arise from this account. The first is that it requires us to ascribe to poetic man a degree of rationality which is implausible, given Vico's whole description of his way of life. This objection would, however, be beside the mark. For while it is true that Vico attributes the *original* character of human institutions to beliefs which derive from the vast imagination of poetic man, he ascribes the *change* in the character of those institutions to the unmasking of those original beliefs. The heroic commonwealths, for example, which protect the huge interests of the nobles, are sustainable only as long as there exists a belief in the semi-divine origins of the heroes. As soon, however, as that belief comes to be questioned and, indeed, its falsity is discerned, the conceptual basis for the form of government which could protect those interests is undermined and the way laid open for a new form of government capable of satisfying new beliefs about the nature, standing and powers of different classes of citizens. Thus, at some point, men's critical capacities develop sufficiently to bring about the overthrow of their original false beliefs and to necessitate the replacement of the institutions which presuppose them.

THE BARBARISM OF REFLECTION

The second difficulty is much more serious and its resolution requires an extended discussion of the concept of the barbarism of reflection. The problem arises from the fact that if, as is implied above, a rationality which evinces itself in the development of new forms of social wisdom or common sense is so fundamental to Vico's conception of the determinants of the historical process, it becomes difficult to understand why he should believe that it is at the very height of the development of that rationality that social disintegration should set in and that the 'barbarism of reflection' should ensue, leading to the recurrence of the whole cycle.

The problem of the 'barbarism of reflection' has been a long-standing difficulty in Vico interpretation.[1] The barbarism which is referred to here is that state of moral corruption into which men fall towards the end of the third age. There is no doubt about the strength of Vico's feelings of revulsion concerning it. He lavishes some of his

---

[1] See 'The Barbarism of Reflection' by Stephen Taylor Holmes, in *Vico: Past and Present,* edited by Giorgio Tagliacozzo, Humanities Press, Atlantic Highlands, N.J., 1981, vol. II, part II, pp. 213–22.

most vitriolic rhetoric upon it and asserts that it is, in fact, a worse form of barbarism than the original primitive barbarism of the senses. In the passage in which he approaches the necessity for the recurrence of the whole cycle of events in the life of a nation, he writes:

But should the nations waste away in this ultimate civil malady, in which they neither consent to a native monarch from within nor are conquered and preserved by better nations from without, then for this most extreme of diseases providence avails itself of the ultimate remedy. For such people have, like beasts, become accustomed to each individual thinking solely of his own particular utilities, and succumbed to that extreme of indulgence or, more accurately, of pride in which, [again] like wild animals, should they fall out over a mere trifle, they grow resentful and wild. Thus, at the height of their fame and the peak of their numbers, they live hideous and beastly lives in the deepest solitude of spirit and will, where scarcely two can agree, since each is bent on his own personal pleasure or whim. [And when such a state is come to pass, providence must apply this remedy]: that, with their ever continuing factions and reckless civil wars, these peoples must turn their cities into forests and the forests into human dens and in this mode, over long centuries of barbarism, rust will blunt the misbegotten sharpness of that malicious wit which has turned them into beasts made even more appalling by the barbarism of reflection than they had been in the first barbarism of the senses. For the latter was an open savagery, against which the rest could defend themselves by flight or by being on their guard, whereas the former is a vile savagery of flattery and embraces, which lays snares against the lives and fortunes of confidants and friends.[1]

The problem of the 'barbarism of reflection' is why, as Vico makes plain in the above passage, such a state should arise when humanity is at the height of its powers and bring about the recurrence of the whole historical pattern. The difficulty could, of course, be met in a number of *ad hoc* ways. One might note, for example, that Vico was the inheritor of a series of cyclical theories of history and that he may have been influenced by them in a manner which was incompatible with features of his own theory of historical development. The weakness of this explanation, however, is that it would make the whole theory of recurrence extraneous to the main doctrines of the *Scienza Nuova*, whereas it is clear that Vico did not himself take it in this way.

An alternative *ad hoc* explanation might be that he was over-impressed by the parallels which he claimed to discern between the

[1] S.N. 1106.

pattern of institutional development in the ancient classical nations and that in Europe during and after the Dark Ages. But if this were so, his position would still be untenable. For his methodology requires a hypothesis in which the necessity for the different stages in the life of nations, including their dissolution, is internal, before he can make meaningful recourse to empirical claims to establish its truth. To adopt this explanation would be, effectively, to ascribe to him the inductive approach discussed in chapter 8 above and rejected as inadequate in relation to his own understanding of the requirements of his project.

Such *ad hoc* explanations cannot entirely be ruled out, including the further possibility that the 'barbarism of reflection' is simply an expression of Vico's own undoubted sense of disappointment with the circumstances of his own life. It would nevertheless be more satisfactory to find a reason which is internal to his general theoretical approach to resolve the difficulty. Such a reason might possibly be found in the pattern which he held to be basic to the notion of human development as such: the progression from infancy to maturity and from maturity to death. But this, of itself, could not be sufficient, for the question would remain as to what grounds he could have for believing not only in the necessity for the death of a nation but for its death after, rather than before, it has reached full rationality. For if, as Vico explicitly claims, a nation will, at the height of its intellectual powers, have the capacity to understand the real nature of things, including its own nature – and this is what the *Scienza Nuova* is itself supposed to provide – one would surely expect such knowledge to support its capacity to protect itself against such dissolution rather than to be a contributory cause of it.

There is another obvious, and plausible, internal reason, for which there is considerable textual evidence. This is that Vico took such a basically pessimistic view of human nature, and of the *primacy* of individual self-interest, that he believed that social progress could occur only under a series of beliefs which would act as an external constraint even upon social activity, by concealing the nature of reality from man – i.e. that, ultimately, he could be responsible for his own social development, in a fully self-conscious way – and by substituting for this knowledge the belief that his behaviour was subject to punitive sanctions wholly beyond his control. Thus, in the age of fully developed reason, when man realises that there are no constraints other than those he may freely choose to impose upon himself as a social being, the element of self-interest is too strong to prevent him from abusing this knowledge and leads ultimately to his social destruction.

This is the position to which Vico's insistence upon the merits of an instinctive morality based upon false beliefs, as against those of a rational morality, confined largely to the educated and with little power to affect their behaviour other than by releasing them from the constraints of the instinctive morality, would seem to point. Before accepting this solution, however, it must be noted that the situation is considerably more complex than this appears to suggest. It is not, for example, clear that Vico believed that social disintegration *is* absolutely inevitable in the fully rational age. Nor is it clear precisely how he understood the relation between the triumph of reason and the decline of religious belief. Since his more theoretical remarks on these important issues are ambiguous, I shall begin this discussion in a somewhat indirect manner, by raising the question of the general *practical* lessons which he thought might be derived from his Science. For, if he believed that one could learn from it that the destruction of society could be averted by some form of action, this would provide good evidence for the view that he did not believe that the recourse of history was made inevitable by the ultimate dominance of self-interest over all other factors. It would then be a further question whether he was justified in what he believed. If answers to these questions can be established, they will in turn have consequences for the interpretation of this important theoretical aspect of his Science.

Vico addressed the question of the practical implications of his Science a number of times, although never in such detail or with such clarity as one might like. One important reference occurs in the *Scienza Nuova Prima*, in a passage in which he distinguishes two 'practical' aspects: a 'new art of criticism which serves as a torch by which to discern what is true in obscure and fabulous history' and an 'art of diagnosis which, regulated in accordance with the wisdom of mankind, gives the stages of necessity which belong to the order of human things and hence provides the principal end of this Science, which is recognition of the indubitable signs of the state of the nations'.[1] The first of these refers to a methodological aspect of the *Scienza Nuova*, i.e. to the help which it can provide in establishing rules for the critical interpretation of a part of the past. This plainly has no implications for the present problem, which concerns the practical implications of the work as a whole.

The second aspect is, however, relevant to the problem. In the succeeding paragraphs Vico makes the following claims. First, that we can learn from his Science how certain human institutions come into being. Second, and as a result, that we can learn what are their 'eternal', i.e. necessary, properties. His conclusion here is that adherence to the three first principles is a necessity for any nation which does not wish to relapse into bestiality. Third, that if it is to be useful, recondite wisdom should serve vulgar wisdom, from which it is born and by which it is kept alive, by correcting it when it is weakened and guiding and leading it when it goes astray. The final claim is that the rule for judging the state of the nations is whether the three maxims – i.e. the beliefs upon which the three first principles are founded – are drawing people closer together or driving them further apart and whether philosophers are assisting them in the former or abandoning them to the latter.

These remarks, which recapitulate claims made in an earlier passage in the same work,[2] are relatively brief and hardly seem developed sufficiently to justify the claim that there is an important practical lesson to be learnt from the *Scienza Nuova*. They amount in essence to little more than asserting that philosophy, which is born of common sense, should assist common sense in supporting social cohesion, by emphasising the importance of the three first principles, and that a nation is in an unhealthy state when this is not being done. But they offer no guidance as to what course of action to adopt in the latter case, whereas this is what one might have expected had Vico believed that there was anything to be done. The implication of his silence could be, therefore, that he did not believe that anything was in practice possible, i.e. that by the time the stage has been reached in which philosophy offers no support to the three first principles and when common sense itself is departing from them, the decline of civilised life is already inevitable.

---

[1] *S.N.P.* 391.   [2] *S.N.P.* 11.

The later versions of the *Scienza Nuova* are at least fuller on this subject. Here two passages are of particular importance. The first occurs in the concluding chapter of the work, entitled 'On an Eternal Natural State, Ordered by Divine Providence, Containing the Best of Each Kind [of Thing]'. This is a difficult chapter to follow. It opens with a reference to Plato who, Vico asserts, conceived of a fourth kind of state 'whose supreme lords would be men of worth and honesty: this would be the true natural aristocracy'.[1] Any suggestion that this might be some sort of utopian state in which the history of the nations might culminate is, however, quickly ruled out. For, having introduced the idea of government by men of worth and honesty in a true natural state, Vico immediately asserts that this is what providence has always ensured, from the moment when it first brought the giants down from the mountains to the caves and subjected them to the power of Jove. Thus, it transpires, the 'eternal natural state' of the title of the chapter is simply the sequence of states delineated in the 'ideal eternal history', each of which, of course, is both appropriate and necessary in the circumstances which give rise to it.

Vico's mode of argument from this point on is highly unstructured. In the initial stages he proceeds by outlining the history of some unidentified nation which has conformed to the phases of the 'ideal eternal history', with the barest of references to any known histories at all. Thus, in effect, he simply delineates the phases of the 'ideal eternal history' by means of a narrative account of the history of some imaginary nation in the past. Since the phases of the 'ideal eternal history' are presented here as though providence has ordained in each era the best state of its kind, there is practically no reference to the need to remedy any features of any particular kind of state. The first such reference, indeed, is not made until we reach the stage at which the free commonwealths arise and in which philosophy is born. For here, since religion is no longer able to rouse people to virtuous action, it is suggested that philosophy should do so by rendering the virtues intelligible in idea and, having done so, enable eloquence to 'inflame the people to command good laws'.[2]

---

[1] *S.N.* 1097.   [2] *S.N.* 1101.

This might seem to recapitulate the idea, expressed in the *Scienza Nuova Prima*, that philosophy should 'support vulgar wisdom when it is weakened and goes astray'. But this is improbable since, if understood in this sense, it would severely constrain the range of that claim. For Vico immediately returns to the narrative mode and, introducing an actual historical reference, asserts that this is what happened in Rome at the time of Scipio Africanus. Moreover, he continues, because it fell into scepticism, philosophy was unable to sustain this role. Eloquence was therefore put to bad use as people sought to seize power through it, thus producing a state of anarchy or unbridled liberty. Thus, the remedial effects of philosophy and of the philosophically informed eloquence, which have so far been mentioned, would appear to be internal to one period of the stages of the 'ideal eternal history' and, therefore, just as constrained by their place in the total pattern as any of the other features mentioned in it. There seems to be no possibility, and certainly no mention is made of one, that their remedial role can be promoted beyond that which they have in virtue of the social position which they occupy at this one stage in the 'ideal eternal history'.

This is further confirmed by the fact that it is at the point where he has reached the state of anarchy that Vico abandons his narrative version of the 'ideal eternal history', and explicitly introduces three remedies, each more drastic than its predecessor, of which providence can avail itself to cure 'this great sickness'. These are: a monarchy based on force, such as he ascribes to Augustus, which can succeed only if it limits itself by offering the people religion and liberty; conquest from outside, so that a nation which is not fit to govern itself should be governed by its betters; or a return, under the influence of the 'barbarism of reflection', to that original state of barbarism, in which the whole cycle is founded.

A notable feature of these final suggestions is that there is a distinct lack of any obvious remedial characteristics in the proposed remedies. This is perhaps less so in the case of the first, where one might accept that a monarchy based on force, but offering the people religion and liberty, would be preferable to a state of anarchy. The difficulty here, however, is that it is impossible to see how it is open to Vico to suggest, in the circumstances, that religious belief could be re-awakened in a nation. For here the imagination has atrophied as reason has developed, while reason itself has been unable to avoid the decline into scepticism. Thus neither is available, in an appropriate form, to perform the task of re-introducing people to religion. In the case of the other remedies, however, their remedial character is less obvious. It is highly dubious that conquest by a foreign nation would be preferable to a state of anarchy, since it would simply substitute one form of oppression for another; and it is almost bizarre to suggest that a return to the original 'open savagery' can be thought of as a remedy relative to anything, even to that vile state which Vico describes as the 'barbarism of reflection'. Finally, however, although he suggests that each remedy in the sequence is more drastic than its predecessor, he does not explicitly commit himself as to whether any of them will or will not occur. It is true that, although the passage has lost almost any historical character it ever had, Augustus is mentioned as an exemplification of one of the three remedies. But it is clear from Vico's earlier account of the Dark Ages and their after-history that he did not believe that Augustus ultimately prevailed in shoring up Roman civilisation, for the cycle is supposed to have recurred. Thus it would look as though the decline from the barbarism of reflection to the original natural barbarism is inevitable, irrespective of whether or not it is dressed up as a remedy.

Both the tone of the passage, and the inconsistencies which it involves, give the impression that Vico is trying either to avoid or to conceal the deterministic character which his view of history derives from the emphasis which it places upon social conditioning. But if the *Scienza Nuova* were truly deterministic, of course, even were it to enable us to diagnose our state of health as a nation, it would be unable to offer any serious practical suggestions as to how to avoid our ultimate fate. Certainly, nothing that Vico has so far offered can be thought of as a serious practical suggestion, since none seem to be in our power to control.

The second passage which might help to throw more light upon this ambiguous area in Vico's thought does not occur within the published version of the *Scienza Nuova* itself. The latter ends with some paragraphs in which Vico exhorts us to admire the work of providence, in the various ways in which it reveals itself, and in which he emphasises the indispensability of religion, be it false as in the case of the pagan nations or true as in the case of Christianity, as the only enduring support for social life within a political framework. But these were not his last thoughts on the subject of the practical lessons which might be drawn from his work. These are to be found in a number of further paragraphs – the *Pratica*[1] – which he excluded from publication but in which he returned to the question. His reasons for omitting these passages from the final published work are obscure and have been discussed in a number of articles.[2] But since they represent his final thoughts upon the matter, it is worth examining them to see what further light they may throw upon it, even if they cannot, in the circumstances, be treated as definitive.

It might be useful to commence with a brief summary of the main claims of the *Pratica*. It begins on a promising note, by conceding that the *Scienza Nuova* would seem so far to have offered no advice as to how to delay, if not prevent, the ruin of the nations in their state of decay. But, it continues, this omission can easily be rectified. For once the course of the nations has been contemplated, the wise and the rulers will realise that their task is to 'recall the nations to their *acme* or perfect state'. Philosophers will have a part to play here, moreover, for if they look backwards from their vantage point in their human age, at the figurative frontispiece to the work, which contains, in symbolic form, all the contents of the *Scienza Nuova*, they will realise that their task must be to support not the corruption of the philosophical sects of their times, but the three principles upon which the whole Science has been founded, i.e. that there is divine providence, that human passions must be moderated, since they can be, and that the human soul is immortal.[3] This call for a return to an appreciation of the indispensability of the three first principles is accompanied by the claim that the common sense of mankind is never completely quiescent and, indeed, that it rouses itself to its most vigorous state of reflection in nations precisely when they are most

---

[1] *S.N.* 1405–11. These paragraphs were translated into English, under the title 'Practic Of The New Science', by Thomas G. Bergin and Max H. Fisch, and published in *Giambattista Vico's Science of Humanity*, edited by Giorgio Tagliacozzo and Donald Phillip Verene, The Johns Hopkins University Press, Baltimore and London 1976, pp. 451–4.

[2] See especially '*Vico's Pratica*' by Max H. Fisch, and 'Prudence and Providence: The *Pratica della Scienza Nuova* and the Problem of Theory and Practice in Vico', by Alain Pons, both in *Giambattista Vico's Science of Humanity*, pp. 423–30 and 431–48 respectively.

[3] *S.N.* 1406.

corrupt. For it is when they are in this state, rather than in one in which they instinctively conform to the three principles, that people talk most of decency and justice, because it is natural to talk of what one affects to be but is not. In this corrupt state, moreover, men sense the lack of the benefits which conformity to the three principles brings and, in an attempt to assuage this sense of loss and to quieten their conscience, they try to use religion to consecrate their evil actions.

On the basis of these claims, Vico arrives at his remedy: that the young should be taught how to descend from the world of God and of minds to the world of nature, in order to live a life of decency in the world of nations. The role of the academies is to teach them to do so. This means that, given the three principles and the criterion of truth, i.e. the common sense of man, they should teach the young that the civil world, which is the world made by man, has the same nature as man himself. This, he continues, consists of two principles, matter and form, which, in man, are the body and the rational soul. The properties of matter, he suggests, with direct reference to Plato, are those of being 'formless, defective, dark, sluggish, divisible, mobile', while those of a rational soul are 'perfection, luminous, active, indivisible, constant'. The final suggestion to come from this is that those who are the form and mind of this world of nations should exert themselves, in every walk of life, to preserve their different orders and thus seek to preserve their states. This means that the enlightened in all walks of life, 'the wise men and princes of the commonwealths... the philosophers in the academies... the knight in knightly arts, the scholar in studies of the sciences, the statesman in the practices of the court, and every artisan in his own craft',[1] should engage in trying to bring about this recall. Nevertheless, it will be beyond them, because of their weak and corrupt nature, unless, as is the case, providence has so arranged the form of society – the orders of human institutions by which religions and laws, assisted by the force of arms, may move them to it – that those who are strong by nature will naturally be drawn to it by their [platonic] affinity with features of that form, and those who are weak will be bound by it, despite themselves, if they do not wish human society to dissolve.[2]

[1] *S.N.* 1410.   [2] *Ibid.*

Despite the greater length of these remarks, there is considerable overlap with the suggestions attached to the idea of a diagnostic art contained in the *Scienza Nuova Prima*. One of the principal recommendations remains that the nations may, even in their last state of decline, be recalled to the conditions of their *acme*, by a firm realisation of the necessity to observe the three first principles. What is new is the rather sketchy idea of the two parts of the state, matter and form, identified in turn with the body and the mind, and the suggestion that the mind, in the form of the enlightened in all walks of life, should endeavour to recall the nation to its perfect state. But this hardly adds to the original suggestion that the way of salvation lies in a return to an appreciation of the necessity for the three first principles.

The more optimistic of these remarks provide a clear echo of one of Vico's early ideals: the suggestion, expressed most notably in *De Nostri Temporis Studiorum Ratione*,[1] but also in the *Scienza Nuova*,[2] that philosophy should inform the practice of the politician and, also, the content of civil wisdom. The crucial question which must be raised, however, is whether it is open to Vico consistently to propose that this ideal can be implemented under the conditions operative during the 'barbarism of reflection'. The answer must surely be that it is not. For his general view is that certain kinds of institutional structures are necessary to certain forms of cohesive social life because they are appropriate to the social natures of the members of a given society. But the 'barbarism of reflection' arises precisely at the point where such an appropriate set of conditions fails to obtain. The possibility that, at this stage, therefore, where the appropriate institutional conditions are absent, men can somehow become philosophers or philosophical politicians, imbued with the highest ideals of public service and capable of introducing new beneficial institutions in place of those which are defective or modifying that which is defective in them, is incompatible with the whole notion that society is supported by, and changes in accordance with, changes in the underlying common sense of the nation. If Vico's claim that the 'principles of metaphysics, logic, and morals, issued from the market place of Athens'[3] and if his rebuke to Polybius for having claimed that had there been

---

[1] Part 7, *Vico: Selected Writings*, p. 44. [2] *S.N.* 129, 1101. [3] *S.N.* 1043.

'philosophers in the world there would be no need of religions'[1] are to be accepted, it is impossible that, in the absence of the appropriate social and cultural conditions, philosophers and men of good conscience could arise to give birth to those very same conditions upon which they themselves depend.

It would appear, furthermore, that this must have become apparent to Vico himself. For, when allowance has been made for any natural wish to finish upon a note of optimism, as is revealed in some of the remarks in the *Pratica*, it remains true that the passage ends upon a strangely confused note. On the one hand we are told that even the virtuous are too weak to do what they must, hence providence has provided the order of institutions which will move them to it. On the other hand, the young are to be taught that a good state is so composed that in it the body serves and the mind commands, so that they may decide whether they wish 'to take the road of pleasure, with baseness, scorn, and slavery for them and for their nations, or the road of virtue, with honour, glory, and happiness'.[2] But if the rest of Vico's theory of social and historical conditioning is to be believed, the die has already been cast and the optimistic option is no option at all. For, if the 'barbarism of reflection' can arise, as it would seem that it has, then already the form of the state is such that the mind does not command and the body is unruly and undisciplined, and in these circumstances only social collapse is possible. Hence, the reason for Vico's failure to publish the *Pratica* is almost certainly to be found in his realisation that its more optimistic prescriptions are incompatible with the basically deterministic character of the rest of the *Scienza Nuova*.

REASON AND IMAGINATION

The foregoing discussion points towards a pessimistic reading of Vico's thoughts about the future of the nations. It has, moreover, strengthened the suggestion that a basic reason for this pessimism is to be found in Vico's conviction that reason alone can never be strong enough to overcome the vicious tendencies within human nature. It remains, therefore, to consider why he should believe this and whether he was justified in so doing.

---

[1] *Ibid*.   [2] *S.N.* 1411.

There exists, in fact, one line of thought which runs through most of Vico's work which can fairly easily explain this distrust of reason and his consequent pessimism. This lies in the dichotomy between thought and the emotions and the way in which he construes it. Thought, he consistently maintains, can lead us towards the truth, but has only a limited capacity to affect behaviour. The emotions, on the other hand, are the ultimate determinants of behaviour, but the direction in which they lead us depends upon that by which they are themselves influenced. It is possible, he concedes, that in certain unusual cases, the mere knowledge of what is right will lead men to act in accordance with this knowledge, but in the majority of cases – for the masses – this is not a possibility. The masses have no such capacity to understand the truth and their passions are open to the influence of eloquence and rhetoric. Hence his early plea that the courtier or politician should possess philosophical wisdom and the orator should know how to direct the passions of the masses in directions the reasons for which the latter are not capable of grasping.[1] Thus the orator occupies a crucial position. For he alone can exercise an influence sufficient to draw the masses towards activities which will strengthen, rather than destroy, their civil environment.

These thoughts, which are expressed quite clearly in the early works, are never wholly abandoned. They are, however, modified in the later works. The reason for their modification is the fundamental importance which Vico comes to ascribe to religious belief, even when the religion in question is, by his own lights, false: religion alone can bring about the context in which men first engage in the struggle to master their most basic and destructive passions; again religion alone can support the pretensions upon which the whole structure of the heroic state depends; and, finally, religion alone can confine the wills of those monarchs who might try to stabilise states when they are in the final stages of disintegration: 'hence, when religion is lost among the peoples, they are left with nothing for their life in society: no

---

[1] *De Nostri Temporis Studiorum Ratione*, Part 7: 'Two things alone can convert to good use the perturbations of the soul, those inner evils of man which spring from appetite, as from a single source: philosophy, which regulates them in wise men, so that virtues may emerge; and eloquence, which fires them in the common people so that they perform the duties of virtue.' *Vico: Selected Writings*, pp. 44–5.

shield of defence, nor means of advice, no basis of support, no form of any existence in the world at all'.[1]

But religion, as Vico describes it, is the greatest of all rhetorical forces, beginning with the sublime religious ceremonies of poetic man and continuing with the positively physical presence of religion in the legal and political practices of heroic man. It is only in the third, rational age that it ceases to be a powerful force for directing the passions. For here reason acts in a double capacity. On the one hand, it continues the work of the unmasking of the religious illusions, upon which past social structures have depended. On the other, it can lend support to true religious belief by philosophical and theological reasoning. But the fruits of this are available to comparatively few, i.e. to those skilled or capable of becoming skilled in highly abstract reasoning, and the general effect of this is certainly not sufficient for religion to retain the hold which it formerly had over the passions of the masses. In addition, as Vico constantly repeats, reasoning cannot of itself create arguments. It presupposes a body of argument derived from another source, the imagination, which is itself the font of the earlier false religions. Reason can, perhaps, support a religion by showing that it is free from rational defects to be found in others – Vico himself occasionally pauses to point out ways in which, in his view, Christianity can be shown to be rationally more acceptable than, say, Mohammedanism – but it cannot, of itself, either invent a religion or invent features which are alternatives to those which, by criticism, it can destroy. Thus if rationality is the primary influence upon conduct in a given age, as it is in the third age, it will work towards the destruction of religious belief, without being able to offer any positive alternative, by which human passions can be directed in socially progressive ways.

It is clear, however, that behind this line of thought there lies a further assumption: that the imagination, which is both the original source of religion and of its later forms in history, is either absent in the fully rational age or is so etiolated as to be incapable of creating the world of belief to be found in the early history of the nation. This is certainly Vico's view. For a primary assumption, throughout the whole of his writings, is that the imagination grows weaker as reason

[1] *S.N.* 1109.

grows stronger.[1] The reason which he gives for this belief is that the imagination is stronger, in the sense of being able to affect people's behaviour, when its imagery is more corporeal and vivid. This capacity for corporeal and highly affective imagery is progressively lost, however, more or less in proportion to the degree to which people come to be capable of the abstract and refined thought which is required for reason. This is presented as an almost polar contrast, the powers of the imagination declining as those of reason strengthen. As a result, the religious beliefs, which imagination alone can produce, and which are necessary to the maintenance of society, also decline and cannot be replaced by anything which reason can produce.

A principal reason for Vico's final pessimism lies, therefore, in an assumption made much earlier in his thought: that there is an antinomy between reason and the imagination. It is this which, allied to his basically pessimistic view of man's individual nature, leads to the conclusion that, as man becomes more rational, he loses the capacity to accept the false beliefs which have prevented his individual vice from producing social destruction, without, in the process, acquiring a capacity to put anything socially supportive in their place.

Given these assumptions, it seems clear that Vico was justified in arriving at pessimistic conclusions about the future, however hard he may have tried to avoid them. It is not so clear, however, that the assumptions are themselves justified. It would be too large an undertaking, and one which is not strictly necessary in offering an interpretation of Vico's thought, to begin upon an exhaustive examination of them at this point. But since they are basic to some important claims in his Science, I shall conclude with some brief critical comments on each.

THE THEOLOGICAL PREMISE

First, with regard to Vico's biblical view of man as fallen and weak and, ultimately, incapable of accepting the responsibility for his own social well-being, it is worth noting that this is not fully supported by the account which he offers of man's historical development. There is no doubt, of course, that he makes this claim about human nature,

---

[1] *S.N.* 185, 218–19.

but whether he adheres to it in quite the simple manner in which it is enunciated is another matter. For, if the interpretation advanced in chapters 3 and 4 above and developed further in this chapter is at all acceptable, the individual man whom Vico posits at the start of a nation's history, is increasingly socialised. He requires a sense of self-interest, if there is to be any historical development at all, for such a sense is necessary as the *occasion* of social and cultural change. But as this sense is increasingly socialised and the conception of self-interest extends to an identity of interest between the individual and the family, or the nation or, possibly, the whole of mankind, it becomes increasingly difficult to see how it is to be distinguished from the common sense which, in the earlier stages, operates in opposition to it and directs legal, constitutional and social change in rationally progressive ways. For, when we arrive at the stage where man's self-interest involves his identification with the interest of mankind in general, the possibility of that form of conflict which is required as the *condition* of change would appear not to exist. The fundamental point here is that the ontological space required for individual self-regard of the sort which could disrupt the deliverances of common sense would seem to have been removed by the identification of that regard with the interests of mankind as such. This might well have the result that, as suggested earlier, there would be no more social development in history, but it would certainly not entail that society should therefore disintegrate. In fact, one would expect that it would have precisely the opposite effect and leave us with some sort of social utopia.

If, therefore, the notion of an *expansion* of the concept of the self has ontological validity – if, that is to say, it characterises a necessary feature of human nature – at a certain point one's self-interest should become wholly identical with one's social interest, as subsumed under common sense. In these circumstances it would no longer make sense to set the one off against the other by assuming the continued existence of the initial contrast and opposition between them. This does not mean that one would not have particular self-interests, which pertained to one as the specific individual one was and which might well not be shared with any other specific individual. It would mean, however, that these were ontologically secondary to those which were socialised and, by virtue of which, one was a constitutive part of

216

society. The assumption must therefore be that, at least in the vast majority of cases, should a conflict arise within one between one's self-interests as a specific individual and as a socially conditioned individual, the former must give way to the latter. For unless this were so, the relationship between the two kinds of interest would remain purely contingent. In this case, however, any changes in their relationship would also be purely contingent. But this would be incompatible with the thesis that there is a necessary pattern in the development of the nation and would be destructive of Vico's claim that what he is offering is an account of the nature of nations.

The fact that Vico holds on to the distinction, when generating his final pessimistic view, must therefore be looked upon as a failure to work out the full implications of his theory of social and historical development. The explanation for this is most probably that he failed to realise that the account which he had offered of the progressive socialisation of human nature must lead to the conclusion that the biblical view of fallen man, with which he had started, should be regarded as, at best, appropriate only to some specific stage of the development of human nature, but not as ontologically ultimate, in the sense of being a necessary and ever-present basis for the development of social well-being. A recognition of this factor alone would have gone a long way towards undercutting the grounds for his final pessimism. It would be possible, of course, to argue that he realised the ontological consequences of his theory but that he chose not to emphasise them solely for reasons of prudence. Such a view would, however, require that one treat his pessimism, and his abandoned attempts to avoid it, as much less sincere than seems plausible.

CONCLUSION

Finally, with regard to his conception of the incompatibility between reason and the imagination, it remains to be noted that, here also, Vico neither needed, nor indeed managed, to remain faithful to it. Again, it is not necessary, in considering this point, to deny his many expressions of belief in the incompatibility. As we have seen, his problems about whether or not there would be a recurrence hinge partially upon it. But despite the stark terms which he uses when offering explicit statements of it, he never makes clear the status of the contrast which he has in mind.

In most cases of its use, however, it is impossible that he could be thinking of it as a logical or strict antinomy. His claim would seem to be not that it is logically impossible for somebody to have both a powerful imagination and also acute critical capacities, but simply that there is a tendency in human nature for the one to weaken as the other strengthens. It is, for example, one of his frequent complaints that, as a result of educational trends in his own times, the capacity of children to develop their powers of imagination at an age when it is best possible for them to do so is being sacrificed on behalf of too early an inculcation of reason. But this is not accompanied by the suggestion that at no stage of their careers should they be taught to reason. All that he maintains is that the latter should come after the former, thus implying that they can co-exist as capacities of the one person. Unless, in fact, he were prepared to allow that the two *can* work alongside and in collaboration with each other, it is wholly unclear what he could say either about the status of his own Science or about his own capacity to construct it. If the opposition were understood in the sense of a strict antinomy, his capacity to construct his Science would render him incapable of criticising it, or his capacity to criticise it would render him incapable of constructing it. The same would hold true, moreover, of every work of literature or thought at any time in human history. These results are obviously unacceptable, however, since, to take only his own example, Vico not only knows that the *Scienza Nuova* is a construction, since it is a *new* science, but also that it satisfies the demands of reason, since it has been subject to critical evaluation.

The opposition between reason and the imagination must therefore be understood as a relative but not exclusive psychological feature or, as in the case of Vico's account of the careers of nations, psycho-historical feature. In this case, there is no good reason why it should be impossible in the rational age for religion to be adapted in such a way as to provide those particular supports for society which, given the influence of his biblical conception of man, Vico would believe to be necessary. Even were it the case that, as a result of the development of reason, man came to believe that all religion was false and that no religious conceptions ought to be accepted, this would not preclude the possibility that his powers of imagination, though they would be less corporeal than those of other ages, could produce other kinds of belief which reason could examine and some of which could be accepted in the light of their capacity to support the well-being of society. Vico was plainly correct in holding that the creation of belief comes before the assessment of its truth or of its social value, but he was wrong if he thought that, because one is a pre-condition of the other, they could not operate jointly for the benefit of society. The important point here is that, even if the creation of belief is ascribed to the imagination, it does not follow that a belief which is imaginary in this sense is false in the sense in which we often indicate that a belief is false by asserting that it is imaginary. In the way in which Vico is using the term, an imaginary belief may be either true or false. Thus, we can accept his account of the corporeal nature of the imagination at certain points in the history of a nation, and of that particular kind of imagination becoming less powerful in us as we develop rationally, without being driven to deny that the imagination, in a less corporeal or imagistic mode, can be present in the fully rational age and that it can there, and in that new mode, fulfil some of the functions which, in a different psycho-historical age, were fulfilled by a different mode of the imagination.

If this is so, it would follow that a further reason for Vico's final pessimism would be not that his theory had shown that the imagination must decline beyond the point at which it can serve any socially or, indeed, epistemologically, useful function, but that at this point in his theorising he conflated the notion of a logically antinomial contrast between them with that of a psycho-historical tendency. This conflation, had he made it consistently, would, in fact, have completely destroyed many of the principal features of his Science. Once made, however, it would seem impossible to him, if he were right about the genesis and career of religion, that the latter could retain its hold over people's minds. On the other hand, for the reasons given above, he was reluctant to abandon the claim that, unless religion could retain that hold, society would survive. Given the combination of the two mistakes, his pessimism is both understandable and inescapable.

These considerations suggest the following conclusions. First, Vico did not see clearly enough that the element of social and historical conditioning in his over-all theoretical framework precluded the sort of remedies to avert a final catastrophe for which he appeared to be seeking but which he was unable to find. His theory is not completely deterministic, in the sense that what will happen will do so in complete independence of human will. But it is deterministic in the sense that what is possible depends upon certain social and historical conditions and that what happens will be a result of what common sense sees as rational in the light of this situation. Hence his search for remedies the grounds for which do not lie in the existent socio-historical situation could not fail to be unsuccessful.

Secondly, he was incorrect in believing that the 'ideal eternal history' need contain such a state as the 'barbarism of reflection' and that, accordingly, there would be a need for the 'unnatural' remedies for which he sought. The belief that such a state as the 'barbarism of reflection' must arise, to be followed by the death and recurrence of the nation as a social and cultural entity, is not necessitated by his general theory of social and historical conditioning. On the contrary, its roots lie in two different assumptions, both of which are mischaracterised when he comes to consider their function in the third, fully human age. The first is his theological view of man as 'weak and fallen'. This is adequate as a description of the individual in the poetic age. It becomes increasingly inadequate, however, as the sense of self which it involves, becomes increasingly socialised until, in the third age, one's self-interest is identical with the common sense of mankind. If any of the original sense of self-interest were left by then, Vico would have required two histories of the self and its interests, in one of which it remained in its original primaeval state throughout and in the other of which it was gradually transmuted into a socialised self, whose interests were identical with the common sense of mankind. But he did not produce two such histories. In these circumstances, it makes no sense to suggest that the original brutish self can suddenly resurrect itself as though mankind had had no historical development, and act, to all intents and purposes, as though we were already back in the conditions of the first primitive barbarism. For this is to give the 'fallen and weak' self an ontological status which is inconsistent with Vico's whole account of its historical and social development. By the third age there should be no 'fallen and weak' man who requires to be saved by 'remedies', the action of which is quite impossible within the framework of Vico's general theory.

The second assumption, the contrast between reason and the imagination, involves a similar mistake. As required and developed in Vico's account of the changing structure of the social and historical life of a nation, this distinction must be a relative one, indicating a non-exclusive tendency within human nature and allowing for reason and the imagination to co-exist and complement each other in different ways at different phases in the 'ideal eternal history'. At no point could they perform their different tasks in Vico's account of history if it were thought that, as differently characterised in the different ages, they were not equally necessary if there were to be any sort of social and cultural development. Yet this is precisely what is denied when, in the age of reason, the contrast is treated as though it were both logically antinomial and ontologically necessary and, hence, a determining feature of *all possible* phases of human existence. For this would entail that mankind could never be both imaginative and reasonable at once. But not only is this a mistake, it is incompatible with the complementary roles which Vico assigns to them as two of the most important structural elements in his Science. If the mistake is rectified, however, and the perfection of reason is seen not as entailing the destruction of the imagination, but simply as requiring that it adapt new, less corporeal forms, there would be no reason why higher forms of social and cultural life should not develop, as a result of the development of the basic tendency towards rational self-understanding upon which the *Scienza Nuova* ultimately rests.

Vico's reasons for making the 'barbarism of reflection' a feature of the 'ideal eternal history', which then forced him into an unsuccessful search for remedies to prevent the final dissolution of society, rest therefore upon mistaken implications drawn from various features of his Science. This is not to say that his acceptance of these consequences may not have been influenced by some of the contingent factors mentioned earlier. Such possibilities cannot be ruled out, although they can, at best, only offer external reasons why Vico may have been inclined to accept some of the mistaken lines of argument. It is much more important, however, to note that the implications *are* mistaken and that they can be corrected – indeed, *must* be corrected, if the rest of Vico's account is to remain internally coherent – without harm to the rest of his Science. One can, therefore, accept the rest of his Science, without being committed to either the 'barbarism of reflection' or the theory of the recourse of the nations.

18

Appendix: humanist interpretations

The general position for which I have argued in this book is that Vico's *Scienza Nuova* was intended both to provide the philosophical foundations of a science of human history and at least a partial exemplification of what such a science would look like. I have not denied – indeed, I have emphasised – that, because of the centrality within it of a commitment to certain humanist insights, it may well be a rather unusual science. For no such commitment would be permissible in most modern conceptions of science. But if this concession were treated as implying a criticism, it would have little force. For, despite his prior commitment to these insights, Vico would still appear to be trying to introduce into historical research principles of economy and consistency, which have been the hall-marks of almost anything which, historically, has been thought to be a science.

In the previous chapter I have argued, in addition, that his Science recognises the indispensable role which the processes of argument and persuasion play in social and historical affairs. My aim there was to show that there is no incoherence in his claim that he can demonstrate the necessity which he ascribes to certain features of the process of historical development and allow for the importance of such apparently contingent factors as the effects of rhetoric and topics in human affairs. A number of commentators have, nevertheless, denied that this is how to understand his work, on the grounds that it still assimilates it to a conception of science which is too close to Descartes', to which, in his earlier work, he had become increasingly opposed, and fails to allow for the full extent of the humanist influence by which, in his capacity as Professor of Rhetoric, he was affected. This criticism can take two forms, resulting either in a difference over what

222

sort of a science Vico intended to produce or a denial that it was any sort of a science at all. It is not my intention in this concluding chapter to rehearse the reasons which I have given earlier for thinking that a proper understanding of the *Scienza Nuova* requires recognition of its scientific character. What I shall do, instead, is examine three relatively recent over-all interpretations of the character of Vico's thought, each of which, in some or other way, denies that it is a science of the sort for which I have argued, to see what sorts of difficulties arise if that character is not acknowledged.

The three principal comprehensive interpretations which I shall discuss have, in their different ways, almost exclusively stressed Vico's place in, or at least his indebtedness to, the juridical and rhetorical traditions of which he knew so much. This is not the correct place to give an account of the whole of any of these interpretations, which contain much valuable material which is not germane to the present issue. My remarks will have the limited aim, therefore, of showing why, in my view, we cannot make sense of Vico, at such comprehensive levels, if we take him either as doing nothing more than restating certain elements in these traditions or as simply developing insights in them in a new way. What I shall do, in other words, is explain why I believe that, after due allowance has been made for the influence of these traditions upon him, we cannot understand his enterprise as a whole, if we do not give serious weight to his wish to establish a science.

The first of these interpretations to appear was Sir Isaiah Berlin's *Vico and Herder*.[1] Although it was published after this book, one of its principal theses – that Vico's theory of knowledge is based upon the primacy of *verstehen*, i.e. of our imaginative capacity to enter into the thoughts of others and, hence, with appropriate methodological safeguards, into that of agents in the past – had been developed in earlier essays and is discussed in the main text above. In *Vico and Herder*, however, Berlin allied this thesis to a number of others, some of which appear not dissimilar to those in the present account. Thus, for example, he stresses the fact that, for Vico, human nature can express itself only in a social context, with its own internal standards and norms of thought and behaviour, which are intelligible only in

---

[1] *Vico and Herder: Two Studies In The History Of Ideas,* The Hogarth Press, London 1976.

relation to it as a whole. Similarly he stresses the importance for Vico of the 'ideal eternal history', i.e. of the idea that human nature is not static but changes as it expresses itself in 'a pattern of development which human society, wherever it is found, must obey'.[1] A central claim here is that, influenced by the development in the French and Italian juridical traditions of the concept of law as a self-creating and self-transcending body of knowledge, Vico extended the Renaissance concept of the individual man as self-creator to that of man as the creator of his collective social and cultural experience in a series of self-transcending decisions.[2]

Despite these similarities, however, there are also some fundamental differences of view. These can best be located by attending, on the one hand, to the status of the phases involved in the 'ideal eternal history' and, on the other, to Berlin's account of how we are to come to know of these phases, if they involve a social context which is structured by standards and norms which are internal to the historical society in question.

With regard to the first point, Berlin's view would seem to involve Vico in an inconsistency. For while he accepts that the 'ideal eternal history' is a statement of a pattern of development which follows from the existence of *laws* which govern the history of every nation in its rise, development, maturity, decline and fall,[3] he denies that this commits Vico to a mechanistic or deterministic conception of the process through which this occurs, preferring to describe it as an organic process. His grounds for this denial rest upon an alternative thesis which he ascribes to Vico: that human nature is plastic and that men have the capacity to transform themselves by their own creative efforts.[4] But these claims are incompatible. If, as seems unarguable, Vico is committed to the existence of a series of laws, which are responsible for an unalterable pattern to be found in the histories of all nations, including, of course, features of the human nature expressed in the different phases of that pattern, what may seem like men transforming themselves by their own creative efforts can only be the operation of the laws in question *through* the activities of men. If this is so, Vico cannot fail to be committed to a deterministic,

---

[1] *Ibid.* p. 64.   [2] *Ibid.* p. 25.
[3] *Ibid.* p. 81.   [4] *Ibid.* pp. 39, 136.

although not necessarily a mechanistic, account of the careers of nations.

In trying to avoid this conclusion, the point has often been made – and is made, indeed, by Berlin himself – that providence, which, if not identified with these laws, is very intimately related to them, operates with the *co-operation* of man, so that it provides a context within which his activities can take on their self-transforming character. But this response is insufficient. For it ignores the fact that it is only *within* the world of human activities and institutions that the laws can operate. They must, therefore, operate *through* the activities of man, with the result that, at a certain level, those activities will necessarily have whatever character they have as a result of being the vehicle for the operation of the laws. They will thus, *at that level*, themselves be determined. There is only one way in which an appeal to the unarguable importance of the activities of man could be used to support the conclusion that Vico does not believe that the historical process is determined. This would require that the relevant activities be construed as not being conditioned by the operation of the laws. For this to be possible, however, they would need to have characteristics which were independent of their place in the socio-historical context in which they occur. It is not, in fact, the case that Vico denies that there are such characteristics, for he insists that individual humans have free will. But these are not the relevant characteristics. The human activities with which he concerns himself when talking of the direction of historical change always turn out to be activities based upon shared beliefs, desires and ideals. The reason why they are shared is that they are manifestations of the operation of those very laws from the influence of which this defence would require them to be immune.

Apart from introducing a gratuitous inconsistency into Vico's thought, this attempt to save him from the charge of wishing to establish a science, with the character of necessity, makes it very difficult to make much sense of many of his more general methodological and theoretical claims. A particular problem which arises is how to understand the whole section on method, which is usually ignored by those who wish to deny, or at least to modify, the claim that Vico is providing the philosophical basis for an historical science of man, if the latter is understood to have deterministic connotations incompatible with his humanistic orientation. Since this section is discussed in chapter 14 above, however, I shall not pursue the point here.

The second general difficulty which arises from Berlin's way of construing Vico's debt to his juridical predecessors concerns the question of the method whereby we can come to know the beliefs of former ages, which are necessarily different from ours, and, through that, advance to a reconstruction of the whole social and cultural pattern of which we are a part. The great jurists of the Renaissance understood the importance of the fact that human products – in their case, human laws – are produced at specific times and places and for specific purposes or to meet specific needs. Thus they were themselves able to expose earlier false beliefs about the nature of Justinian's code and to restore a more historically accurate understanding of its variously derived parts, just as the humanist philologists were able to restore a correct understanding of many other political and cultural documents which had come to light with the awakening of interest in the classical world. As Berlin notes, the extent of Vico's debt to various different scholars is difficult to establish, although it is impossible to doubt that there was a significant general influence. Nevertheless, despite their actual achievements, the humanists certainly did not think of themselves as producing anything as systematic as a natural science. They concentrated upon the placing of documents in concrete historical contexts and trying to establish their purpose and meaning within those contexts.

In this respect, on Berlin's account, Vico both assimilated what the humanists had achieved but went beyond it. He assimilated it by acknowledging the role of inductive and deductive techniques in scholarly research, above all in the process of sifting historical fact from fiction. But he went beyond it in his emphasis upon the necessity to use our imaginative understanding, *fantasia*, in the attempt to grasp the world of intentional, intelligible purposes which are the causes of actions and to place this world in the dynamic historical process of which it is a part.[1] Berlin agrees that there is a tension here between two theses: that because, in the course of their history, men create their cultural world, they can, by the use of the creative or reconstructive imagination, re-enter that world; and that the 'ideal eternal

[1] *Ibid.* pp. 107, 114.

history' is the product of the laws which providence provides, which then becomes not just a matter of human making.[1] But he is clear that, despite this, the reconstructive imagination, the use of which is essential for the selection, classification and interpretation of material, is ultimately a subjective capacity, dependent upon our own experience and what we can learn from our investigation of the modifications of our own minds.[2] This may include insight into an intelligible structure to be found within our own lives, upon which Vico models the main phases of the lives of nations as explicated in the 'ideal eternal history'.[3]

Since the suggestion that Vico may be relying upon a conviction about the nature of an intelligible developmental human pattern as one of the philosophical bases of his science is one which I share, albeit with a difference of emphasis, I shall not comment further upon it here. Much more contentious is the emphasis which, in stressing Vico's humanist connections, Berlin comes to lay upon the centrality of the reconstructive imagination, which gives rise to a number of difficulties.

The first, as noted by Berlin himself, concerns how, on this view, Vico can lay any claim whatsoever to knowledge of the phases of the 'ideal eternal history' which is not itself of human making. It is not merely the case, however, that Vico claims such knowledge. He both does so frequently, referring to it as one of the principal aspects of the *Scienza Nuova*, and associates it firmly with the concept of the operation in history of laws which transcend the things which men propose to themselves and what they do in pursuit of those purposes. It could be, of course, that he had simply overlooked the fact that the 'ideal eternal history' is not a human production and, therefore, that his theory of knowledge, as construed in Berlin's account, actually denies him knowledge of it. But if he were guilty of so gross an error on such a fundamental point, we should have to conclude that the *Scienza Nuova* was epistemologically flawed and that there was little point in looking for some reasonable degree of coherence in this aspect of it. It might enable us to know what people in the past were thinking about and what they thought was occurring but it could not tell us, nor explain, what was really occurring, if, as Vico claims, the latter went beyond the views of past agents.

[1] *Ibid*. p. 113.   [2] *Ibid*. p. 107.   [3] *Ibid*. pp. 33–4.

It is not necessary to go to any such lengths, however, if the thesis of the reconstructive imagination is given up. This does not mean that Berlin is wrong in insisting upon the fact that we must use our imagination in pursuing historical research and in understanding historical cultures. But it is to suggest that he is wrong in thinking that Vico's distinction between knowledge of the natural world, which we cannot reach because we have not made that world, and knowledge of the world of history, which is accessible because we have made it, rests upon the employment of the imagination in one case but not the other. For all knowledge requires the use of the imagination, at least in the sense that it requires the creation and application of methods, hypotheses and theories. This is as true of natural knowledge as of human knowledge and there is nothing in Vico's statements about science, especially empirically based science as he approves of it in his earlier works, to suggest that he was not fully aware of this fact. Berlin is, of course, correct in emphasising that Vico claims a superiority in the intelligibility of the human world as against the natural world. The present point is only that it does not depend upon the use or lack of use of the *reconstructive* imagination. I shall not, however elaborate my own suggestion for the solution to this problem, which is given in the main text above.

It is important to notice, however, that the text of the *Scienza Nuova* does not lend much support to Berlin's stronger thesis. It is clear enough that Vico believed that it would be historically valuable to be able to enter the minds of former ages. But when, for example, we come to the barbaric mind of primitive man, with which he was so concerned, it is the impossibility of so doing to which he often draws attention. It is in this connection, indeed, that he draws a distinction between the incapacity of the imagination to enter those minds and the possibility of an *understanding* of their thought which, albeit with the greatest difficulty, he claims to have reached.[1] If he is willing to accept the impossibility of entering the imagination of men in an age so important to the whole of his research, it is difficult to believe that the necessity of so doing is as fundamental to his account as Berlin suggests.

[1] For a more extended discussion of this issue, see my 'Imagination in Vico', in *Vico: Past and Present,* edited by Giorgio Tagliacozzo, Humanities Press, Atlantic Highlands, N.J., 1981, vol. I, pp. 162–70.

Berlin's thesis gives rise to further problems, which turn upon differences in the structure of the concepts of imagination and knowledge. Since these are, however, raised, if anything in a more acute form, by the next work to be considered, I shall discuss them in that context.

The influence of the rhetorical, rather than the more exclusively juridical, tradition upon Vico has been given great emphasis in the work of Professor Donald Phillip Verene, both in a series of articles published in the last ten years and in his major work *Vico's Science of Imagination*.[1] Although the latter is not intended primarily as a contribution towards strictly historical research upon Vico, it does in fact place him very firmly in the rhetorical tradition and interprets his work almost solely from this perspective.

As the title of the book suggests, Verene's aim is to investigate the place and importance of the theory of the imagination in Vico's work and, indeed, to defend the results which are produced, not merely as representing a correct interpretation of Vico but as being true in themselves. One of his declared intentions, in fact, is to show how a correct appreciation of this aspect of Vico's work can alert us to certain dangers present in the modern world, which he identifies as a rebirth of the arid and anti-humanist spirit of Cartesianism in the form of an over-estimation of the importance of the continuous development of modern technology. Although I do not propose to discuss the latter thesis here, it is worthy of mention in so far as the danger which Verene identifies is that of an over-intellectual approach to life, in which it is assumed that all that matters in it is what can be brought under general concepts and categories, and that all the rest of our experience is peripheral and unimportant. This approach is thus seen as hostile to art, care for the individual, and to the many other matters with which humanism has traditionally been concerned. As a consequence, the Vico for whom Verene argues is one who is also hostile to categories and to conceptual thinking in general and who wishes to show, in contradistinction to the over-riding importance which many philosophers have attached to the notion of rationality, that the primary human capacity is the imagination. This, it is claimed, is fundamental in two ways. On the one hand, it is the source both of meaning itself and of its historical development; on the other, it is

[1] *Vico's Science of Imagination*, Cornell University Press, Ithaca 1981.

the source of our capacity to recapture and relive that development and thus to regain a sense of our real natures. It is primary, therefore, both in an ontological and in an epistemological sense. As a result, Vico is presented as a thinker for whom there is a polar contrast – indeed, an incompatibility – between reason and imagination, and for whom most of what is normally attributed to reason, and certainly all that is essential to our capacity to live together in society and to our understanding of that capacity, is properly the work of the imagination.

Verene's book is a major contribution to Vico studies, particularly in its detailed exposition of different aspects of the imagination and of such difficult Vichian concepts as the imaginative or fantastic universal. Verene himself sees it as closer to the approach to be found in Berlin's work than that in the present study.[1] Although this is clearly true, his account is nevertheless in many ways very different from Berlin's. For, although Berlin also lays great emphasis upon the role of the imagination, both in the early phases of the 'ideal eternal history' and as at least a necessary condition of historical knowledge, he recognises that Vico seems to think that he has access to the laws which govern history, which he more or less identifies with the activity of providence. Verene, on the contrary, makes little or no mention of these laws and gives an entirely different account of providence.

It is not possible here to give a detailed account of the whole of Verene's book nor, indeed, would it be pertinent to do so, since much of it deals with matters which raise no difficulties of principle for the present approach. I shall confine my remarks, therefore, to those over-all points of interpretation which do produce such difficulties, i.e. Verene's claims for the centrality of imagination, memory and invention, both in the production of the substance of human experience and history and in the understanding of it.

There would be no difficulty with regard to the first of these claims, were it the case that Verene wished to argue solely for the primacy of imagination, memory and invention as the source of the social and cultural world in which early man lives. A recognition of the importance of the human imagination in the life of poetic man is common to most interpretations of the *Scienza Nuova*, including my own. Verene, in fact, carries the analysis of this period further than anyone

[1] *Ibid*. p. 10.

else, by offering an interesting account of how it is that the imagination can introduce fixed points of meaning in a world which would otherwise consist merely of a flux of sensations. Although I am not persuaded that Vico held such a theory, it would be compatible with his general view of this phase of human development and with the account which I give of it here. My main reservation would merely be that it takes him to be offering a more explicit theory on this metaphysical point than the text seems plausibly to support.

Difficulties in principle arise, however, when, having emphasised the importance of the imaginative faculties, and their role in the original production of common sense – the shared body of belief which is built into our culture and institutions and upon which we draw continuously in our everyday activities – Verene suggests that for Vico any form of conceptual thinking, or conceptually based criticism, is inevitably to be seen as a corrosive and malign force, tending only to the destruction of society. Although he does not use the expression, he seems to be ascribing to Vico a 'Manichaean' view of history, in which the benefits of the imagination are necessarily in contention with the evils of reason.

It is true, of course, that Vico constantly emphasises that the creation of belief is both logically and historically prior to its criticism and that an art of topics, which draws upon and systematises the contents of common sense in various areas of life, is therefore both logically and historically prior to an art of criticism. It is true, furthermore, that he locates the ultimate decline of each society into the 'barbarism of reflection', in the third, fully human, age, i.e. in the very age in which man is credited with the capacity to understand the nature of things and to employ such understanding in his daily life, in place of the less rational, more natural – but also more superstitious – beliefs which govern earlier periods. If the argument of the last chapter is correct, however, neither of these points can be used in support of the view that Vico believed that reason is, *in itself*, an innately corrosive or evil capacity. Were he to have believed that, he could hardly have maintained his general thesis that the quality of law and of civil life improves as a result of man's growing capacity to discern what is false in his general set of beliefs.

Apart from this, however, it must be noted that, while extolling the incomparable power of the poetic imagination, Vico is far from being an admirer of many of the institutions to which this gives birth. He shows no great regard, apart from recognising its propriety and necessity, for the first form of law, for example, in which men believe themselves and all their institutions to depend upon the gods, because they hold that everything is a god or an act of god, and he shows a distinct preference for the human law of the third age, dictated by fully developed human reason.[1] Similarly, much though he admires some of the characteristics of 'heroic man' who, as a natural development of those earlier false beliefs, is believed to be noble in virtue of descending from unions of gods and men, it is nevertheless through the exposure of the *falsity* of the belief in their allegedly divine descent that he explains how the heroes come to lose their privileged place in society and, indeed, how the form of society which can offer them such a place is superseded. There is not, in fact, to be found in Vico any such one-sided attitude towards the respective merits of imagination and reason as Verene suggests. Vico's many admiring comments about the virtues of the third, fully rational kind of human nature leave little doubt that he thinks of the sequence unfolded in the 'ideal eternal history' as largely progressive, even though, as suggested above, he does not think of it as a simple and continuous progression towards better states of affairs and is well aware of the many valuable capacities and characteristics of human nature which are lost along the way.

The first of Verene's theses, therefore, which is incompatible with the argument of the present study, is that a large part of the substance of human history depends solely upon the *imaginative* creation and continuous transformation of the world of human meaning in which human activity takes place. It is necessary to note the qualification that it is only a large part of human history of which this is true, for Verene accepts that many human activities do not achieve their intended aims and recognises that there is in Vico a role to be played by providence. Nevertheless, disregarding the latter for the moment, it is evident that if, contrary to what I have argued, Vico does not think of reason as giving us access to truth, some other account must be given as to how he thinks that we do reach it.

It is at this point that Verene's other major thesis comes into play. There are, he claims, two senses of imagination to be found in Vico,

[1] *S.N.* 324–7, 918.

although they are not both explicitly distinguished by him.[1] The first is the original and ever-present imaginative capacity to *create* meaning, which is discussed above. The second is the power to *rediscover* meaning in virtue of the *recollective* imagination, through which we can recreate and understand from the inside the imaginative origins of humanity and, similarly, the other developments traced in the *Scienza Nuova*. On this view, Vico is urging us to revive this basic capacity, in the third age, in the interests of epistemology, in order to gain an internal understanding of our own imaginative origins and development. This would be denied us if we adopted an approach based upon concepts which, at best, would merely allow us to formulate truths about it. The recollective imagination, it is suggested, enables us to recreate the original imaginative world because it contains within itself, in a one-to-one correspondence, the principal features of the original power of imagination, of which the most crucial is, perhaps, the ability to create images. On this account, the 'ideal eternal history' itself becomes a master image, in which we see ourselves in the third age as the end of a process which, both as a whole and in all of its parts, moves from a beginning, through a middle to an end.[2] Nevertheless, although the 'ideal eternal history' is a master image, within the confines of which all historical understanding must take place, it is not itself limited to the products of the original imagination. For, as Vico endlessly insists, the human will is constantly being thwarted. One of the primary functions of the 'ideal eternal history' is, therefore, to enable us to see how, in virtue of this very fact, there is a providential force at work in history, revealing itself in the way in which men's intended actions always issue an unintended but beneficial results.

This account of the recollective imagination and of the 'ideal eternal history' is plainly incompatible with the view for which I have argued earlier. The incompatibility does not hinge upon the weight which it lays upon the use of the imagination, for, as mentioned above, Vico stresses the need to use the imagination to create beliefs before using the art of criticism to pronounce judgement upon them. It lies rather in the function which is to be ascribed to the imagination. For, if Vico really believes that the world of meaning is wholly a product of

---

[1] *Vico's Science of Imagination*, p. 99.   [2] *Ibid*. pp. 108–10.

233

the imagination and that the only way in which we can come to understand it is by its internal recreation, there would be no way in which he would be entitled to describe, as he so often does, some of its contents as wholly false. To judge something to be false becomes an idle claim if one is not in a position to appeal to notions of truth, falsity and warrant and to substantiate one's use of these in cases of dispute. If, however, as Verene maintains, the world in which Vico's historian lives is itself simply a product of the imagination and, hence, not founded upon, for example, a commitment to such fundamentally rational notions as that incompatible propositions cannot all be true, it is impossible to see how Vico's remarks about the falsity of primitive belief and the truth of present belief can be taken seriously or, indeed, how he could think that he was entitled to make them.

The basic point here is that the logic of the concepts of imagination and knowledge is entirely different. It is internal to the concept of knowledge that, when claims to knowledge are made, it is always in order to ask how the claim has been arrived at and what reasons there are for accepting it. This is not so, however, with regard to the concept of imagination. When something is said to be a product of the imagination such questions are inappropriate and, if asked, would simply betray a misunderstanding of the nature of the assertion. We admire an artist or a novelist, for example, for the imaginative qualities by which he can give us new insights into human and social affairs, just as we admire a scientist for the imaginative qualities involved in producing new and bold hypotheses. But we accept neither the insights nor the hypotheses as true merely on the strength of the fact that they are new or bold. Their application to a further range of experience is still in order and it is only when we have assured ourselves that this supplies sufficient warrant for them that we can accept them as true.

It should be added that Verene himself accepts that, on his interpretation, Vico's science offers no guarantee against the discovery of *false* origins. Indeed, he asserts that there is no answer to the question of a proof of the *Scienza Nuova* apart from the work itself and the imaginative experience we can gain through it.[1] But this is implausible, at least as an explication of Vico's intentions. When we turn to the

---

[1] *Ibid*. pp. 156–7.

text of his work, the language which he employs and the requirements which he claims to have met are wholly those appropriate to knowledge and not to the immediate internal creation and grasp of an image. He makes frequent use, for example, of the concepts of inconsistency and absurdity and of falsity and truth when discussing and criticising the fruits of the work of other historians, philologists and natural law theorists. Some of the less plausible of these are, in fact, described as the results of *confused* imaginations. The burden of his charge is often that they do not make historical sense or that they are anachronistic, but his method of supporting his claim is usually by showing that they cannot be made part of a coherent or internally consistent interpretation of the beliefs of some society or, again, as in the case of the social contract theorists, that they involve the philosophical *mistake* of believing that societies can rest upon contracts whereas, he claims, contracts require societies. The weight which he lays upon the role of argument and evidence and the importance which he attaches to consistency and coherence in supporting claims to knowledge provides strong reason for rejecting Verene's account of the role of the imagination in knowledge.

A further difficulty which arises concerns Verene's explanation of Vico's notion of providence. If this is correct, Vico would be guilty of claiming a knowledge to which he was not entitled. On Verene's view, the 'ideal eternal history' is a master image, in which there are two components: the actions of men under their imaginative beliefs, and the activity of providence, evincing itself in the beneficial character of the unintended consequences of these actions. If the account of the recollective imagination were acceptable, we would understand the first of these by recreating their imaginative content. We could not, however, in the same way, come to an understanding of the second. The aim of providence, as Vico often asserts, is not an aim shared by primitive man. Nor, however, could it be an aim which could be grasped by any of his more sophisticated successors, if all that they possessed was the power of recollective imagination. For all that the latter can do is to recollect that which the original imagination created, in virtue of the one-to-one correspondence between the features of the two kinds of imagination. Since providence's end is not something created by the original imagination, however, it cannot be recreated or recaptured by the recollective imagination. It is not an aim, therefore, which can be portrayed and grasped in the 'ideal eternal history' as a master image. It would therefore be impossible for Vico to have that knowledge of it which he constantly asserts.

Despite the generally accepted obscurity of Vico's notion of providence, it must be emphasised that the particular character of the difficulty which Verene's account creates arises from the feature commented upon above, namely his insistence that it is the imagination, rather than reason or the understanding, which is fundamental to Vico's epistemology. Once the imagination has been substituted for the understanding, it becomes difficult to make sense of Vico's many claims to knowledge in the various areas of research which fall within the scope of his enterprise. The difficulty about his knowledge of providence is just one such example.

The third and final humanistic interpretation of Vico which I shall discuss is that which Dr B. A. Haddock has produced, in which it is suggested that Vico's primary aim, by the time of the *Scienza Nuova*, was to provide the criteria and canons of a theory of historical interpretation. Haddock has developed this thesis progressively in a series of articles, in a chapter of his book *An Introduction to Historical Thought*[1] and, finally, in his book *Vico's Political Thought*.[2]

Taking his cue initially from Berlin, Haddock is concerned to stress Vico's relation, on the one hand, to the Renaissance jurists and the methods developed in their discovery of the real nature of Justinian's code and, on the other, to the natural law theorists, to whose anachronistic accounts of the origins of society he is constantly opposed. Since Haddock lays great weight upon Vico's grasp of the difficulty posed by the problem of conceptual anachronism in any adequate approach to history, there is much in his account which is compatible with the conclusions of my own study, in which this problem is also seen as one which troubled Vico. There is, however, also considerable divergence between the two views, the most important of which lies in Haddock's contention that the *Scienza Nuova* does not contain, as is claimed in my own account, an explanatory theory about the necessary stages through which the historical development of a nation

---

[1] *An Introduction to Historical Thought*, Edward Arnold, London 1980.
[2] *Vico's Political Thought*, Mortlake Press, Swansea 1986.

must go, i.e. 'a hypothetical predictive theory about the conditions under which institutions will develop in certain ways'.[1] For Haddock, on the contrary, the more theoretical parts of the *Scienza Nuova* are largely concerned with providing a methodological canon for the interpretation of human history, based upon the insights that institutions are human artefacts created to satisfy human needs, that needs vary according to the nature of the people whose needs they are, and that ultimately, therefore, to understand a society through an interpretation of its artefacts, we must understand the minds of its people, which requires that we penetrate or 'enter into' them. Haddock accepts that this is not all that Vico needs and suggests that the three ages of gods, heroes and men, as explicated in the 'ideal eternal history', should be regarded as historical paradigms which determine the range of interpretations of what is conceptually possible. This would provide Vico with a way of guarding himself against the possibility of misinterpretations of the past of the positively global proportions of which he accuses his opponents. I shall return to this point shortly.

It will be seen that there is some agreement here with the accounts offered by Berlin and Verene, particularly in the stress given to the requirement that we be able to enter the minds of the people who create human institutions. Since I have already expressed my reservations both about the textual support for this claim and about its compatibility with Vico's view that his science must go beyond telling us of the way in which men have thought of themselves and give us knowledge of the patterns which emerge from the largely unintended consequences of their actions, I shall not pursue it further here.

The basic weakness in Haddock's account is that, in emphasising Vico's concern over interpretation, it fails to offer an adequate explanation of his further claim to have provided the truth about the human past. It does not matter here whether we believe that he achieved this or that he had good grounds for thinking that he had done so. It is important, however, that we can see how and why he might have thought that he had done so. Haddock's thesis, however, leaves this unresolved, for he does not believe that Vico's paradigms have or require any grounding. If this is so, however, they can, at most, be among a set of merely possible interpretative schema. The best that

---

[1] 'Vico's *Discovery of the True Homer*: A Case Study in Historical Reconstruction', *Journal of the History of Ideas*, 40, 1979, footnote 14.

Vico could do in this case, *vis-à-vis* his opponents, would be to show that his interpretations were more consistent than theirs, in so far as they were controlled by a self-consistent paradigm. He could not, however, as he claims, show that they were correct, nor, indeed, that they were in any way preferable to other equally consistent interpretations, if the latter in turn derived from other self-consistent paradigms.

This point is obscured because Haddock sets the problem up in such a way as to imply that Vico was concerned primarily with the fact that the anachronistic character of the accounts to which he objected derived from the unconscious character of the assumptions made by their authors.[1] It is true, of course, that Vico draws attention frequently to the fact that there is a natural tendency to make such assumptions unconsciously. But it does not follow, nor is there any evidence that Vico believed that it did, that the move from unconscious to conscious assumptions entails the adoption of cognitively superior paradigms. The connection between conscious and unconscious assumptions and well and badly grounded assumptions is only contingent. It may be a necessary condition of *satisfying* oneself of the superiority of some new paradigms that one can articulate them consciously, but this will not establish what it is about one paradigm which makes it superior to some other. There must be some further reason why the adopted paradigm is seen to be preferable to any rivals. But this is what Haddock's neglect of the possibility of enquiring into the grounding of the relevant paradigms rules out. In this case, however, the problem of global misinterpretation – the misinterpretation of the thought and artefacts of a whole historical society – will remain unresolved.

In *An Introduction to Historical Thought*, Haddock goes some way to resolving these difficulties. There he accepts that Vico holds that there is a *necessary* succession in the genesis of modes of consciousness, and suggests that the three ages of gods, heroes and men as specified in the 'ideal eternal history' be regarded as 'paradigms to define the parameters of meanings which can be attributed to the artefacts of a

---

[1] '[Vico's] contention was that without a self-conscious and articulated theory of interpretation, historians were liable (by default) to read into the pronouncements of other places and peoples the modes of thought, rules and conventions which gave these sorts of utterances meanings within their own world of ideas', *An Introduction to Historical Thought*, p. 66.

particular period'.[1] He remains reluctant, however, to accept that, in order to support this particular paradigm, Vico has invoked a prior claim about a determinate, necessary sequence which will be displayed in the histories of all nations, if their development is not obstructed by some external factor. The suggestion is, therefore, that Vico realised the need to make use of an interpretative paradigm and, indeed, of one involving the idea of a necessary sequence in the generation of modes of consciousness, but not that there should be any independent grounding for the necessary sequence involved. This remains, although Haddock does not put it thus, a matter of mere hypothesis. But if Vico is advocating a procedure in which we are free to adopt any paradigm whatsoever, provided only that it is internally consistent and has some hypothetical claims to necessity built into it, it is difficult to see how he can claim to have overcome the danger that his paradigms may themselves be faulty, if not false, instruments of historical interpretation. The fact that he is conscious of his employment of them and can test them for internal consistency will certainly not suffice to show that they are capable of generating true accounts of the past.

These difficulties arise, I believe, because like Berlin and Verene, Haddock has been so impressed by Vico's rejection of Cartesianism as to think that it carried with it a rejection of any notion of necessity in human history and, therefore, of the possibility of producing a science with some, at least, of the necessity involved in a natural science. The 'science' which Haddock ascribes to Vico is, therefore, one which is more closely connected to the methods of the jurists, in which a body of rules and knowledge is appealed to in order that, through the interpretation of human motives in known circumstances, facts can be established. He recognises, of course, that a more elaborate methodology is required if we are to advance from a science of this sort to one in which we can establish unknown kinds of motives and actions in unknown conceptual circumstances, hence the introduction of the notion of a necessary sequence in the development of the modes of human consciousness as an internal feature of the 'ideal eternal history' and of the latter as a substantial paradigm to delineate the range of interpretative possibilities. But this is insufficient. Unless we are provided with some grounds for the necessity claimed for the

---

[1] *Ibid.* p. 71.

structural connections within each of the three ages within the paradigm and for the over-all sequence which it contains, there will be nothing to force us to apply it in its parts or as a whole. We shall be free to accept such parts of it as we wish piecemeal, dependent upon external or incidental factors or to dispense with it altogether. In this case, however, it will not be able to serve the function of specifying a 'logical (and not merely empirical) limit to the conceptual range of any particular phase of development'.[1]

Thus, when it comes to the question why we should adopt one paradigm rather than some other, no satisfactory answer is forthcoming. Haddock appeals, it is true, to Vico's constant comparisons between phases of the 'ideal eternal history' and phases to be found in the sequence of the life of an ordinary individual from infancy to death. But unless, in addition, we believe that we have access to a theory to support the claim that one phase *must* lead to the next, either in the case of the individual or of the society, there is no reason why we should accept the sequence delineated in the 'ideal eternal history' as a correct guide to the interpretation of the history of any nation whatsoever in the past. If this is so, however, the suggestion that the *Scienza Nuova* be regarded as setting out the requirements of an interpretative theory without recourse to any explanatory theory[2] must be rejected.

This point can be supported in a different way. It was noted, in connection with Verene's interpretation, that he accepted that Vico did not believe that human history consisted solely in the thoughts, activities and institutions of men. There is, in addition, the influence of providence, detected primarily in the beneficial character of the unintended consequences of human action. Verene was unable to show, however, how our knowledge of this feature of history was possible since, on his account, the historian could know, by the use of the recollective imagination, only what men had created by use of the original imagination. In a similar way, however, Haddock also is unable to show how we can know it. If we accept that an empathetic identification with an agent's mode of thought and, through that, a knowledge of the correct way in which to interpret his institutions is

---

[1] *Ibid.* p. 70.
[2] 'Vico's *Discovery of the True Homer*: A Case Study in Historical Reconstruction', p. 600.

all that the *Scienza Nuova* purports to establish, a knowledge of these wider features of history is excluded. For this further knowledge requires cognitive access to the way in which providence is responsible for patterns of development which *transcend* the understanding and actions of those who are involved in them. But if this is not accepted as part of Vico's intention then, as argued above,[1] it will not be possible to make sense of his fundamental distinction between *scienza* and *coscienza*.

The major difference between the interpretation for which I have argued and those discussed above lies not so much in the question whether what Vico has produced is humanistic in character but more in the way in which human insight plays its part in his theory. On the view put forward in this monograph, there is a crucial reliance upon commitment to a determinate, necessary sequence which governs the course of development of human mentality and, through that, of human history. This cannot be reached by an empirical science but it provides constraints which any attempt to put history upon a scientific foundation must observe. On the three alternative interpretations discussed, his humanism enters in an entirely different way. For, despite the many differences between them, they agree in emphasising the importance of our capacity to enter imaginatively into the mind of past peoples as an indispensable aspect of the method to be employed in history. Ultimately, therefore, the difference is between the view that Vico takes historical knowledge to involve the capacity imaginatively to be as, or to identify with, minds in the past and the view that he requires us to be able, more theoretically, to construct true and defensible accounts of the past, including explanations of what caused people to be as they were.

---

[1] Pp. 160–1.

Bibliography

The number of works on various aspects of Vico's thought is now very large. The following bibliography is confined to a selection of the more important of those relevant to the themes dealt with in the present monograph.

A. EDITIONS, ENGLISH TRANSLATIONS AND BIBLIOGRAPHIES

G. B. Vico, edited by F. Nicolini in the *Scrittori d'Italia* series, Laterza, Bari 1911–41. This is the definitive edition of Vico's work. *La Scienza Nuova* was published in 1928 in this edition.

Giambattista Vico: Opere, edited by F. Nicolini, Riccardo Ricciardi, Naples 1953.

Giambattista Vico: La Scienza Nuova, edited with notes by P. Rossi. Rizzoli Editore, Milan 1963.

Giambattista Vico: Opere Filosofiche, edited by P. Cristofolini with an Introduction by N. Badaloni. Sansoni Editore, Florence 1971.

The New Science of Giambattista Vico. Revised translation of the third edition (1744) by T. G. Bergin and M. H. Fisch. Cornell University Press, Ithaca 1968. With new introduction by M. H. Fisch.

The Autobiography of Giambattista Vico. Translation by T. G. Bergin and M. H. Fisch. Great Seal Books (Cornell University Press), Ithaca 1963. With an Introduction by M. H. Fisch.

On The Study Methods Of Our Time. Translation with Introduction and Bibliography by E. Gianturco of Vico's *De Nostri Temporis Studiorum Ratione*. Bobbs-Merrill, Indianapolis 1965.

On The Most Ancient Wisdom Of The Italians. Translation with Introduction and notes by Lucia M. Palmer of Vico's *De Antiquissima Italorum Sapientia* and his two *Risposte* of 1711 and 1712 to objections published in the *Giornale de' letterati d'Italia*. Cornell University Press, Ithaca 1988.

'Practic of the New Science'. Translation of Vico's *Pratica*, by Thomas G. Bergin and M. H. Fisch, in *Giambattista Vico's Science of Humanity*, edited by Giorgio Tagliacozzo and Donald Phillip Verene. The Johns Hopkins University Press, Baltimore 1976.

'On the Heroic Mind: An Oration Given at the Royal Academy of Naples October 20, 1732', translated by Elizabeth Sewell and Anthony C. Sirignano, in *Vico and Contemporary Thought*, edited by Giorgio Tagliacozzo, Michael Mooney and Donald Phillip Verene. Macmillan, London 1980.

Vico: Selected Writings, edited and translated with an Introduction and notes by Leon Pompa. Cambridge University Press, Cambridge 1982.

Bibliografia Vichiana, by B. Croce and F. Nicolini. Riccardo Ricciardi, Naples 1947–8.

A Selective Bibliography of Vico Scholarship (1948–68), by E. Gianturco. *Forum Italicum*, Supplement. Florence 1968.

Contributo alla Bibliografia Vichiana (1948–70), by M. Donzelli. Studi Vichiani No. 9. Guida Editori, Naples 1973.

'Critical Writings on Vico In English', by Molly Black Verene, in *Giambattista Vico's Science of Humanity*, edited by Giorgio Tagliacozzo and Donald Phillip Verene. The Johns Hopkins University Press, Baltimore 1976.

Vico In English: A Bibliography of Writings by and about Giambattista Vico (1668–1744), by Robert Crease. Humanities Press, Atlantic Highlands, N.J., 1978. *Supplement*, 1978–1980, 1981.

Nuovo Contributo alla Bibliografia Vichiana (1971–80), edited by Andrea Battistini. Guida Editori, Naples 1983.

A Bibliography Of Vico In English: 1884–1984, edited by Giorgio Tagliacozzo, Donald Phillip Verene and Vanessa Rumble. Philosophy Documentation Center, Bowling Green State University, Bowling Green, Ohio, 1986. Supplemented annually in *New Vico Studies*.

Terzo Contributo Alla Bibliografia Vichiana (1981–1985), edited by Roberto Mazzola. Supplement of the *Bollettino del Centro di Studi Vichiani*, *1987–1988*, Bibliopolis, Naples 1988.

B. JOURNALS OF VICO STUDIES

Bollettino Del Centro Di Studi Vichiani, Centro di Studi Vichiani, Naples 1971–88.

New Vico Studies, edited by Giorgio Tagliacozzo and Donald Phillip Verene, The Institute For Vico Studies, New York 1983–6.

C. COLLECTIONS OF ARTICLES

De Homine 27–8. Istituto Di Filosofia Della Università Di Roma, 1968.

Forum Italicum, vol. 2, no. 4, edited by M. Ricciardelli. State University of New York at Buffalo, N.Y., 1968.

Omaggio a Vico, edited by P. Piovani. Morano, Naples 1968.

Quaderni Contemporanei, no. 2, edited by F. Tessitore. L'Istituto Universitario di Salerno, Naples 1968.

Giambattista Vico: An International Symposium, edited by Giorgio Tagliacozzo and Hayden V. White. The Johns Hopkins University Press, Baltimore 1969.

Giambattista Vico's Science of Humanity, edited by Giorgio Tagliacozzo and Donald Phillip Verene. The Johns Hopkins University Press, Baltimore 1976.

Social Research, vol. 43, nos. 3 and 4. New School for Social Research, 1976.

Vico And Contemporary Thought, edited by Giorgio Tagliacozzo, Michael Mooney and Donald Phillip Verene. Macmillan, London 1980.

Vico: Past and Present, edited by Giorgio Tagliacozzo. Humanities Press, Atlantic Highlands, N.J., 1981.

Leggere Vico, edited by E. Riverso. Spirali, Milan 1982.

Vico and Marx: Affinities and Contrasts, edited by Giorgio Tagliacozzo. Humanities Press, Atlantic Highlands, N.J. and Macmillan, London 1983.

D. BOOKS, SUBSTANTIAL CHAPTERS IN BOOKS AND ARTICLES NOT CONTAINED IN THE COLLECTIONS LISTED ABOVE

Adams, H. P. *The Life and Writings of Giambattista Vico*. Allen and Unwin, London 1935.

Amerio, F. *Introduzione allo Studio di G. B. Vico*. Società Editrice Internazionale, Turin 1947.

Auerbach, E. 'Vico and Aesthetic Historism', in *Journal of Aesthetics and Art Criticism* 8, 1949.

Badaloni, N. *Introduzione a G. B. Vico*. Feltrinelli, Milan 1961.
  Introduzione a Vico. Laterza, Rome–Bari 1984.

Bellofiore, L. *La Dottrina della Providenza in G. B. Vico*. Cedam, Padua 1962.

Berlin, I. 'On Vico', in *The Philosophical Quarterly* 35, 1985.
  'The Philosophical Ideas of Giambattista Vico', in *Art and Ideas in Eighteenth-Century Italy*. Edizione Di Storia E Letteratura, Rome 1960.
  Vico and Herder: Two Studies In The History Of Ideas. The Hogarth Press, London 1976.

Berry, T. M. *The Historical Theory of Giambattista Vico*. Catholic University of America, Washington, D.C., 1949.

Bianca, G. A. *Il Concetto di Poesia in Giambattista Vico*. Casa Editrice G. D'Anna, Florence 1967.

Brown, R. *The Nature of Social Laws: Machiavelli to Mill*. Cambridge University Press, Cambridge 1984.

Burke, P. *Vico*. Oxford University Press, Oxford 1985.

Cantelli, G. *Mente Corpo Linguaggio: Saggi sull'interpretazione vichiana del mito*. Biblioteca Di Studi Filosofici. Sansoni, Florence 1986.

Vico and Bayle: Premesse per un Confronto. Studi Vichiani no. 4. Guida Editori, Naples 1971.

Caponigri, A. R. *Time and Idea. The Theory of History in Giambattista Vico*. University of Notre Dame Press, Notre Dame 1968.

Chambliss, J. J. *Imagination and Reason in Plato, Aristotle, Vico, Rousseau and Keats: an Essay on the Philosophy of Experience*. Martinus Nijhoff, The Hague 1974.

Chaix-Ruy, J. *La Formation de la Pensée de G. B. Vico*. Jean, Gap 1943.

Child, A. R. *Making and Knowing in Hobbes, Vico and Dewey*. University of California Press, Los Angeles 1953. Translated and published as *Fare e Conoscere in Hobbes, Vico e Dewey*. Studi Vichiani no. 2. Guida Editori, Naples 1970.

Collingwood, R. G. *The Idea of History*. The Clarendon Press, Oxford 1946.

Corsano, A. *Bayle, Leibniz e la Storia*. Studi Vichiani no. 8. Guida Editori, Naples, 1971.

G. B. Vico. Laterza, Bari 1956.

Croce, B. *Aesthetic, As Science of Expression and General Linguistic*, translated by D. Ainslie. Macmillan, New York 1909.

La Filosofia di G. B. Vico. Laterza, Bari, 6th edn, 1965. Translated by R. G. Collingwood and published under the title *The Philsophy of Giambattista Vivo*. Howard Latimer, London 1913.

De Mas, E. 'On the New Method of a New Science – A Study of Giambattista Vico', in *Journal of the History of Ideas* 32, 1971.

Donagan, Alan and Barbara. *Philosophy of History*. Macmillan, New York 1965.

Fassò, G. *I 'Quattro Autori' del Vico. Saggio sulla Genesi della 'Scienza Nuova'*. Guiffre, Milan 1949.

Vico e Grozio. Studi Vichiani no. 7. Guida Editori, Naples 1971.

Fisch, M. H. 'Vico on Roman Law', in *Essays in Political Theory Presented to George H. Sabine*, edited by M. R. Konvitz and A. E. Murphy. Cornell University Press, Ithaca 1948.

Flint, R. *Vico*. Blackwood, Edinburgh 1901.

Fubini, M. *Stile e Umanità di G. B. Vico*. Riccardo Ricciardi, Naples 1965.

Gianturco, E. *Joseph de Maistre and Giambattista Vico: Italian Roots of De Maistre's Political Culture*. Columbia University Press, New York 1937.

Giarrizzo, G. *Vico, La Politica E La Storia*. Guida Editori, Naples 1981.

Haddock, B. A. *An Introduction to Historical Thought*. Edward Arnold, London 1980.

'Vico's *Discovery of the True Homer*: A Case Study in Historical Reconstruction', in *Journal of the History of Ideas*, 40, 1979.

Vico's Political Thought. Mortlake Press, Swansea 1986.

Hutton, P. H. 'The New Science of Giambattista Vico: Historicism in Its Relation to Poetics', in *Journal of Aesthetics and Art Criticism* 31, 1972.

Iannizzotto M. *L'Empirismo nella Gnoseologia di Giambattista Vico*. Cedam, Padua 1968.

Jacobelli, I. *G. B. Vico, La Vita e Le Opere*. Cappelli, Bologna 1960.

G. B. Vico: Per Una 'Scienza Della Storia'. Armando Editore, Rome 1985.

Lifshitz, M. A. 'Giambattista Vico (1668–1744)', in *Philosophy and Phenomenological Research* 8, 1948.

Löwith, K. *Meaning in History: The Theological Implications of the Philosophy of History*. University of Chicago Press, Chicago 1949.

Manson, R. *The Theory of Knowledge of Giambattista Vico*. Archon Books, Hamden 1969.

Manuel, F. *The Eighteenth Century Confronts the Gods*. Harvard University Press, Cambridge, Mass., 1959.

Mazlich, B. *The Riddle of History: The Great Speculators from Vico to Freud*. Harper and Row, New York 1966.

Modica, G. *La Filosofia Del 'Senso Commune' in Giambattista Vico*. S. Sciascia Editore, Rome 1983.

Mondolfo, R. *Il Verum-Factum Prima di Vico*. Studi Vichiani no. 1. Guida Editori, Naples 1969.

Mooney, M. *Vico In The Tradition of Rhetoric*. Princeton University Press, Princeton, N.J., 1985.

Nicolini, F. *Commento Storico alla Seconda Scienza Nuova*, vols. I and II. Edizioni Di Storia E Letteratura, Rome 1978.

La Giovinezza di G. B. Vico. Laterza, Bari 1932.

Pasini, D. *Diritto Società E Stato In Vico*. Editore Jovene, Naples 1970.

Piovani, P. *Giambattista Vico – Our Perennial Standard*. Istituto Italiano di Cultura, New York 1969.

Pompa, L. 'Vico's Science', in *History and Theory* 10, 1971.

Randall, J. H. Jr. *The Career of Philosophy*, vol. I. Columbia University Press, New York 1962–5.

Robertson, J. C. *Studies in the Genesis of Romantic Theory*. Cambridge University Press, Cambridge 1923.

Rossi, P. *Le Sterminate Antichità*. Nistri-Lischi, Pisa 1969.

Severino, S. *Principi e Modificazioni della Mente in Vico*. Il Melangelo, Genoa 1981.

Toulmin, S. and Goodfield, J. *The Discovery of Time*. Harper and Row, New York 1965.

Tristam, R. J. 'Explanation in the *New Science*: On Vico's Contribution to Scientific Sociohistorical Thought', in *History and Theory* 21, 1983.

Vaughan, C. F. *Studies in the History of Political Philosophy Before and After Rousseau*, vol. I. Manchester University Press, Manchester 1925.

Vaughan, F. *The Political Philosophy of Giambattista Vico*. Martinus Nijhoff, The Hague 1972.

Verene, B. P. *Vico's Science of Imagination*. Cornell University Press, Ithaca 1981.

Whittaker, T. *Reason and Other Essays*. Cambridge University Press, Cambridge 1934.

Zagorin, P. 'Berlin on Vico', in *The Philosophical Quarterly* 35, 1985.

'Vico's Theory of Knowledge: A Critique', in *The Philosophical Quarterly* 34, 1984.

Index

Pufendorf, 39, 46–7
Pythagoras, 80, 98

rationale of institutions, 40
reason, 47, 74, 121, 123, 189, 197, 212–15, 217–19, 232; Hegelian concept of, *see* Hegel
reflection, *see* self-reflection
religion, of primitive man, 44, 115; *see also* principles, three first
rhapsodes, 5, 139
rhetoric, Vico's theory of, *see* topics
Rossi, P., 98, 105, 148

Salutati, 19
scienza, 72, 82–3, 160–1, 165, 168
Scipio Africanus, 69, 125–6
Selden, 35–6, 39, 46–7
self-interest, 26, 198–200, 203, 216
self-preservation, 200
self-reflection, 165–9, 183
Servius Tullius, 187
Siciliana, 87
Smith, Adam, 176
social: change, 25, 37, 42; conditioning, 27–8, 30; rôles, *see* institutional rôles; structure, 55–7, 62, 112–19
Spencer, 9–10, 36
Spengler, O., 172, 174
Socrates, 89
Spinoza, Spinozism, 22–3, 52, 54–5, 76, 78, 85, 158
Stoics, 17–18, 22, 27, 51–2, 54, 142, 158; *see also* metaphysical determinism
substance, 44, 86

Tacitus, 107, 110
Tagliacozzo, G., 76, 105, 123, 148, 201, 209, 228
Tarquin tyrants, 12

theoretical commitment, 171–6
theory: epistemological, *see* theory of knowledge; metaphysical, 4, 15–16, 23, 29, 31, 45, 70–1, 85, 93, 115, 134, 137, 141–2; sociological and historico-sociological, 4–6, 23–4, 103, 116–27, 131–4, 137, 140–2; of knowledge, 4, 6, 15, 72, 75–84, 152–85; *see also* creative theory of knowledge
Tiberius, 69, 126
times, of institutions, 42, 45–9
topics, Vico's theory of, 186, 190–5, 231
Toynbee, A., 171–2, 174, 178
transmission theory of civilisation, 2, 41
true, the, 92–3; *see also* vero
truth, causal theory of, 78–81

unintended consequences, 24, 198–9
utility, *see* human needs or utilities; private utilities

Valla, 19
Van Heurn, 9, 35
Varro, 110
Vaughan, F., 51, 61
Verene, D. P., 209, 229–37, 240
verification, 4, 81, 147; *see also* proofs, philological
vero, 73
verstehen, *see* imagination
vices, *see* human vices

White, H., 76, 105, 123, 148
wisdom: poetic, 4; matchless of the ancients, 11
Wits, 35
Wittgenstein, 181

Zeno, 52, 59–60, 89, 105